The

Vegetarian

Bistro

THE VEGETARIAN BISTRO

« 250 »

AUTHENTIC FRENCH
REGIONAL RECIPES

BY MARLENA SPIELER

ILLUSTRATED BY PIERRE LE-TAN

CHRONICLE BOOKS

SAN FRANCISCO

Library of Congress Cataloging-in-Publication Data:

Spieler, Marlena
        The vegetarian bistro: 250 authentic French regional
recipes/by Marlena Spieler; illustrated by Pierre Le-Tan.
                p.   cm.
        Includes index.
        ISBN 0-8118-1376-2 (pb)
        1. Vegetarian cookery. 2. Cookery, French. I. Title.
TX837.S696 1997
641.5'636'0944–dc21   96-51122
                                                                        CIP

Printed in the United States

Cover and book design by Rebecca S. Neimark, Twenty-Six Letters

Distributed in Canada by Raincoast Books
8680 Cambie Street
Vancouver, British Columbia V6P 6M9

10 9 8 7 6 5 4 3 2 1

Chronicle Books
85 Second Street
San Francisco, California 94105

Web Site: www.chronbooks.com

Contents

. . . .

Preface

. . . .

Sitting at a paper-topped table with lace curtains framing the window, a glass of red wine in your hand and the sound of French ringing lyrically in your ears, it is easy to think you are in a movie instead of simply sitting down to dinner. And if the voices are a wee bit too loud, and you are elbow to elbow with your fellow diners, this only adds to the flavor.

And if you are open to whatever comes your way, the food will taste better, the ambiance will be more intense, and you will be nourished in more than just your body.

You might find yourself sitting next to an elderly philosopher, as I did in Paris recently; halfway through the meal the waiter brought out a guitar and my philosophical table neighbor played a song about bubble bath and the meaning of life, very eccentric and very Parisian. "He does this every Saturday night," said the waiter indulgently, proudly. The famous ex-movie star sitting at my other side agreed, then dipped her crusty bread into the sauce on her plate and took a big lusty bite.

There was a time in a Calais bistro when I got caught up in the celebrations at the next table and was soon arm in arm with a group of lively World War II veterans, singing "La Marseillaise" and crying "Vive la France!" And there was a couscous dinner in Nice at which the chef brought out a special couscous *pour les chiens* at the next table. And the dogs ate so politely, probably more politely than myself. (My husband swears they smoked cigars afterwards–I'm not so sure.)

Though dishes of vegetables have always been my favored choice, I have tended towards omnivorous eating, choosing from whatever is on the menu. But when my daughter went to university, she acquired a vegetarian boyfriend, and our family eating tours of France haven't been the same since. Now we search the country for France's most delicious vegetarian specialties.

In writing this book I've crossed the Channel and boarded planes at the drop of a hat. I've explored Paris by métro and foot, and I've driven along winding countryside roads. Delicious bistro meals have been mine in an old train station, a refurbished *bergerie* (sheep barn), and in farmhouses with whitewashed stone walls. One bistro stretched into a cave in the back.

I've spooned up *pipérade* in a tiny hole-in-the-wall, and somewhere outside of Gourdon, I ate in a village bistro that provided shelter from the rain and dazzled me with their wild mushrooms and truffles.

I ate so many meals in that

La confiture

peculiar French style of having little dogs sitting alongside me that when I returned home to my own dogless table, I felt bereft. Did the proximity of dogs make everything taste better? Perhaps. An elegant poodle and its stylish mistress amused me in a Saint-Tropez bistro, each with her own plate of chic sundried tomato pizza. A bichon frise nibbled on the bits of my choucroute that fell to the ground as I lunched in the sunny square at Saint-Paul-de-Vence, and a tiny basset hound puppy stationed himself next to Picasso's favorite seat in Paris's Café de Flore, lapping up errant spills from my cup of chocolate and chasing croissant crumbs.

Le jardin potager

My pursuit of delicious vegetarian dishes for this book was also accompanied with a hefty helping of adventure. There was the time I was attacked by bears near Perpignan–in the car, in a *réserve africaine,* Jurassic Park style. And in the Jura, in pursuit of the perfect gratin, I spent one potato-filled week snowed in (I found the gratin, and more; see *"Pâtes, Riz, et Pommes de Terre"*). In Nice I spent a week in the Pasteur hospital with a strep infection; not only did they heal me, but doctors, nurses, patients, and visitors alike all offered advice on where to eat and shared recipes as well.

This book reflects the traditional bistro fare I've sampled in trips through France as well as dishes I've created in my own kitchen, inspired by dishes I've been lucky enough to eat on French soil.

I've often avoided naming specific bistros for a reason: The dish may have been inspired by a restaurant, but often I have changed or adapted the recipe substantially. This may have been done

to make it vegetarian, to streamline preparation, or simply because I felt the dish would be improved. However, I have endeavored to keep the dishes always in the spirit of bistro food: down to earth, robust, satisfying.

I admit that many of my recipes include large amounts of garlic, often more than the original. My explanation is that I can't help myself, I love it so.

Bistro dishes traditionally contain large amounts of cream, eggs, butter, and cheese. Many of the recipes in this collection do, too, for you cannot do justice to this hearty way of French cooking without these rich, traditional ingredients. I have often cut down on the amount of these ingredients, however, and have tried to balance the amount of rich dishes with lighter ones. (There are times, though, when a luscious cream-enriched sauce ladled over poached eggs soothes the soul as does no steamer full of vegetables. Let your own dietary needs be your guide.)

Bon appétit!

Introduction

. . . .

Dining in a formal Michelin-starred restaurant is a thrilling experience, one that amplifies life's special occasions and turns even an ordinary meal into an event.

But in the texture of everyday French life, it is the bistro that is woven into the daily pattern of meals and celebrations. The bistro is that little neighborhood restaurant where they know who you are, greet you warmly, and serve you satisfying foods that change with the seasons and define regional, homey French cuisine.

I was smitten my first time as I sat at a little table in Paris, unfurled my red-checked napkin, and ate what was the best, most satisfying meal of my life so far. And it was vegetarian: a tart of herby cheeses followed by a soft and unctuous *pipérade* and a salad of wild greens.

While the French do love all kinds of animal foods, their love of vegetables is legendary. Vegetable dishes form the basis of much French cookery, since a diet of vegetables, herbs, legumes, and grains has been the mainstay during lean times.

But French appreciation of vegetables goes beyond necessity; it is also part of the country's love of its regions, its connection with the soil, and its culinary largesse.

And its history! During the Middle Ages a great variety of vegetables were for sale in the streets of Paris: carrots, sorrel, chervil, leeks, turnips, beets, peas, fava beans, lentils, parsnips, cabbage, watercress, onions, asparagus, cucumbers, garlic, and many more. During the Renaissance interest in vegetables grew. There might be nearly 20 varieties of spinach available

at a time; red cabbage, broccoli, and pumpkin were being cultivated for the first time, and a young bride, Catherine de' Medici, brought her retinue of chefs and a variety of new vegetables to France from her Italian homeland. Many of our contemporary artichoke dishes reflect her chefs' ways with this gray-green thistle.

The New World added its bounty to France's vegetable basket: tomatoes, eggplants, potatoes, squash, white beans, Jerusalem artichokes, and corn.

A hero in France's history of vegetable cultivation is La Quintinie, King Louis XIV's gardener at Versailles. He developed methods of fertilizing, sheltering, and breeding that are still used today.

Traditionally, a separate vegetable course was served, often a selection of three or four dishes, carefully prepared and sauced. It was not until this century that meat became more readily available and affordable, and the French began to eat more animal products, relegating vegetables to mere accompaniment.

Today, however, vegetables are once again at the center of the meal. More and more young people in France are eating in a vegetarian or semi-vegetarian way. Still, eating well as a vegetarian in France takes a bit of work. Vegetarian restaurants exist, especially in Paris and the larger cities, but they often serve international "vegetarian whole food" rather than the traditional French specialties we yearn for.

Instead, we head for the bistro. There, among the specialties of the regional *cuisine du terroir* and the homey *cuisine de grandmère*, we feast.

The Bistro Defined

A bistro can be either a restaurant or a café. Often owned by a family or couple, it offers a cozy, casual atmosphere, and serves food that is close to the owners' heart, reflecting their regional and family traditions.

The menu might be printed on a sheet of paper, but often it is scrawled on a blackboard or a mirror. Sometimes the owner or waiter won't bother with a menu at all, and will decide for you, bringing whatever he or she has decided you *really want.*

Sometimes bistros are just a few tables tucked into the back of a noisy, smoky bar or café, looking like a vignette snipped from the pages of Pagnol or Zola.

Some, especially in Paris, might have a whimsical theme, such as La Cafetière (The Coffeepot), which boasts a beautiful collection of antique coffeepots, or Au Chien Qui Fume, literally translated as At the Smoking Dog, in honor of the talents of the two dogs that belonged to the original owner (the griffon smoked a pipe, the poodle, a cigar).

Or a bistro might be a chic little restaurant owned by a famous chef as a sort of gastronomical plaything to amuse the overstressed kitchen staff and relieve the tensions of running the serious gastronomical temple up the street.

Bistros are small (unlike the huge brasseries). The smallest bistro I have eaten in consisted of three little tables. (The food was superb, and their desserts made me literally tremble with desire.)

Until recently a bistro could be counted on to have traditional decor: lace curtains at the window, red banquettes along the wall, paper or checked cloths on the tables, gleaming brass fittings, wine in carafes–and indeed, many still do.

But in recent years a new style of bistro has appeared, especially in Paris: contemporary in design, with a modern style that is influencing the cuisine as well as the surroundings. And they take their vegetables seriously. Some of these restaurants offer an *assiette végétarienne,* or vegetarian plate. Others even offer a *dégustation,* or a tasting of many courses, all vegetarian.

But while there might be a whiff of exotic spices in a vegetable ragout or a ratatouille, a traditional eggplant *daube,* or nuggets of tropical fruit in your *salade composée,* some things never change.

The largest and most important meal is at midday; the evening is traditionally a time for soup, and perhaps a light main course. The main meal will follow a progression of three basic courses, opening with a small first course, then proceeding on to a main dish and finishing with either dessert or cheese. There might be an additional plate of nibbles or hors d'oeuvres before the first course, perhaps a salad at some point, and you might enjoy both cheese and dessert, but the shape of the meal is the same. For a special occasion such as Sunday lunch, the number of courses served will be a festive four or five, and the meal will stretch deliciously throughout the afternoon.

And always there is crisp, crusty bread on the table, eaten with each course, employed in sopping up delectable sauces and for nibbling with the cheese.

A Little History of the Bistro

The origin of the word *bistro* is a bit vague. No one is even sure as to how to spell it: *bistro* or *bistrot*–both are used interchangeably.

In the most colorful story, the word is said to date from 1815 when the Cossacks occupied Paris. The soldiers were camped out at the Champs-

Elysées and, Cossacks not being known for their manners, pushed their way into the cafés, shouting *"Bystro! Bystro!"* meaning, "Quick, quick! We are hungry! Bring us food and drink *fast!"*

Others say the word comes from the verb *bistrouiller,* to dilute fruit juices with alcohol and serve it under the guise of wine in restaurants of dubious character. Still others say it was *bistouille*, a mixture of coffee and eau-de-vie offered in the little restaurant-cafés that gave the establishments their name.

These bistros served as a home away from home, offering a warm welcome in addition to a warming meal. Many of the first bistros clustered around Paris's Les Halles area, catering to the needs of the hardworking locals. By the mid-1800s bistros were springing up in every neighborhood and arrondissement of Paris, and in the provinces as well.

Intellectuals and artists who flocked to Paris and the south often found themselves sustained by bistros, sitting night after night absorbing big helpings of atmosphere along with the hearty meals. These great artists and writers drew upon their time spent at these restaurants, creating vibrant portraits in words on paper and in paint on canvas, establishing the bistro as an icon of French culture.

REGIONAL CUISINE AND THE VEGETARIAN

The garden-based regional cooking of France offers a wide array of vegetable specialties.

In Normandy and Brittany, silvery green artichokes are rolled into tender omelets, soups are puréed from simmered earthy vegetables, and green beans are sprinkled with fresh herbs. Rustic greens are offered alongside local goat cheeses or tossed with delicate warm potatoes, and meals are often finished with creamy Camembert, Brie, Pont-l'Evêque, or a deliciously stinky Livarot.

Brittany is the land of buckwheat and crêpes, often combined into sweet or savory street snacks or bistro specialties.

The Dordogne and Périgord can be difficult for vegetarians, as foods are often cooked in duck or goose fat–but oil is squeezed from the walnuts whose groves dot the countryside, and you'll often find salads of greens and vegetables dressed in this fragrant oil. Breads are hearty and taste of baking in wood-burning ovens–perfect along with the inky local wines and luscious farmyard goat cheeses.

The nearby Auvergne grows France's most famous lentil, the nutty little gray-green lentil de Puy. Bleu d'Auvergne, bleu des Causses, and the world-famous Roquefort find their way into salads and dishes of potatoes and pasta, or are simply eaten with bread. And tangy Cantal cheese, along with warm mashed potatoes, is whipped into the ultimate comfort dish, *aligot.*

Through the Jura and Savoy you'll find more potatoes: gratinéed with wild mushrooms, baked with onions and pungent cheese, or sliced and pan-fried to golden, then tossed with parsley and garlic. Walnuts, grown in the Val d'Isère, are tossed into salads, pastas, or tarts. Saint-Marcellin is made in the same valley, and throughout the region you'll find creamy Reblochon and the elegant Beaufort.

The area also has a pasta specialty, *raviole,* tiny square pasta filled with cheese. Delicate and irresistible, they need no sauce, only a puddle of butter or a splash of herby broth.

Because this area is so close to Switzerland, fondue dishes are on the menu. You can find the classic fondue, or a garlicky cheese and tomato mixture, as I did last autumn sitting at a table full of singing grape-pickers who had just finished working in the local fields.

South through the Alps, in the sunny land of Provence, you enter the Mediterranean world. Here vivacious vegetable dishes cook in local olive oil, fragrant with herbs and dripping garlic. Because of the area's history of poverty, the hot climate that favors lighter eating habits, and the fact that so many vegetables grow so easily here, the local tradition of vegetable specialties has always been strong.

Nibble on artichokes sliced raw with fava beans or braised in white wine, sliced tomatoes tossed with puréed basil, pasta with fragrant basil pistou; wipe it all up with breads studded with herbs, nuts, or olives.

In the Languedoc you might sample a *pipérade* of melting red peppers and tomatoes scrambled with eggs, or a salad of wild asparagus , and goat cheeses or blue cheeses from the famous caves to the north, all sweetened with sips of the local Muscat dessert wines.

A BISTRO EXPERIENCE

A frisson of excitement is in the air, with an edge of expectancy as the staff bustles about, tending each diner. As the diners sip aperitifs, they anticipate the delights to come.

As each plate is carried out, all eyes discreetly follow it with interest. How does the soup look, is the warm salad perhaps what I would like? How beautiful that plate looks! How wonderful its aromas!

The pre-meal chatter gently subsides, leaving only the sound of cutlery and contented murmurs. As the meal unfolds, the chef pokes his head out from the kitchen, checking the expres-

sion on the face of each diner. A smile lights his face as I take a bite and smile blissfully to myself.

Yet when I ask him for a recipe, he says "*Non!* Certainly not! It is my secret!"

"Don't worry," says the waitress. "He is always like that." She consoles me. "Chefs are jealous, you see; and anyhow, he hopes to write his own book."

She continues, "Most of us learn to cook from our mothers, as I did. I, in turn, teach my recipes to my daughter and son. Cuisine is part of our culture, not simply what we will eat that day."

And when I praise the meal and the superb wines, she says it is an honor to have me as a guest in the bistro.

But indeed, the honor is mine, to be allowed to partake in a society that so venerates the ties of food and culture.

ORDERING VEGETARIAN MEALS IN BISTROS

Salads are deliciously dependable, as restaurant owners can understand the passion for fresh vegetables. The farther south you travel, the more luscious the salads.

Vegetable soups, often made with water instead of stock, can be a wonderful vegetarian choice. The *soupe des légumes* in the Pas de Calais, Normandy, and Picardie will either be green from leafy vegetables, orange from carrots and rutabagas, or creamy white from leeks, turnips, and potatoes. And the niçoise *soupe au pistou* will taste of garlic and sweet basil, and almost always contain only vegetables.

From north to south, bistros offer appetizers of raw and cooked vegetables. What could be more classic than a composed salad of spindly frisée surrounding a nugget of Roquefort pâté, or celery root in mustardy mayonnaise, tiny potatoes in walnut oil, asparagus in a light vinaigrette, or artichokes in caper mayonnaise? At Paris's Chardenoux, sample the poached leeks in a creamy beet purée–it is no less than wonderful.

Eating habits in France have relaxed and become more casual over the last decade. The progression of a meal is less rigid, and the line between what to eat as a first course or main plate has blurred. Since many of the traditional first courses are vegetarian, you can choose your meal entirely from the list of first courses and it will not raise the eyebrows–or ire–of the waiter as it might have in the not too distant past.

Crêpes, egg dishes, omelets all make a splendid start to the meal, as do savory pastries–a flaky turnover oozing pungent Roquefort onto a bed of bitter greens, a crisp little galette of red peppers and tomatoes, or a rustic round of bread dough with a whole disc of fresh cheese–a Maroilles–lopped on top and baked in. All make a hearty main course.

Pasta, of course, is always a succulent plateful, and the French often sauce it so seductively.

Sometimes we request–always politely, always in French–that the kitchen prepare a vegetarian dish, whatever the chef or *patron* wishes. Without exception they comply gracefully, helpfully, though with varying results. We have been served soul-satisfying dishes of lovingly cooked vegetables, soufflés, and gratins, but we've also been served lackluster plates of dowdy steamed vegetables.

Do scan the menu for accompaniments. Sometimes the pasta, rice, or gratin offered as a side dish is just what you'd like for a main dish.

WHAT TO DRINK?

Bistros often have their own house drink to be sipped before the meal.

Kir is a distinctive bistro choice as an aperitif.

It comes in a wide variety of guises, from the Dijonnaise dry white wine enriched with a shot of crème de cassis, to the *kir royal,* in which the white wine is replaced by Champagne. In other areas, the black currant flavor of cassis is replaced by any fruity liqueur–peach, pear, strawberry, raspberry, or orange are especially refreshing. In some cafés, a kir becomes a *communard,* the cassis added to red rather than white wine.

Other drinks to consider are anise-flavored pastis, such as Pernod or Ricard, or the bitter tonics such as Suze, Picon, and Mandarin (the latter two tasting of orange as well).

Sometimes a sweet fortified wine will be served, such as Cognac's Pineau des Charentes, or in the south, a Muscat such as Beaumes de Venise or Muscat de Frontignan.

Choosing wines to complement your meal adds piquant interest to your dining. Everyday food is fine with *vin ordinaire.* Most bistros have an arrangement with a specific vineyard, usually from the region that they hail from, and offer an absolutely delicious table wine. Ask for *vin de la maison;* it may not be listed on the menu. The *vin de la maison* may be bottled, bearing the label and name of the bistro, or it may be poured from the barrel into a carafe. Beaujolais, Chinon, and Brouilly are quintessential bistro wines.

For a special meal such as Sunday lunch, where the dishes are carefully chosen, your choice of wine should be given special attention. If you have questions, ask the advice of your waiter or waitress; his or her enthusiasm will be contagious and you will likely be rewarded sip after enticing sip.

As a general rule, try to pair a wine with a dish by the intensity of flavors. Often matching by regions works well, as over the years wines have usually been crafted that complement the dishes of the area. White wines are the traditional choice for the first course. A fruity or spicy Gewürztraminer is best with a spicy dish or one with a pungent cheese such as Roquefort, a crisp white such as a Sancerre best with lighter offerings. Red wines such as the fruity Beaujolais nouveau of late autumn, a Chinon, or Brouilly are often my first-course choice, and sometimes I'll continue to drink it, or switch to something lush and robust for the heartier main course, such as a Bordeaux, a Côtes-du-Rhône, or an inky rough Cahors.

Beer is less likely to be served in bistros as it is less compatible with the food. Rather it is drunk on its own as an afternoon refreshment, or served with the sauerkraut and Alsatian-style dishes usually served in brasseries.

Coffee is served at the end of the meal–*after*, not *with*–dessert. Unlike breakfast, when it is served *au lait* or *crème*, after a meal coffee is traditionally served black, a tiny cup of utterly strong essence of coffee (though milk is increasingly available on request). Most bistros have decaffeinated coffee, *décaféiné*.

A tiny glass of eau-de-vie, such as Cognac, Armagnac, Calvados, or marc, is the traditional ending to many a bistro meal. Strong and fiery, it gives a warm glow as it slowly slips down the throat. Fruit-based spirits such as raspberry *(framboise)*, prune *(prunelle)*, pear *(poire)*, strawberry *(fraise des bois)* are classic, too. My favorite, however, is a few sips of any of the lyrical sweet wines based on the Muscat grape, such as Beaumes de Venise or Muscat de Frontignon.

Chez Nous: The Bistro at Home

The memories of meals enjoyed in bistros–savored course by course, accompanied with hunks of crusty bread, sips of rustic wines, and lively conversation–make me want to eat this way at home, too.

It is as much an attitude and style as it is a way of cooking: a glass filled with wildflowers set on a bright cloth-covered table, a carafe of wine, and casual plates, wineglasses and cutlery. Don't worry about formalities; nothing need even match–this will only enhance the charm of the meal.

Begin with a little plate of something simple for nibbling: pungent black olives, crisp toasted almonds, or a little pot of fresh cheese enlivened with garlic and parsley. Crisp bread-based canapes are good, too, to dawdle over while you ready yourselves for the rest of the meal.

The first course can be as simple as raw vegetables–crudités–served in a little communal plate for everyone. A composed salad is beautiful and elegant, and since the plates can be arranged beforehand, the cook can enjoy the meal with the rest of the diners. Or, have a warming soup, ladled into large shallow soup bowls.

Many bistro main courses are long-cooked casseroles or gratins that bubble away happily in the oven or simmer on the stove while everyone is eating the first course.

After the main course, offer cheese instead of–or just before–dessert. It is a delectable time to sip the last of your wine, deliciously prolonging the meal. Offer a selection of several or simply one well-chosen cheese, but stay with tiny portions. Use a plate, a board, or as they do in Burgundy, a flat basket and serve individual portions from that. If edible unsprayed leaves are available, arrange your cheeses on them. (Vine leaves are classic, but lemon leaves are lovely too.)

If served at all, dessert should be simple. Perfectly ripe, utterly fragrant fresh fruit can hardly be bettered, unless it is macerated in a little liqueur and spooned over ice cream. Chocolate mousse and simple cakes, grandmotherly fruit tarts and eggy custards are all classic finales to lunch or dinner in most any bistro. If, like me, you haven't the talent or patience for preparing such sweets, it pays to be on cordial terms with your local pâtisserie.

Serve a small cup of strong, fragrant coffee as its own course after the cheese or dessert. If you haven't had dessert at all, offer a tiny chocolate or two along with the coffee. Then there is that sip of eau-de-vie–*ô-là-là*. What a nice way to live.

MERCI BIEN

To Rev. Jon Harford, for being a very good sport, especially when we were attacked by a bear in the Pyrenees.

To my daughter Leah, studying medicine in Liverpool, England. And to my stepdaughter Gretchen, of San Francisco, California: I'm already planning next year's spring vacation!

To our friends in Nice: Susie Morgenstern, who hosted the most memorable dinner party I've ever attended. And to her daughter, Dr. Maya Morgenstern, who saved my life that same night. It isn't many dinner parties that end with the guest leaving for the hospital (nothing to do with Susie's delicious cooking; I still regret that I couldn't stay for dessert). Thank you, Professor Dan Ostrowsky and Professor Nicole Ostrowsky, for sharing the Nice marketplace with us, and Alice and Max Tubiana, for helping me research Nice's Jewish community.

To Jerome Freeman and Sheila Hannon, Ian Robertson, and Marie Helley for a winter weekend in Calais, all of us with forks and corkscrews in hand, ready for anything edible. To Peter Milne, for potato-filled visits to Grenoble and good-natured forays to Provence and Picardy.

To Kathleen Griffin and Benjamin Ergas, for sharing their expertise in French; to Sue Kreitzman, food writer and East End neighbor, who shares my gastronomic passions. To Amanda and Tim Hemmeter, Dr. Esther Novack and Rev. John Chendo, Madame Noelle Hubau and "Eliot" of Paris and Provence, Paula Aspin, Vivien Milne, Kamala Friedman, Sandy Waks, and Rabbi Jason Gaber, a true friend.

To my colleagues at the *San Francisco Chronicle* who commissioned the article that this book became: Michael Bauer, Maria Cianci, Fran Irwin, M. A. Mariner, and Karola Saekel. To British wine writer Fiona Beckett, Trevor Vibert, and their family for a delicious wine-filled week in their cottage in the Languedoc.

To Melissa, Steven, Alison, and Lexie Opper, enthusiastic eaters and good cooks, too. To my esteemed grandmother, Sophia (Bachi) Dubowsky, my parents Caroline and Izzy Smith, and Aunt Estelle and Uncle Sy Opper.

To Freud, kitty extraordinaire with a passion for pain Poilâne. And to Bella (Chrisp Street), Bunny (Brick Lane), Fred (Nice), Elvis (Sacramento), Lucy (Marin County), Imogen (Calais), Davidoff (Bar-sur-Loup), Hypolyte (Antibes), Flore (Paris), Pigalle (Paris), Lovey (New York), and of course, Gaston (Nice) and Barney (Capetown, South Africa).

To Alan McLaughlan: agent, food shopper, dishwasher, potato peeler, map reader, and–oh, and husband. He ate these dishes all doggedly and is still cheerful when the word *gratin* is mentioned.

And to Bill LeBlond, Leslie Jonath, and Sarah Putman at Chronicle Books: Thank you for commissioning *The Vegetarian Bistro*.

Hors d'Œuvre

✦✦✦

Appetizers

The phrase itself literally means "outside the main work," referring to the role of this course as tidbits to be nibbled on before the real eating begins. Hors d'oeuvres are meant to amuse rather than to seriously fuel, and are sometimes referred to as *amuse-gueules* or *amuse-bouches*.

Eating even the simplest hors d'oeuvre sets aside a space in time that forms a bridge between the work and bustle of life, and the enjoyment of the meal to come. It is a custom that dates from Roman times, when herbs, eggs, cheese, olives, and/or nuts were laid out before the meal began.

La table de ferme

An hors d'oeuvre shouldn't be large or filling; it should whet your appetite and titillate you, coax you into the rest of the meal. It might be no more than a pot of savory herbed cheese or butter redolent of garlic for spreading onto small slices of bread or, in the Loire Valley, onto puffy breads called *foue*. Aioli or tapenade might make an appearance, or a vegetable mixture such as spinach rillettes, with a little basket of raw vegetables for dipping.

Many bistros bring several little plates of hors d'oeuvres to the table before you even look at the menu. One of my favorites is the simple combination of briny green olives and freshly toasted almonds. Radishes alongside unsalted butter is a treat in spring when the radishes are juicy and crunchy and just spicy enough to excite.

And regional specialties in tiny portions are great fun to nibble on. Little squares of *trouchia*, strips of *socca*, or crisp-fried *panisses* are delightful alongside a pre-dinner rosé. And once along the Côte d'Azur I was served miniature *pan bagnats:* tiny one-bite marvels of crusty roll filled with peppers, tomatoes, onions, slivers of eggs and olives, and a dusting of herbs.

SOCCA

THIN CRÊPES OF SIZZLING CHICKPEA BATTER

– Serves 4 –

This specialty of Nice is most often found in the little shops and bars that punctuate the streets of the old town–Vieux Nice and its picturesque Cours Saleya market–and in the market that winds around the streets surrounding the old train station. It serves as a mid-morning snack, or *casse-croûte*, vendors and manual workers sip a glass of chilled rosé and nibble on this rather unrefined huge crêpe of chickpea flour cooked in hot olive oil and served hot in wide strips.

Homemade *socca* makes a good hors d'oeuvre, too. It is at its best prepared over a wood-burning fire in a covered grill, the faint whiff of smoke perfuming the nutty, vegetal flavor of the chickpeas.

1 to 1½ cups cold water or more as needed
1 teaspoon salt
4 to 5 tablespoons olive oil
1 cup chickpea flour
Freshly ground pepper to taste

♦♦Preheat the broiler. Slowly whisk the water, salt, and 2 tablespoons of the olive oil into the chickpea flour, mixing until it forms a batter the thickness of crêpe batter. It will still have a few lumps; strain to smooth out the lumps if desired, or just leave the lumps, to add a rustic quality to the *socca*.

♦♦Heat a 12- to 18-inch heavy cast-iron, steel, or lined copper pan over medium-high heat, then drizzle 1 tablespoon of the olive oil into it and swirl the oil around to coat the pan.

♦♦Pour or ladle in ¼ to ½ cup batter and swirl around the hot oiled pan, letting the batter roll up onto the sides then back down again.

♦♦Cook the thin layer of batter until crusty brown on the bottom; take care that it does not burn.

♦♦At this point, the top of the pancake will probably still be damp. Place it under the hot broiler for a minute or two to cook the top until no longer moist.

♦♦Using a metal spatula, cut the *socca* into squares or wide strips and scrape out of the pan (it will stick a little in spots). Serve at once, sprinkled with pepper.

♦♦Continue until the batter has been used up, or you have enough *socca* for the time being.

♦♦Leftover batter can be stored, well covered, in the refrigerator for 3 to 4 days.

TROUCHIA

NIÇOISE FLAT OMELET OF SPINACH AND CHEESE

– Serves 4 –

Green with chopped spinach or chard, *trouchia* is one of Nice's classic simple little dishes (farther down the coast, in Cannes, it is known as a *cannoise*). You may find *la trouchia* scrawled onto the chalkboard menu as a first course, such as at Nice's Lou Pistou, but it's utterly charming cut into bite-sized chunks for nibbling with a chilled rosé or a white Côtes-du-Provence.

The following *trouchia* is scented with lots of garlic and the grassy freshness of chervil. Sometimes I stir the chervil into the spinach mixture; at other times I sprinkle it on afterwards–each way is subtly different and both are lovely. If fresh chervil is unavailable, sweet basil or chopped chives are delicious instead.

> 1½ pounds spinach or chard, cooked, chopped, and squeezed dry (2 cups)
> ¾ cup (3 ounces) shredded Gruyère, Beaufort, or Fontina cheese
> ¼ cup grated Parmesan, pecorino, or aged Asiago cheese
> 3 garlic cloves, minced
> 2 shallots, minced
> 6 eggs, lightly beaten
> 1 to 2 tablespoons milk
> Salt and pepper to taste
> 2 tablespoons coarsely chopped fresh chervil
> 1 to 2 tablespoons olive oil

✦✦Preheat the broiler. Combine the spinach or chard, shredded cheese, grated cheese, garlic, shallots, eggs, and milk. Season the mixture with salt and pepper, adding the chervil now if desired.

✦✦Heat the oil in a heavy 12-inch skillet over medium-low heat, then pour in the spinach mixture. Cook until the bottom lightly browns, but the top is still somewhat runny.

✦✦Place the omelet under the hot broiler and cook until the top lightly browns, about 5 to 7 minutes.

✦✦Serve either hot or cool; if the chervil has not been added to the spinach or chard mixture, sprinkle it on top.

EGGPLANT AND CHEESE "PÂTÉ"

– Serves 4 to 6 –

A slab of chopped eggplant and mushrooms baked with cheese makes a delicious pâté-like starter.

Serve cold, as a nibble, along with a plate of whole lightly toasted blanched almonds.

> 2 eggplants, halved lengthwise
> 2 tablespoons olive oil
> Salt to taste
> 8 ounces mushrooms, diced
> 1 onion, chopped
> 3 garlic cloves, minced
> ½ cup fresh bread crumbs
> 3 tablespoons heavy cream
> 1 teaspoon minced fresh tarragon, or ¼ teaspoon dried tarragon
> 1 cup (4 ounces) grated Gruyère, Emmenthal, Comte, or Cantal cheese
> 2 to 3 tablespoons freshly grated Parmesan cheese
> 4 to 6 tablespoons minced fresh chives

✦✦Preheat the oven to 375°F.

✦✦Score the flesh of the eggplants, going up to the skin but not through it. Brush the cut sides with some of the olive oil, sprinkle with salt, and place skin-side down on a baking sheet.

✦✦Bake until the eggplants are lightly browned and tender, about 30 minutes. Let cool.

✦✦When cool enough to handle, scrape the eggplant flesh from the skins. Arrange the skins, shiny-side out, in a buttered 6-cup terrine or loaf pan so that it completely lines the pan. Set aside.

✦✦Heat the remaining oil in a large skillet or sauté pan over medium-high heat. Sauté the mushrooms, onion, and garlic until the mushrooms are lightly browned and softened, then add the eggplant flesh, bread crumbs, and cream. Heat through, then stir in the tarragon and half of each cheese.

✦✦ Heap the mushroom-eggplant mixture onto the eggplant skins and press firmly to even it out. Sprinkle the top with the remaining cheese.

✦✦ Bake until the cheese melts and sizzles, about 20 to 25 minutes.

✦✦ Let cool, then cover and refrigerate until ready to serve.

✦✦ To serve, cut into squares or slices, arrange on a plate, and sprinkle with chives.

PANISSES

PANISSA

– Serves 4 to 6 –

Li *Panissa* is Niçoise for *panisses,* the firm polentalike porridge of chickpea flour left to cool, then cut into strips and fried to a crisp.

Drying the strips of *panisse* in the oven before frying makes the task easier and gives a crisper result.

2½ cups water
Pinch of salt, plus salt to taste
1 teaspoon olive oil
1 cup chickpea flour
Olive oil for frying
Pepper to taste

✦✦ Combine half of the water, salt, and olive oil. Pour half in a saucepan and bring it to a boil. Reduce heat to medium.

✦✦ Stir the remaining water into the chickpea flour and mix well, then slowly stir this mixture into the boiling water, stirring as it cooks until the mixture thickens and boils, about 10 minutes. The plop-plop sounds are distinctive of this thick bubbling mixture. Take care that your hands do not get burnt as each bubble pops.

✦✦ Oil 6 saucers, pour the chickpea mixture into them, and let cool for at least 2 hours or up to 2 days at a cool room temperature.

✦✦ Preheat the oven to 300°F. Cut the chickpea cakes into ½- to 1-inch strips and place on a wire rack in a roasting pan. Bake for about 15 minutes on each side, or until slightly dry and crunchy.

✦✦ In a large, heavy skillet, heat 2 inches of the oil over medium-high heat until it begins to smoke. When a cube of bread dropped into the hot oil fries to a golden crisp it is ready. Fry the strips of *panisse* in batches without crowding the pan until they are golden and crunchy. Using a slotted spoon, transfer to paper towels to drain. Sprinkle with salt and pepper and serve at once.

CANAPÉS "À LA PICASSO"

TOASTS WITH TAPENADE

AND FRESH HERBS

– Serves 4 –

I will always associate these little morsels with the Picasso museum at Antibes. On the terrace once, I noticed masses of herbs growing: tender rosemary, basil, thyme, and *sarriette* (summer savory). So I picked enough to fill my pockets, thrilling as I did so: Perhaps Picasso himself had planted these very herbs, or at least their ancestors.

Of course, I got caught by security. At first

they were quite stern, but then in true Gallic style, smiled and let me off when I waxed lyrical about how delicious these herbs would be with our dinner. They even offered culinary suggestions.

When we began our meal with these little canapés, I reached into my pocket and sprinkled everything with Picasso's herbs!

12 diagonally cut thin slices baguette
½ cup (1 stick) unsalted butter at room
* temperature*
3 garlic cloves, or to taste
3 tablespoons tapenade, or to taste
Fresh sprigs of tiny-leafed basil, and minced
* fresh rosemary, savory, and thyme*

✦✦ Arrange the baguette slices on a serving plate. Mix the butter with the garlic and tapenade, then spread onto the bread. Garnish the top of each canapé with the herbs and serve.

PAPETON D'AUBERGINES

SAVORY EGGPLANT "CAVIAR"

– Serves 4 –

Chopped eggplant spreads are, of course, eaten throughout the Middle East, Balkans, and Mediterranean. This one was inspired by a similar dish at a bustling bistro in Saint-Tropez. The bistro was tucked into one of the little streets down by the old port, and the eggplant was served to look like a flower, plopped in a mound onto the middle of the plate and surrounded by a circle of tomato "petals." It tastes equally good, if less fanciful, heaped onto a plate and accompanied with crisp little toasts.

Preparing the eggplant by two different meth-

ods, then combining them, gives the mixture a complex character and texture: creamy smooth purée of baked eggplant mixed with chunks of browned eggplant, combined with garlic, tomatoes, and olive oil.

4 long eggplants or 3 round ones, halved
* lengthwise*
4 to 6 tablespoons olive oil, or as desired
Salt to taste, plus a pinch of salt
4 garlic cloves
5 fresh or drained canned tomatoes, diced
Sugar to taste (optional)
Dash of balsamic vinegar
Large pinch of herbes de Provence
1 teaspoon minced fresh parsley
Crisp crackers or toasts and tender lettuce
* leaves for serving*

✦✦ Preheat the oven to 375°F.

✦✦ Take half of the eggplants and score the cut side not quite all the way through to the skin.

✦✦ Drizzle with 1 tablespoon of the olive oil, sprinkle with the salt, and arrange on a baking sheet. Bake until the eggplant flesh is lightly browned in spots and the flesh is tender, 30 to 40 minutes. Let cool.

✦✦ Dice the other half of the eggplants. Heat a large skillet or sauté pan over medium-high heat, add 2 tablespoons of the olive oil, and cook the diced eggplant until tender-firm and lightly browned. Remove from heat and season with salt.

✦✦ When the eggplant halves have cooled, remove them from their skins. Mash the tender flesh coarsely with a fork.

✦✦ In a large mortar or a food processor, or using a large chef's knife on a cutting board or a curved chopping knife (mezzaluna) in a wooden bowl, crush the garlic with a generous pinch of salt, then work in the diced tomatoes and the eggplant pulp. Work in the remaining 1 to 3 tablespoons olive oil.

✦✦ Lightly mash the browned eggplant dice, then mix it with the tomato mixture; season with salt, sugar, balsamic vinegar, and herbes de Provence.

✦✦ Serve heaped on a plate, sprinkled with parsley and accompanied with crisp little crackers or toasts, and tender inside lettuce leaves.

RILLETTES D'EPINARDS

AU CITRON

LEMON-SCENTED

SPINACH SPREAD

– Serves 4 –

Rillettes is a soft, spreadable savory meat paste, served in a little crock for spreading, or spread thinly onto a thick slice of sour pain levain. This spinach pâtélike spread has a similar consistency.

Other greens such as chard and arugula give a nice complexity to

Les poivrons

the spinach, but if they are unavailable, simply omit and double the amount of spinach.

1 bunch spinach, cut into ribbons, or
  1 pound frozen spinach
6 or so chard leaves, coarsely chopped
  (reserve the stalks for another purpose)
3 shallots, minced
3 garlic cloves, minced
2 tablespoons butter
Handful of arugula leaves, coarsely
  chopped
Freshly grated nutmeg to taste
2 tablespoons crème fraîche
1 tablespoon minced fresh dill
3 tablespoons minced fresh parsley
⅛ teaspoon grated lemon zest
Juice of ½ lemon, or to taste
Salt and pepper to taste
Thinly sliced pain levain or sour rye coun-
  try bread for serving

✦✦ Blanch the fresh spinach and the chard until just bright green, then rinse with cold water and squeeze dry. Let drain in a colander for a few moments. If using frozen spinach, defrost and squeeze dry (save the liquid for soup or another use).

✦✦ Meanwhile, in a medium 2- to 3-inch-deep sauté pan or skillet over medium heat, sauté the shallots and garlic in the butter until they have softened, then add the arugula, spinach, and chard and cook a few minutes until the greens have absorbed the butter.

✦✦ Remove from heat and stir in the nutmeg, crème fraîche, dill, parsley, lemon zest, and lemon juice. Season with salt and pepper.

✦✦ Serve with thin slices of bread.

BRANDADE AUX LÉGUMES

PURÉE OF BEANS AND POTATOES

WITH OLIVE OIL

– Serves 4 –

This specialty of the Provençal town of Nimes is so evocative of the area that Gaston Doumerue, president of France from 1924 to 1931, said that whenever he ate it, he could hear the crickets chirping in the pine trees near Nimes's historic Magne Tower. Though most commonly prepared with salted cod, a *brandade* of vegetables is also traditional. Here it is prepared with potatoes and white beans; in artichoke season, slices of crisp green artichoke hearts are served alongside to dip into the garlicky spread.

The name *brandade* comes from the Provençal word *brandado,* meaning stirred, since the olive oil and seasonings are vigorously stirred into the vegetable mixture. When haricots verts, those pencil-thin green beans, are in season, I like to serve a mound of them alongside, dressed with a garlic vinaigrette.

In the Luberon, this dish came to my table surrounded by stewed artichokes–*barigoule*–that had been drained of their marinade and had just a whiff of cinnamon about them. "Come back in truffle season," said Madame enthusiastically, "and I give you this dish with grated truffles!"

1 cup cooked white beans (such as lingots, cannellini, or butter beans), drained (reserve the cooking liquid for puréeing the beans)
1 large baking potato, peeled and cut into chunks
1 bay leaf
1 onion, chopped

3 garlic cloves, minced
2 to 3 tablespoons olive oil
Pinch of herbes de Provence
Dash of fresh lemon juice
Salt, black pepper, and cayenne pepper to taste

✦✦ Drain the beans, mash them coarsely, and set them aside.

✦✦ Meanwhile, boil the potato with the bay leaf until the potatoes are tender. Drain, discard the bay leaf, and mash the potatoes.

✦✦ In a medium sauté pan or skillet over medium-low heat, sauté the onion and 2 of the garlic cloves in 1 to 2 tablespoons of the olive oil until softened, about 8 minutes. Add the puréed beans and mashed potato and warm them all together.

✦✦ Remove the mixture from heat and beat in the raw garlic and remaining 1 to 2 tablespoons olive oil; season with lemon juice, salt, black pepper, and cayenne.

✦✦ Serve in a little crock or mounded onto a plate, surrounded by the vegetables as described above.

Poivrons Rouges Farcé au Brandade (Red Peppers Stuffed with Brandade) One afternoon I was served small red peppers filled with *brandade,* served in a puddle of herby vinaigrette. If you have small fleshy red peppers that have lots of flavor and a tiny hit of heat, use them; if not, use ordinary red bell peppers.

Roast and skin the peppers (see page 210). Remove their seeds by cutting a slit into each pepper, but leave them whole with their stem attached. Stuff each pepper with *brandade.* If the peppers are large, cut each one into several wide strips and wrap the strips around a few tablespoons of *brandade* instead of stuffing them.

Arrange each stuffed pepper on a plate alongside a handful of mixed greens, mâche, or watercress, and on a pool of vinaigrette to which you've added a few tablespoons of minced fresh herbs such as basil, rosemary, parsley, chives, and so on.

"Caviar" de Lentilles de Puy

Puy Lentil Salad-Spread

– Serves 4 to 6 –

A mixture of lentils and hard-cooked egg, dressed in an olive oil vinaigrette, is nice to nibble on, piled onto crisp little toasts, along with a glass of a good strong Côtes-du-Rhône or a Cahors.

> *1 recipe warm cooked lentils (see page 209)*
> *1 small onion, finely chopped*
> *1 garlic clove, minced*
> *2 ripe tomatoes, diced*
> *1 tablespoon minced fresh parsley*
> *1 tablespoon minced fresh chervil*
> *1 to 3 tablespoons olive oil, as desired*
> *1 to 2 teaspoons wine vinegar or to taste*
> *Salt and pepper to taste*
> *2 hard-cooked eggs, diced*
> *Toasts (see page 211), for serving*
> *Frisée leaves for garnish*

✦✦ Combine the lentils with the onion, garlic, tomatoes, parsley, and chervil. Season the mixture with the oil, vinegar, salt, and pepper, then add the eggs.

✦✦ Pile onto a small plate and set out with the toasts and a handful of frisée.

Aïoli

Garlic Mayonnaise

– Makes 1 cup –

A good and proper aioli is a thing of beauty: reeking deliciously of garlic, oozing the fragrant richness of olive oil, it can be slathered onto most anything. Known as *le beurre de Provence*, the butter of Provence, for its omnipresent golden richness, it has been eaten in the area for over two thousand years.

In homey bistros from Saint-Tropez to Avignon, Aix to Menton, aioli might be brought to the table in a little pot to munch on while you decide on your meal, spreading the garlicky sauce on bread and raw vegetables, with perhaps a few egg wedges and wisps of herbs alongside.

Sauces made from raw eggs are eaten with great delight and gusto in France. Alas, in the United States, salmonella poisoning has become a problem and any dish that uses raw eggs is too dangerous for me to recommend. (If you have access to organic eggs from salmonella-free chickens, prepare your aioli from the first recipe. If you don't, make your aioli from storebought mayonnaise. Though it is not as rich and flavorful as the original, it is fine for adding to salads or for spreading.)

> *3 to 5 garlic cloves*
> *Large pinch of salt, plus salt to taste*
> *1 egg yolk*
> *¾ to 1 cup olive oil*
> *Fresh lemon juice to taste*
> *Cayenne pepper to taste*

✦✦ Crush the garlic with the pinch of salt in a mortar or food processor until it forms a paste. Add the egg yolk and mix well.

♦♦Slowly add the olive oil, drop by drop at first until it emulsifies, then in a thin steady drip, then a drizzle, until the mixture is thick and a mayonnaise has formed.

♦♦Season with lemon juice, cayenne, and salt. Cover and refrigerate until ready to serve.

AÏOLI À LA MINUTE

QUICK AIOLI

– Makes about ½ cup –

This is not as silky and richly flavored as classic aioli, but it is delightful for salads, sandwiches, and as a spread, and it eliminates the danger of salmonella poisoning.

2 to 3 garlic cloves
Large pinch of salt, plus salt to taste
3 tablespoons olive oil
⅓ cup mayonnaise
Fresh lemon juice to taste
Cayenne pepper to taste

Les pains

♦♦Crush the garlic and pinch of salt together in a mortar or food processor until it forms a paste, then gradually add the olive oil to form a smooth creamy mixture.

♦♦Stir into the mayonnaise and season to taste with lemon, salt, and cayenne. Cover and refrigerate until ready to serve.

TAPENADE

BLACK OLIVE PASTE WITH

HERBES DE PROVENCE

– Makes ½ to ¾ cup –

Pungent purées of black olives, salty and tasting of antiquity, are so evocative a flavor of the Mediterranean that one bite can transport me to Vence or Antibes or Monaco, or anyplace where I have sampled this oh-so-flavorful spread.

It is delicious spread onto buttered bread for open-faced sandwiches (*tartines*), savory pastries, or vegetable omelets, or spooned onto sautéed mushrooms or atop savory white bean casserole, but it is also lovely just set out in a little pot to dip into at will, along with a bowl of crunchy radishes, sweet cherry tomatoes, and pungent green onions, as well as crisp little olive oil–spread toasts.

You can buy tapenade throughout Provence, in delis, markets, and in jars, but it often includes anchovies. To be sure of a purely vegetarian spread, purchase olive paste (*olivada*) or prepare it yourself.

1 cup halved pitted black olives,
preferably strongly flavored ones such as
Nyons, niçoise, or Italian oil-cured olives
2 tablespoons olive oil, or as needed

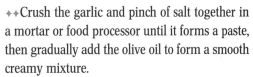

1 garlic clove, minced
1 teaspoon brandy
¼ teaspoon dry mustard
Large pinch of herbes de Provence

✦✦Purée the olives in a blender or food processor and slowly add the olive oil until it forms a spreadable emulsion.

✦✦Continue to purée and add the garlic, brandy, mustard, and herbes de Provence. Cover and refrigerate for up to 2 weeks.

TAPENADE VERTE

GREEN OLIVE AND ALMOND TAPENADE

– Makes ½ to ¾ cup –

The combination of green olives and crunchy almonds is a quintessentially Provençal one, tasting of a summer afternoon as it drifts into evening.

1 cup halved pitted green olives
3 tablespoons almonds, toasted and
   coarsely chopped (see page 211)
1 garlic clove, chopped
2 teaspoons capers, drained and rinsed
½ to 1 teaspoon chopped fresh rosemary
Fresh lemon juice to taste
2 tablespoons olive oil, or as needed

✦✦In a blender or food processor, combine the olives, almonds, garlic, capers, rosemary and lemon juice and purée until chunky.

✦✦Gradually blend in the olive oil until you have a thick, slightly chunky mixture. Cover and refrigerate for up to 1 week.

BEURRE ROQUEFORT

ROQUEFORT BUTTER WITH ARMAGNAC OR BRANDY

– Serves 4 –

Roquefort cheese is a strongly flavored sheep milk cheese, shot through with the blue *penicillum Roqueforti* bacteria that gives the cheese its distinctive taste. True Roquefort is aged in the caves near the southwestern village of Roquefort, where the specific spores are rich and inimitable. Other cheeses, such as bleu de Causses, are made in nearby caves and, though less expensive, are often quite good.

This appealing spread of cheese and butter with a hint of brandy is delicious with crusty bread and raw vegetables. Serve with a vigorous red wine such as a Gigondas or a Châteauneuf-du-Pape.

3 ounces blue cheese, crumbled
3 tablespoons unsalted butter at room
   temperature
1 garlic clove, minced
1 tablespoon Armagnac or brandy
Sliced baguette or toasts (see page 211) for
   serving
Watercress sprigs for garnish

✦✦Combine the blue cheese with the butter, garlic, and Armagnac or brandy and mix it well until it forms a smooth and creamy consistency. Spoon the mixture into little crocks. Cover and refrigerate until ready to serve.

✦✦Remove from the refrigerator 10 to 20 minutes before serving. Serve with baguette slices or toasts, with watercress sprigs as a garnish.

Potages et Soupes
◆◆◆
Soups

In France, soup is a seasonal pot. Whatever is in the garden or the market goes into the pot, its flavors dictated by the region and climate, as well as by whoever is stirring the pot.

Soup is usually served at night; in fact the origin of the English word *supper* is the French *souper,* to eat soup.

It might be rich, served in little portions to begin the meal, or it might be hearty and filling enough to be your entire meal. Soup can be light, healthy potions of simmered vegetables and herbs, or rich bowls thickened with egg yolks, cream, and butter.

The term *soupe* refers to all sorts of soups, whether light and lithe or hearty and sustaining. *Potage* refers to a thick robust soup, either puréed or served half puréed, half chunky. *Potages* usually have lots of potatoes, often leeks, lentils, root vegetables, beans, and quite often a generous enrichment of cream.

Les champignons

PURÉE D'ARTICHAUTS

PURÉED ARTICHOKE SOUP

WITH GARLIC

– Serves 4 –

"Madame l'Artichaut," as the artichoke seller in Nice's market is nicknamed, smiled as she stuffed a huge bouquet of artichokes on their stems into my mesh bag. "Today," she said, "I am making soup! It is a nice thing to do with the little artichokes, *n'est-ce pas?*" And so it is: a smooth purée of artichoke, heady with garlic, and enriched at the end with a nubbin of butter.

The flavor chemicals in artichokes interact harshly with the subtleties of wine, but I think a light little summery wine such as a chilled Provençal white, say a Cassis, would be fine with this soup.

6 artichoke hearts (see page 210), or 1 package thawed frozen artichoke hearts
3 garlic cloves, coarsely chopped
3 tablespoons unsalted butter
1 baking potato, peeled and diced
4 cups vegetable stock (pages 201–202)
Salt and pepper to taste

✦✦In a large, heavy saucepan over medium heat, lightly sauté the artichoke hearts with the garlic in 1½ tablespoons of the butter; do not brown, just let them turn golden.

✦✦Add the potato and stock, bring to a boil, then lower the heat. Cover the pan and simmer until the artichokes and potatoes are both tender, about 10 minutes.

✦✦In a blender or food processor, purée the vegetables with just enough of their liquid to achieve a smooth consistency, then return the purée to the pan and stir to combine well. Season with salt and pepper, then reheat. Serve right away, each bowl topped with a little of the remaining 1½ tablespoons butter to enrich the soup.

Soupe d'Artichauts aux Noisettes **(Artichoke Soup with Hazelnuts)** Instead of sautéing the garlic, artichokes, and potatoes, simmer them in the stock. When serving, substitute a sprinkling of hazelnut oil and coarsely chopped hazelnuts for the butter.

SOUPE AU FENOUIL

FENNEL BISQUE WITH ZUCCHINI

AND LEEKS

– Serves 4 –

This creamy, light fennel-scented purée of zucchini and leeks is the essence of the Côte d'Azur: refined flavor redolent of the local fennel that grows on the hillsides, thickened with a little egg yolk and olive oil rather than the cream you'd find elsewhere.

½ fennel bulb, including the tough outer leaves, thinly sliced or chopped
2 leeks, white part only, thinly sliced
1 zucchini, diced
4 to 5 garlic cloves, lightly crushed
5 tablespoons olive oil
½ teaspoon fennel seeds
6 cups vegetable stock (pages 201–202)
2 egg yolks
Salt and pepper to taste
1 to 2 tablespoons fennel leaves for garnish

✦✦Place the fennel bulb, leek, zucchini, and garlic in a saucepan with 3 tablespoons of the olive oil. Cover and cook the vegetables over medium-low heat, letting them simmer gently in the olive oil until softened but not brown, 15 to 20 minutes.

✦✦Add the fennel seeds and stock, increase the heat to medium, and cook for 10 to 15 minutes. The soup should smell splendid at this point.

✦✦Beat the egg yolks with the remaining 2 tablespoons olive oil.

✦✦Put the solids from the soup into a blender or food processor with just enough of the liquid to purée. Whirl until smooth.

✦✦Stir several tablespoons of the hot soup into the egg yolk mixture, then add this to the blender or processor with the puréed vegetable soup. Whirl again until smooth, then return to saucepan with the drained liquid.

✦✦Heat the mixture over medium-low heat until it is warmed through and slightly steaming. Stir the soup as it heats, taking care that the egg yolks don't string or curdle. Season with salt and pepper.

✦✦The yolks should thicken the soup ever so slightly. Serve right away, garnished with a few feathery leaves of fresh fennel.

SOUPE AUX CHOUX
DE BRUXELLES
AU PIMENT D'ESPELETTE
BASQUE CHILI-SCENTED
BRUSSELS SPROUTS SOUP

– *Serves 4 to 6* –

Sprinkling chervil on this mildly spicy soup adds a fresh herbal flourish. Though I've tried it with other herbs, such as cilantro and/or parsley, chervil adds just the right flavor and herbal but unobtrusive taste.

This Basque country soup is even better made a day or two ahead of time, then reheated. Serve with chunks of bread for dunking; if you share my delight in doing so, this is a good soup to *faire chabrot,* that is, to tip a little red wine into your soup bowl.

A southwestern Madiran or a sturdy Bergerac wine would be a nice accompaniment, or even a hearty Morgon.

> *1 onion, chopped*
> *2 carrots, peeled and diced*
> *2 celery stalks, chopped*
> *2 tablespoons olive oil*
> *2 tablespoons minced fresh parsley*
> *2 pounds Brussels sprouts, coarsely chopped*
> *5 garlic cloves, minced*
> *1 tablespoon paprika*
> *1 to 3 teaspoons mild ground French chili*
> *   such as piment d'Espelette or nura (or*
> *   ground New Mexico, California, ancho,*
> *   negro, or guajillo chili)*
> *3 tablespoons tomato paste*
> *2 cups dry red wine*
> *6 cups vegetable stock (pages 201–202)*
> *Pinch of dried thyme or ¼ to ½ teaspoon*
> *   minced fresh thyme*
> *Salt and pepper to taste*
> *3 to 4 tablespoons minced fresh chervil*

✦✦In a large saucepan over medium heat, lightly sauté the onion, carrots and celery in the olive oil until softened, about 5 minutes. Stir in the parsley, Brussels sprouts, and half the garlic and cook a few minutes longer.

✦✦Sprinkle in the paprika and ground chili, stir a few moments to cook out the rawness of the spices and bring out their flavor, then stir in the remaining garlic, tomato paste, wine, and stock. Bring to a boil, then reduce heat and simmer, covered, for 15 to 20 minutes, or until the Brussels sprouts are cooked through and the soup is flavorful.

✦✦Season with thyme, salt, and pepper, and serve hot, each bowlful garnished with a sprinkling of chervil.

Potage Paysanne (Country Soup) Add about ½ cup cooked barley; ½ cup cooked pink beans such as cranberry, Borlotti, or pinto; and ½ cup large white beans such as lingots or butter beans. Simmer for 15 to 20 minutes to meld the flavors.

POTAGE AUX CHAMPIGNONS

MUSHROOM SOUP

– Serves 4 –

Slices of meaty, earthy mushrooms awash in a light creamy broth are sprinkled with chopped chives at the last minute. You can use any combination of mushrooms you like: chanterelles, mousserons, morels, oyster mushrooms, trompettes de la mort, morels, and so forth. Be sure to choose fresh rather than dried mushrooms for this soup, as you want a delicate, rather than pungent flavor.

3 ounces shiitakes, stemmed, or oyster
*   mushrooms*
3 ounces cultivated white mushrooms
3 ounces other mushrooms of choice
3 tablespoons butter

Le chou.

1 small red onion, finely chopped, or
*   5 shallots, minced*
3 garlic cloves, minced
Salt and pepper to taste
Freshly grated nutmeg to taste
½ to 1 teaspoon fresh lemon juice
2 to 3 tablespoons flour
4 cups vegetable stock (pages 201–202)
1 bay leaf
⅔ cup heavy cream
4 to 5 tablespoons minced fresh chives

✦✦Slice all of the mushrooms about ¼ inch thick, then sauté them in the butter in a large, heavy sauté pan or skillet over medium-high heat along with the onion and garlic until browned in spots. Sprinkle with salt, pepper, nutmeg, and lemon juice and cook a few moments more.

✦✦Transfer the mushrooms to a large saucepan. Deglaze the pan with a little water to enrich your soup. Sprinkle the mushrooms with the flour and cook over medium heat, stirring, for several minutes.

✦✦Add the stock, liquid from the pan, and bay leaf, stir well, and cook until the soup is richly flavored and slightly thickened, about 15 to 20 minutes. Remove and discard the bay leaf.

✦✦Stir in the cream and heat through. Taste and adjust the seasoning and serve sprinkled with chives.

SOUPE D'ASPERGES
DU LANGUEDOC

ASPARAGUS AND TOMATO SOUP
WITH BASIL

– Serves 4 to 6 –

Every morning in our little village tiny trucks would come barreling into the main square, screech to a stop, then open their back doors and display their vegetables for sale. One week last spring, it was asparagus, and in the afternoons after "Monsieur Asperge's" visit, the local bistro offered this basil-scented soup.

Try a Côtes-du-Rhône with it.

¾ cup pastina or rice-shaped pasta
4 garlic cloves, coarsely chopped
3 tablespoons olive oil
½ cup dry white wine
1 cup diced fresh or canned tomatoes
1 bunch asparagus, tough ends broken off,
*   cut into bite-sized pieces*
4 cups vegetable stock (pages 201–202)
Salt and pepper to taste
3 tablespoons shredded fresh basil for
*   garnish*
Grated Parmesan cheese for sprinkling

✦✦Cook the pasta in salted boiling water until al dente; drain well and set it aside.
✦✦In a large saucepan over medium heat, sauté half of the garlic in the olive oil until just golden, only a moment or two, then pour in the wine

and bring to a boil. Cook to reduce it to a flavorful essence, then add the tomatoes, asparagus, and stock. Bring to a boil, then reduce heat and simmer until the asparagus is crisp-tender, about 5 to 10 minutes. Season the soup with salt and pepper, add the remaining garlic and the pasta, then ladle it into bowls and serve with a sprinkling of basil and Parmesan cheese.

SOUPE AUX ASPERGES
ET RAVIOLES

GOAT CHEESE RAVIOLI
IN ASPARAGUS BROTH

– Serves 4 to 6 –

Ravioles are little ½- to ¾-inch-square cheese-filled pasta, beloved from the Savoy through Provence–and these days, in Paris, too, where they often float in a light, clear broth. When I prepare them at home, I make large, plump filled pasta. It is easier, true, and perhaps I am a bit lazy, but they are pleasingly generous this way and delicious, too.

In this soup the *ravioles* are filled with delicate goat cheese, and the broth is filled with asparagus.

3 ounces fresh white goat cheese, crumbled
2 to 3 tablespoons freshly grated Parmesan
*   cheese*
½ cup (2 ounces) shredded Comté,
*   Beaufort, or Gruyère cheese*
2 tablespoons minced fresh chives or
*   ½ teaspoon minced fresh thyme*
1 egg, lightly beaten
4 garlic cloves, minced

Salt and pepper to taste

16 to 20 wonton wrappers or 10 to 12
ounces thin pasta, cut into 3-inch
squares

Flour for dusting

5 shallots, minced

1 tablespoon olive oil

1 cup dry white wine

5 cups vegetable stock (pages 201–202)

10 to 15 asparagus spears, cut into bite-
sized pieces

Grated Parmesan or pecorino cheese for
sprinkling

2 tablespoons minced fresh herbs: chives,
basil, marjoram, parsley, rosemary, or as
desired

✦✦ To make the *ravioles:* Mix the goat cheese with grated and shredded cheese, chives or thyme, egg, and half the garlic. Season with salt and pepper.

✦✦ Place 1 or 2 tablespoons of the cheese mixture in the center of a wonton wrapper or pasta square, then wet the edges with a pastry brush dipped in water. Top with a second wrapper or square and press the edges together to seal. Dust a large plate or flat pan with flour, then place each filled pasta on this to dry while you finish filling the rest.

✦✦ In a large saucepan over medium-low heat, lightly sauté the shallots and the remaining garlic in the olive oil until softened, then pour in the wine and cook a few moments to evaporate the alcohol. Add the stock and asparagus, bring to a boil, then reduce the heat and simmer for about 4 to 5 minutes, or until asparagus is just crisp-tender.

✦✦ Meanwhile, cook the *ravioles* in salted boiling water until just tender, about 3 to 4 minutes. Drain gently.

✦✦ Serve 3 or 4 of the *ravioles* in a ladleful of the hot asparagus broth in a shallow soup bowl, each portion sprinkled with grated cheese and herbs.

SOUPE AUX GAUDES

CREAMY ONION

AND CORNMEAL PURÉE

– Serves 4 to 6 –

This Burgundian specialty can sometimes be found in the bistros of that area. At one time the hardworking laborers who spooned up the hearty filling soups of cornmeal were called *gaudes,* or "yellow belts," for the golden pottage with which they filled their stomachs.

Gascony has similar soups and dishes, rich with this New World grain.

2 onions, thinly sliced

1 tablespoon butter

½ cup polenta

5 cups vegetable stock (pages 201–202)

½ cup heavy cream

Salt, black and white pepper, and cayenne
or Tabasco to taste

1 to 2 tablespoons minced fresh chives

✦✦ In a large saucepan over medium-low heat, sauté the onions in the butter until soft and golden, about 10 to 15 minutes. Meanwhile, combine the polenta with half the vegetable stock.

✦✦ Stir the polenta mixture and the remaining vegetable stock into the onions. Cook over medium-low heat, stirring occasionally, until the polenta has thickened the soup, about 30 minutes, though this will vary wildly depending on what sort of cornmeal you use.

◆◆In a blender or food processor, purée the soup, then return it to the pot. Stir in the cream, season with salt, pepper, and cayenne or Tabasco and heat through.

◆◆Serve hot, sprinkled with chives.

GRATINÉE DES HALLES

ONION SOUP WITH GRATINÉED CHEESE TOPPING

– Serves 6 –

This hefty cheese-topped soup is famous from the days when it warmed the souls of traders in the Paris central market, Les Halles. The market is gone, but many bistros remain, and a good onion soup can be found throughout Paris, especially in winter.

Soupe à l'oignon is also known as *gratinée lyonnaise,* a favorite of bistros in that onion-loving city, where it was traditionally served last rather than first, to fill up any still-hungry workers.

Adding a tot of red wine at the table is a southwestern custom called *faire chabrot.* I've been told it is a somewhat déclassé thing to do, something you might apologize for in polite company, but which I cannot resist. Even though it lowers the temperature of the soup, to my mind it makes it even more delicious, and I always find myself tipping my glass over in the direction of my soup bowl.

2½ pounds onions, thinly sliced
3 tablespoons vegetable oil
Salt and pepper to taste

A pinch of sugar
8 cups vegetable stock (pages 201–202)
6 thick slices country bread, toasted or stale
3 cups (12 ounces) shredded Gruyère or
*   mixed Parmesan and Gruyère*
½ cup dry red wine

◆◆In a large, heavy pot, preferably of enameled cast iron, slowly and gently cook the onions in the oil over low heat until lightly golden and meltingly soft, 30 to 40 minutes. Season the onions with salt, pepper, and sugar as they cook; this will help the caramelization. Pour in the stock and bring to a boil. Reduce heat and simmer until richly flavored, 30 to 40 minutes.

◆◆Preheat the broiler. Ladle the soup into 6 deep ovenproof soup bowls or crocks, then top each with a slice of toasted or stale bread and sprinkle with the shredded cheese.

◆◆Broil until the cheese melts and lightly browns, 3 to 5 minutes. Serve at once while the cheese is sizzling hot, and let each person spill a few tablespoons of red wine into his or her soup underneath the cheese-topped *croûte.*

VARIATIONS

A traditional cheese topping in the southwest is a mixture of half Roquefort and half Gruyère spread on the bread.

Another traditional enrichment: Beat an egg yolk and mix it with 1 tablespoon of Cognac and 1 tablespoon of port or Madeira, then "lighten" it with a ladle of hot soup. Pour a little of this into each bowlful by lifting the cheese-topped *croûtes* and slipping the alcoholic mixture underneath.

SOUPE GLACÉE AUX TOMATES ET CITRUS

ICED TOMATO SOUP WITH LIME AND LEMON, SCENTED WITH ROSEMARY

– Serves 4 –

This essence of tomato is sublimely refreshing. In Provence you might find it served in a little bistro set on a stone terrace next to a pool surrounded by fruit trees, but it is equally good, or almost so, eaten in your own summer kitchen.

Since this is the sort of food that depends on the quality of ingredients, you'll probably need to play around with the seasonings somewhat: a pinch more sugar if the tomatoes are acidic, more citrus juice if the mixture is summer-sweet. The last-minute enrichment of olive oil and fresh rosemary is strikingly, inspiringly good.

> 2 pounds ripe tomatoes, diced
> 1 small onion, chopped
> 2 garlic cloves, minced
> ½ to 2 teaspoons sugar
> Pinch of herbes de Provence
> 1½ cups tomato juice
> Juice of ½ to 1 lemon
> Juice of ½ to 1 lime
> Salt, black pepper, and cayenne or Tabasco
>   to taste
> 1½ tablespoons olive oil for garnish
> 1 to 2 teaspoons minced fresh rosemary

♦♦In a blender or food processor, purée the tomatoes with the onion and garlic, then stir in the sugar, herbes de Provence, tomato juice, and citrus juices. Season with salt, pepper, and cayenne or Tabasco. Taste and adjust the seasoning. Since the soup is to be served cold, be sure you add enough salt.

♦♦Cover and refrigerate for at least 2 hours.

♦♦The soup will separate, with solids forming at the top. Stir before serving, then ladle into bowls. Drizzle each with a little olive oil, sprinkle with rosemary, and serve.

SOUPE AUX CHOUX ET ROQUEFORT

CABBAGE SOUP WITH ROQUEFORT

– Serves 4 –

This rustic soup is made from the local ingredients of the Auvergne region: cabbage, Roquefort cheese, and garlic. It is eaten in various guises throughout the region–sometimes with white beans, potatoes, or rye bread (though usually it is not vegetarian).

This version is sleek and flavorful, pared down to the main ingredients of cabbage, aromatics, and Roquefort cheese. It is adapted from a bowl I spooned up in a country bistro one freezing night, accompanied with a bottle of Gigondas and followed by a warming vegetable cassoulet.

> ¼ baguette or country loaf such as pain
>   levain, cut into ½- to ¾-inch slices
> 1 onion, chopped
> 1 carrot, peeled and diced
> 1 celery stalk, diced
> 2 tablespoons butter
> ½ cabbage, thinly sliced
> 1 tablespoon flour

4 cups vegetable stock (pages 201–202)

3 garlic cloves, sliced or slivered

3 tablespoons heavy cream

3 ounces Roquefort or other strong blue
    cheese, crumbled

Coarsely ground black pepper and salt
    to taste

✦✦Preheat the oven to 375°F. Bake the bread until golden brown on both sides, 20 to 30 minutes. Set aside.

✦✦In a large, heavy saucepan over medium heat, lightly cook the onion, carrot, and celery in the butter until the mixture is softened and golden, about 8 to 10 minutes. Add the cabbage, cover, and cook for 10 to 15 minutes longer, or until softened.

✦✦Sprinkle the vegetables with the flour, stir well, and cook a few minutes longer, then stir in the stock. Bring to a boil, then reduce heat and cook for 30 minutes.

✦✦Add the garlic and cook another 10 minutes. Stir in the cream and Roquefort; season with pepper and, if needed, salt. Serve right away in bowls, each with a slice or two of the toasted bread.

PURÉE OF CELERY, CELERY LEAVES, AND CELERY ROOT

– Serves 4 to 6 –

Celery is adored in France, often served as a vegetable and not just an ingredient for soups or sauces. The entire plant is eaten, each part having been developed for its own distinctive celery flavor and texture: the root, the stalks, and the herby leaves.

1 bunch celery, diced, including the leaves

½ celery root, peeled and diced

1 onion, chopped

3 tablespoons butter

2 tablespoons flour

4 cups vegetable stock (pages 201–202)

1 to 2 cups milk

Minced fresh tarragon or chervil to taste,
    or ¼ to ½ teaspoon dried tarragon

Salt and pepper to taste

✦✦Lightly sauté the celery, celery root, and onion in 2 tablespoons of the butter in a heavy casserole or saucepan over medium heat. After about 15 to 20 minutes, when the vegetables are tender, sprinkle in the flour and cook for 3 to 5 minutes, stirring.

✦✦Stir in the stock, then cover and bring to a boil; reduce heat and simmer for 15 minutes, or until the vegetables are tender.

✦✦Purée the vegetables, in small batches, in a blender or food processor with the milk, adding just enough of the cooking liquid to create a smooth consistency. Return the mixture to the saucepan with the hot soup and heat through, stirring to encourage the foam to subside.

✦✦Add the tarragon, salt, and pepper.

Le jardinier

♦♦When hot and steamy, ladle the soup into bowls, swirling each bowlful with a little of the remaining 1 tablespoon butter.

SOUPE AUX LÉGUMES VERTS ET SON BEURRE À L'AIL

PURÉE OF GREEN VEGETABLE SOUP WITH GARLIC BUTTER

– Serves 6 to 8 –

This is my own version of a home and bistro classic throughout the Pas de Calais and Picardy–though the traditional butter enrichment is flavored with only parsley and chives, I have added a handsome amount of garlic to make it deliciously memorable.

Be sure not to overcook this green vegetable purée; its charm lies in its verdant freshness.

4 to 5 garlic cloves, minced
3 tablespoons unsalted butter at room temperature
8 to 10 shallots, minced
1 celery stalk, including leaves, chopped
1 tablespoon olive oil
8 cups vegetable stock (pages 201–202)
1 large baking potato, peeled and diced
1 large zucchini, diced
1 cup frozen or fresh peas
3 cups (about 1 large bunch) raw spinach leaves, coarsely chopped, or one 10-ounce package frozen spinach, chopped (reserve the liquid)
½ cup sugar snap peas

1 teaspoon minced fresh rosemary, or to taste
Salt and pepper to taste

♦♦Make the garlic butter by combining half the garlic with the butter. Set aside.

♦♦In a large saucepan over medium heat, sauté the shallots, celery, and remaining garlic in the olive oil until they are softened, about 5 minutes. Add the stock, potato, and zucchini. Bring to a boil and cook over high heat for about 10 minutes, or until the potato is tender.

♦♦Add the peas, spinach, and sugar snap peas to the pan and heat together.

♦♦Purée the vegetables in a blender or food processor with just enough of the cooking liquid to achieve a smooth consistency. Season with the rosemary, salt, and pepper.

♦♦Return to the saucepan with the rest of the cooking liquid and spinach juice and reheat just until very hot; you do not want to overcook this vibrant green soup.

♦♦Pour into bowls and add a little garlic butter to each. Serve right away.

AÏGO BOUIDO

GARLIC SOUP WITH GARLIC CROUTONS AND EDIBLE BLOSSOMS

– Serves 4 to 6 –

A good garlic soup can have anything in it–tomatoes, rice, pasta, cheese, bread, herbs–as long as nothing obscures the garlic's delicious character. This garlic soup is as good as it gets, with long-simmered whole garlic cloves accented by garlicky croutons, and a surprise garnish of edible flower petals. Either a chilled rosé or a young Cahors would be a good wine choice.

CROUTONS

4 to 6 slices stale country bread, cut into
    bite-sized cubes
1 tablespoon olive oil
Salt and pepper to taste
3 garlic cloves, finely minced

SOUP

Peeled whole cloves from 1 head garlic
4 cups vegetable stock (pages 201–202)
1 bay leaf
Several pinches of minced fresh thyme
1 egg yolk
3 to 4 tablespoons freshly grated mixed
    cheeses such as Gruyère, Parmesan,
    Asiago, Fontina, and pecorino
½ cup dry white wine
Salt, pepper, and cayenne pepper to taste
Edible flower petals: chives, marigolds,
    nasturtiums or other unsprayed non-
    toxic flowers

✦✦Preheat the oven to 375°F. To make the croutons: Toss the bread with the olive oil and bake on a baking sheet until crispy and golden, then turn and bake the second side, a total of about 30 minutes, depending on how stale the bread is. Toss with the salt, pepper, and minced garlic. Set aside.

✦✦To make the soup: Combine the whole garlic cloves in a saucepan with the stock, bay leaf, and thyme. Bring to a boil, then reduce heat and simmer until the garlic is very tender.

✦✦Beat the egg yolk and stir together with the

cheese and wine, then whisk this mixture into the pan of hot soup and heat, stirring so as not to curdle the yolk. Add the salt, pepper and cayenne. Ladle into soup bowls and garnish with lots of garlic croutons and bits of garlic from the baking sheet, as well as a sprinkling of flower petals.

Soupe à l'Ail, Œuf Poché (*Garlic Soup with Poached Egg, Saffron, and Nasturtium Confetti*) Prepare the garlic croutons using sliced baguettes instead of bite-sized pieces of bread and sprinkle them well with Parmesan cheese along with the garlic. Do not add the egg yolk, cheese, and wine to the soup. Poach 4 eggs.

Serve the soup ladled into each bowl and add a few strands of saffron to each one. Place a garlic crouton in the soup, top with a poached egg, and dust generously with Parmesan cheese. Garnish with petals, letting some rest on the egg, others fall into the soup.

Serve right away.

GARLIC SOUP

Garlic soup is the French (and Spanish) equivalent to Jewish penicillin: It's good for whatever ails you, from a nasty flu to a broken heart. In Provence it is eaten the day after overindulging. They say it will save your life (*l'aïgo bouido sauvo la vido*); some say it will raise the dead. Others attribute aphrodisiacal powers to it. In Bordeaux, it is served to newlyweds on their wedding night.

ROASTED EGGPLANT SOUP WITH

SPICY RED PEPPER PURÉE

– Serves 4 –

This flavor-filled soup tastes of the south, with its roasted eggplant, sweet fennel, and peppery rouille. A chilled, slightly fruity rosé balances nicely with the spiciness of the red pepper purée.

ROUILLE

*2 red bell peppers, roasted, peeled, and
    diced (see page 210)*
1 to 3 garlic cloves, minced
½ teaspoon harissa, or to taste
Salt and fresh lemon juice to taste

SOUP

1 tablespoon olive oil
*1 eggplant, cut into bite-sized pieces or
    julienned*
1 onion, cut into quarters
5 garlic cloves
*1 fennel bulb, cut into bite-sized pieces or
    julienned*
3 ripe tomatoes, halved crosswise
2 cups dry white wine
6 cups vegetable stock (pages 201–202)
Salt and pepper to taste
Pinch of herbes de Provence

✦✦To make the rouille: In a blender or food processor, purée all the ingredients to a smooth mixture. Set aside.

✦✦To make the soup: In a large, heavy sauté pan or skillet over high heat, heat the olive oil. Add the eggplant, onion, garlic, fennel, and tomatoes to the pan and cook, without stirring, until slightly charred, about 15 to 20 minutes. Turn and cook for 5 to 10 minutes, without stirring, or until they are sticky, slightly charred, whole yet falling apart a little. (This is important, especially for the tomatoes, as they can easily turn to sauce during cooking.) Reduce heat and cook the vegetables 10 to 15 minutes, or until they are very tender.

✦✦In a large saucepan, heat the wine and the stock, then add the roasted vegetables. Bring to a boil, then reduce heat and simmer until the soup is fragrant and the alcohol of the wine has burned off, leaving behind only a whiff of fragrance.

✦✦Purée the vegetables in a blender or food processor with just enough of the cooking liquid to make a smooth purée. Return to the liquid in the pan and reheat to boiling. Remove from heat and add the salt, pepper, and herbes de Provence.

✦✦Ladle into bowls, drizzle each with some rouille, then serve right away.

PURÉED CAULIFLOWER SOUP

WITH CHERVIL, TARRAGON,

AND CHIVES

– Serves 4 –

The white flesh of the cauliflower is cooked to a tender state, then whirled to a smooth purée, its earthy flavor brightened by a handful of fragrant herbs: chervil, tarragon, and chives.

A chilled Riesling would be good with this northern soup.

1 onion, chopped
2 celery stalks, chopped
3 tablespoons butter
1 head cauliflower, broken into florets
2 tablespoons flour
4 cups vegetable stock (pages 201–202)
1 cup milk
3 to 4 tablespoons minced fresh chervil
Salt and pepper to taste
2 to 3 tablespoons minced fresh tarragon
1 to 2 tablespoons minced fresh chives

✦✦In a large saucepan over medium-low heat, lightly sauté the onion and celery in 1 tablespoon of the butter until softened and lightly golden, about 8 to 10 minutes. Add the cauliflower and stir until lightly colored, about 5 to 8 minutes.

✦✦Sprinkle in the flour, then cook and stir the mixture for 5 to 10 minutes, until the flour is cooked through.

✦✦Stir in the stock, then bring it to a boil. Reduce heat and gently simmer, covered, until the cauliflower and celery are tender, about 20 minutes.

✦✦In a blender, purée the solids with just enough of the cooking liquid to make a smooth consistency, then add 1 tablespoon of the chervil and purée again.

✦✦Return to the pan, stir in the milk, and season with salt and pepper.

✦✦When ready to serve, heat until bubbles form around the edge of the soup. Ladle it into bowls, and garnish each with ½ tablespoon of the remaining butter, the remaining chervil, and the tarragon and chives.

Potage Crécy (Carrot Soup) A lovely chervil-scented purée of carrots can be made using the above recipe. Substitute 2 carrots for the cauliflower and 1 potato for the celery. Omit the flour, and proceed as above.

SOUPE DE CAROTTES ET

TOMATES AU CUMIN

CUMIN-SCENTED CARROT

AND TOMATO SOUP

– Serves 4 –

This soup is at its best when made a little ahead of time, either earlier in the day or the day before; thus it is excellent for entertaining.
Serve a carafe of Beaujolais with this soup.

½ onion, chopped
3 carrots, peeled and thinly sliced
1 tablespoon butter or olive oil
Pinch of sugar
¼ teaspoon cumin seeds
5 garlic cloves, sliced
½ to ¾ cup dry white wine
1 cup diced fresh or canned tomatoes
4 cups vegetable stock (pages 201–202)
Pinch of dried thyme or herbes de Provence
Salt and pepper to taste

✦✦In a large, heavy saucepan over medium-low heat, lightly sauté the onion and carrots in the butter or olive oil with the sugar and cumin seeds until the vegetables are softened and lightly golden in places, about 5 to 10 minutes. Add the garlic, then pour in the wine and cook over high heat until it has reduced by at least half.

♦♦Add the tomatoes, stock, thyme or herbes de Provence, salt, and pepper, and cook over medium-high heat until the carrots are tender and the soup is well flavored.

♦♦Taste for seasoning, then serve hot.

SOUPE AU PISTOU

VEGETABLE SOUP OF PROVENCE WITH FRAGRANT GARLIC-BASIL PURÉE

– Serves 6 to 8 –

S*oupe au pistou* is more than a soup–it is a dish that exudes the very essence of the sun-drenched town of Nice. It is at once history and tradition–Nice having a shared past with nearby basil-loving Liguria–yet as contemporary a dish as you might wish for.

Most bistros in Nice–from the funkiest to the most elegant–serve bowls of fragrant *soupe au pistou*, especially when the tiny white beans known as cocos are fresh. Fresh cranberry beans are good in their place, and when there are no fresh shell beans at all, use dried white beans such as lingots (or the more easily available white kidney beans or Italian cannellini).

Traditionally, *soupe au pistou* is made with water so that the flavors of the vegetables shine through. This only works with consummately flavorful vegetables at their peak of ripeness; I find that, as with most soups, a little stock helps along the way.

Drink a nice sturdy red wine with this; I often find myself tipping a little into my soup bowl.

½ cup dried white beans, or 1 cup fresh
*   or canned shell beans*
1 fresh thyme sprig
1 bay leaf
8 to 10 cups water or vegetable stock
*   (pages 201–202), or a mixture*
2 tablespoons extra-virgin olive oil
2 leeks, including the tender green parts,
*   chopped or thinly sliced*
1½ to 2 carrots, diced
1 celery stalk, chopped
1 zucchini, cut into ½-inch pieces

La boulangerie

1 yellow crookneck squash or golden
    zucchini, cut into ½-inch pieces
½ pound green beans, cut into ½-inch
    pieces
½ cup fresh or frozen peas
1 to 2 small waxy potatoes, peeled and cut
    into ½-inch pieces
¼ cabbage, thinly sliced
6 to 8 ripe tomatoes, diced
2 tablespoons minced fresh parsley
½ to ¾ cup small elbow macaroni
Pistou (pages 208–209)
Grated Parmesan or pecorino cheese for
    serving

♦♦ If using dried beans, soak them overnight and cook them (page 209), adding the thyme sprig and bay leaf to the cooking beans. Drain and discard the thyme and bay leaf. Set the cooked beans aside. If using canned beans, rinse and drain them. Add the thyme and bay leaf to the water and/or stock.

♦♦ In a large saucepan, combine the water or stock with the olive oil, all of the vegetables, and the parsley. Bring to a boil, then simmer for 15 to 20 minutes. Add the macaroni and continue to simmer the soup until the macaroni is cooked through, 15 to 20 minutes.

♦♦ Ladle the soup into a tureen or individual bowls. Top with a generous dollop of pistou and either serve as is, or stir it in. Offer grated cheese alongside.

Soupe au Pistou Toute Verte (All-Green Pistou Soup) Prepare the above soup and include only green and white vegetables: Omit the carrots, yellow squash, and tomatoes and include a handful of chopped spinach.

SOUPE AUX LÉGUMES

VEGETABLE PURÉE

OF THE SEASON

– Serves 4 –

In most any bistro and home kitchen throughout France the daily *soupe aux légumes* is a purée of fresh vegetables, often enriched with leftover vegetables from yesterday's dinner table. Whatever is in season finds its way into this soup: young peas in spring, zucchini in summer, pumpkin and leafy greens in the autumn, earthy roots in winter.

Many versions thicken the soup with only potato, but adding cooked beans gives the soup substantial body, while a handful of pine nuts gives added richness. Adding no butter, oils or fats makes this a true *potage de santé,* "healthy soup."

½ cup drained cooked white beans, chick-
    peas, or split peas
1 leek, diced (include the tender green part
    of the leek)
1 small turnip or ¼ rutabaga, peeled and
    diced
½ carrot, peeled and diced
1 potato, peeled and diced
½ zucchini, diced, or equal amount of
    other seasonal green vegetable
2 stalks celery, diced
2 tablespoons pine nuts
3 garlic cloves, coarsely chopped
2 bay leaves
1 fresh rosemary sprig (optional)
6 cups vegetable stock (pages 201–202)

✦✦In a large saucepan, combine all the ingredients and bring to a boil. Reduce heat and simmer until the vegetables are tender, about 30 minutes.

✦✦Remove and discard the bay leaves and rosemary sprig, then purée the soup, leaving some of the vegetables in chunks. Taste and adjust the seasoning and serve.

SOUPE AUX POIS VERTS SECHES

PURÉE OF GREEN SPLIT PEA

SOUP WITH CARROTS

AND FRESH MARJORAM

– Serves 4 to 6 –

P*ain levain* is, happily, stylish these days in Paris. Delicious it is, too: slightly sour and tasting of yeast and whole wheat, with a whiff of the wood-burning oven it baked in.

Leftovers make wonderful croutons, especially for rustic soups such as this purée of split peas and carrots. The sweet freshness of the marjoram gives the soup its unique and fresh character.

1½ cups cubed whole-wheat country bread

2 tablespoons vegetable oil

2 garlic cloves, minced

2 carrots, peeled and diced

2 celery stalks, including leaves, diced

5 shallots, minced, or 1 onion, chopped

2 tablespoons butter

2 cups water

½ cup green split peas

4 cups vegetable stock (pages 201–202)

Salt, pepper, and cayenne pepper or
Tabasco to taste

1 to 2 tablespoons minced fresh marjoram

✦✦Preheat the oven to 375°F. Toss the bread cubes with the vegetable oil and arrange them in a single layer on a baking sheet. Bake or lightly toast for 10 to 15 minutes on each side, or until the bread cubes are golden brown and crisp. Toss with chopped garlic and set aside.

✦✦In a large, heavy saucepan over medium-low heat, lightly sauté half the carrots and half the celery with the shallots or onion in the butter until softened. Add the water and split peas.

✦✦Bring to a boil, then reduce heat and simmer until the peas are very tender and creamy, adding more water as needed to keep the peas from scorching.

✦✦Purée in a blender or food processor, then return to the pan with the remaining carrots and celery, and the stock. (For a more subtle, elegant texture, strain the soup at this point.)

✦✦Bring to a boil, then reduce heat and simmer until the vegetables are cooked through. If the soup is too thick, add more stock.

✦✦Season with salt, pepper, and cayenne or Tabasco, then stir in the marjoram (see Note) and serve.

NOTE For a more subtle flavor, add the fresh marjoram when you purée the soup.

SUPPA D'ERBIGIE

CORSICAN SOUP OF

TOMATOES, BEANS, POTATOES,

AND LOTS OF FRESH HERBS

– Serves 4 –

T his is a satisfying soup of hearty, pink, fragrant beans and herbs, with a depth of flavor that belies its simplicity.

Like Provence, the rocky hills of Corsica are covered with fragrant herbs. Food there can be very simple, but almost always it is flavored with aromatics.

Whichever herbs you use for the soup will lend their character; as in Corsica, choose whatever is seasonal. Tarragon, marjoram, basil, mint, thyme, rosemary, sage, chervil or cilantro, lots of parsley, chives, or green garlic–all are delicious.

1 onion, chopped
½ leek, thinly sliced
3 to 4 garlic cloves, minced
1 tablespoon olive oil
Salt and pepper to taste
2 potatoes, peeled and diced
2 ripe tomatoes, diced
2 tablespoons tomato paste
1 bay leaf
2 pinches of herbes de Provence
4 cups vegetable stock (pages 201–202)
1 cup drained cooked pink beans such as
  Borlotti, pinto, or cranberry
½ to 1 cup coarsely chopped mixed fresh
  herbs: parsley, mint, chives, marjoram,
  oregano, basil, tarragon, chervil, rose-
  mary, fennel leaves, sage

✦✦ In a large, heavy saucepan over medium-low heat, lightly sauté the onion, leek, and garlic in the olive oil until the vegetables are softened, about 5 to 8 minutes, sprinkling with the salt and pepper as they cook.

✦✦ Add the potatoes and cook for 5 to 8 minutes. Add the tomatoes and continue to cook several minutes, then stir in the tomato paste, bay leaf, herbes de Provence, and stock. Bring to a boil, then reduce heat and simmer until the potatoes are almost tender, about 15 minutes.

✦✦ Add the beans and cook until the potatoes are tender and the beans heated through. Remove and discard the bay leaf. Taste and adjust the seasoning.

✦✦ Just before serving, stir in the herbs, or sprinkle the herbs over each person's bowl.

SOUPE AUX HARICOTS ROUGES ET BLANCS ET SES CHAMPIGNONS FORESTIERS EN CROÛTE

PASTRY-TOPPED SOUP OF RED AND WHITE BEANS, WITH FOREST MUSHROOMS

– Serves 4 to 6 –

The pastry on top of this hearty southwestern soup bakes to form a crust–dig in with your spoon to unearth a cache of fragrant soup. A wine from the southwest, such as a Cahors or a Madiran, would be a good choice; or try a Bordeaux such as Medoc or Saint-Emillion.

Dried mushrooms add their particular woodsy charm. In France you can often buy a mixture of dried forest mushrooms called *garniture forestière;* in many U.S. supermarkets there are similar mixtures. If not, use only one or two types of dried mushrooms.

1 onion, chopped
2 tablespoons butter or olive oil
5 garlic cloves, thinly sliced or coarsely
  chopped
1 cup drained cooked red kidney beans
1 cup drained cooked cannellini beans
5 cups vegetable stock (pages 201–202)

½ cup diced peeled celery root

Large pinch of dried thyme or several
pinches of minced fresh thyme

2 to 3 tablespoons dried mushrooms,
preferably an assortment of types: cèpes,
morels, trompettes de la mort, chante-
relles, and so forth

1 cup hot water

Salt and pepper to taste

2 tablespoons brandy or Armagnac
(optional)

Pastry dough (pages 202–203)

✦✦ In a large, heavy saucepan over medium-low heat, lightly sauté the onion in the butter or olive oil until it turns translucent and lightly golden, about 5 to 8 minutes. Stir in half the garlic and cook for 1 minute.

✦✦ Stir in the beans, stock, celery root, and thyme and bring to a boil, then reduce heat and simmer for 30 minutes.

✦✦ Meanwhile, place the mushrooms in a bowl and pour the hot water over them. Let them soak for 20 minutes, then remove the mushrooms from their soaking liquid. Squeeze the mushrooms, letting the juice run back into the soaking liquid. Place mushrooms in cold water for 5 minutes, then remove them and squeeze them dry. Add the mushrooms and the remaining garlic to simmering soup. Strain the soaking liquid through a cheesecloth-lined sieve or simply let the grit settle, then pour the richly flavored soaking liquid off. Discard the grit that is left behind and add the strained liquid to the soup. Add the salt, pepper, and brandy or Armagnac.

✦✦ Roll out the pastry dough, cut it into 4 squares, and set aside.

✦✦ In a blender or food processor, purée about half of the soup mixture, then return it to the pan with the rest of the soup and heat through. Taste and adjust the seasoning.

✦✦ Preheat the oven to 375°F.

✦✦ Ladle the soup into individual baking dishes or crocks. Cover each with a pastry square and seal the edges around the top of each bowl.

✦✦ Bake until the tops of the pastry are golden brown in places (in the center of the crust it might remain quite pale), about 15 to 20 minutes. Serve right away, letting each person cut into the crust and release the fragrant aroma of the hot, steamy soup.

Tourte aux Haricots et Champignons **(Savory Pie Filled with Mixed Beans and Wild Mushrooms)** Instead of a stew, prepare a bean-and-mushroom pie: Prepare the soup as a thick stew by decreasing the amount of stock from 5 cups to 2 to 3 cups, then top with a pastry crust as above and bake as directed.

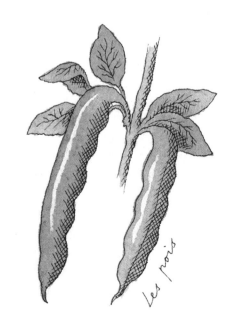

A French meal is like theater. First there is the thrill of anticipation as you find your seat. Then the meal opens with the entrée, or first course (not the main course, as in the United States). The word comes directly from the French word *entrer,* which means "to enter." And so we enter the pleasures and nourishment of the table.

First courses are often the most delightful, as they exist to entice and delight. They should be full of bright colors, interesting textures, and/or irresistible aromas. They should never be so heavy as to overwhelm the rest of the meal–rather they should lure the diner along, as a good plot does.

They must also be small in size, so as not to obliterate the appetite. Even the heartiest dishes of pasta, gratinéd soups, and warm salads can make excellent starters if served in modest enough portions to keep the diner wanting more of the meal to follow.

At its best, the first course sets the stage for the plat du jour.

Salades

...

Salads

Salads in France are so full of freshness that they are usually an irresistible choice on the menu. On a sultry day, what could be more refreshing than a chilled bowl of cooling endive leaves, watercress sprigs, and cheese or sweet grapes? And on a cold night, what is more satisfying than boiled potatoes in a mustardy dressing, or rustic greens topped with warm goat cheese melted onto a garlicky croûte? At the height of summer, sliced tomatoes appear on the table dressed in a sprinkling of salt and chives, or a drizzle of olive oil and basil.

French salads depend on high-quality ingredients such as vegetables, herbs, fruits, and cheeses, as well as excellent oils and vinegars.

Salads of vegetables, greens, cheese, and/or fruit can be eaten as a first course, embellished with crisp croûtes, sautéed vegetables, and the like. As a last course, you may find a simple salad of greens on its own or sharing a plate with the cheese course.

· · · · · · · · · · · · · · · · · · · ·

SALADE D'ENDIVES, FROMAGE, ET NOIX

BELGIAN ENDIVE SALAD WITH CHEESE AND WALNUTS

– Serves 4 –

A big glass bowl filled with slices of crisp endive, its bitter-fresh flavor balancing the decadent, slightly rank scent of rich Roquefort and the crunch of walnuts, is a classic of the Auvergne and of bistros throughout the area, and in Paris as well.

At La Tour de Montlhéry, also known as Chez Denise, a classic brass-fitted etched-glass bistro a few steps from Paris's former Les Halles, eaters sit *coude à coude,* or elbow to elbow, at paper-topped tables listening to stories of the old days, tales of meals eaten and events that have taken place at the tables. The walls are covered with sketches and drawings, and the waiters seem to have been there since the moment time began. The menu is scrawled on a huge blackboard and toted around; I think there is only one, and it can be a challenge to come into possession of it for long enough to order your meal before it is grabbed away again.

Portions are huge, quality varies, flavors are lusty, and this is one of the few dishes on the menu that is vegetarian. If you can get both red and white endive, use a combination of the two.

Serve with a Brouilly or Chinon.

6 Belgian endives, cored
1 tablespoon olive oil
3 ounces Roquefort or other blue cheese
*   such as fourme d'Ambert, cut into bite-*
*   sized pieces*

¼ to ½ cup walnut halves
1 teaspoon walnut oil
2 teaspoons raspberry or sherry vinegar
Pepper to taste

✦✦ Cut the endives crosswise into ¼-inch slices, then toss with the olive oil, letting the endive pieces separate from each other, to make a ribbon-like effect.

✦✦ Add the cheese and walnuts, then toss them once again, this time adding the walnut oil and raspberry or sherry vinegar. Season with pepper to taste (you won't need salt, as the cheese is so salty).

SALADE VIGNERONNE

WINEMAKER'S SALAD

– Serves 4 –

I ate this refreshing salad in a restaurant set out on the edge of a vineyard as an extra business for the winemaker and his family.

The salad of bitter Belgian endive and crisp green watercress had sweet grapes added, a bonus from living in a vineyard. Balsamic vinegar, though Italian in origin, is used in many French salad dressings these days, especially in the south. It adds a winey flavor without the harshness of wine vinegar, and is thus less disruptive to whatever you're drinking with the meal.

8 Belgian endives, cut crosswise into thin
strips
Several handfuls of watercress
2 shallots, minced
1 cup mixed grapes, such as Red Flame
and Muscat or green seedless

2 to 3 tablespoons olive or vegetable oil
1 teaspoon balsamic vinegar
1 teaspoon fresh lemon juice
Salt and pepper to taste

✦✦ Toss the endive and watercress with the shallots in a chilled bowl.

✦✦ Cut the grapes into halves, removing the seeds from any varieties that have them. Place the grapes in the bowl with the vegetables. Chill until ready to serve.

✦✦ Dress the salad with the remaining ingredients. Serve right away.

SALADE MARAÎCHÈRE

MARKETPLACE SALAD

– Serves 4 to 6 –

T his is adapted from a salad my family and I ate at Paris's Baracane-Bistrôt de l'Oulette near the Place des Vosges: a feast of vegetables, tossed with a tangy dressing, then heaped onto the plate in a pyramid shape. Despite the fact that we set fire to the menu (accidentally, I swear), the staff was helpful and eager to please.

Slices of crisp pain levain accompanied the meal, and we ended with a fabulous plate of cheeses from the southwest and a glass of breathtakingly good Poire Williams. But it was the salad that was so remarkable, full of varied vegetable tastes and textures, and easy to make at home.

4 beets
¼ pound haricots verts, baby Blue Lake
green beans, or fresh peas in the pod
4 to 6 tomatoes, diced

½ *English cucumber (or 1 American cucumber, peeled and seeded), halved lengthwise and sliced into half moons*

½ *head tender green leaf lettuce, cut into thin slices*

3 carrots, peeled and sliced very thinly

8 to 10 mushrooms, cut into halves, then thinly sliced

2 celery stalks, sliced

1 Belgian endive, cored and sliced crosswise

3 to 5 shallots, minced

1 to 2 garlic cloves, minced

1 to 2 tablespoons chopped fresh chives

1 to 2 tablespoons chopped fresh parsley or tarragon

1 to 2 tablespoons chopped fresh chervil

3 tablespoons Dijon mustard

1 to 2 tablespoons white wine vinegar

¼ *teaspoon sugar*

4 tablespoons vegetable oil

2 to 3 tablespoons heavy cream or sour cream

Salt and pepper to taste

Country bread for serving

✦✦ Cook the beets by steaming them for 30 to 40 minutes, or by baking them in a preheated 350°F oven for about 1 hour, depending on the size and age of the beets. Let cool.

✦✦ Slip their skins off the beets and cut the beets into bite-sized pieces. (Beets can be cooked up to 3 days ahead of time and stored in the refrigerator.)

✦✦ Boil the beans or peas until they are just tender, 5 minutes or so. Refresh them by draining, then plunging them into ice cold water for a moment. Drain and set aside.

✦✦ Combine the tomatoes, cucumber, lettuce, carrots, mushrooms, celery, endive, shallots, gar-lic, chives, parsley or tarragon, and chervil, then toss in the green beans.

✦✦ Mix the mustard with the wine vinegar and sugar, then whisk or stir in the oil until it emulsifies.

✦✦ Stir the cream into this dressing, then toss it with the mixed vegetables and coat well. Add the beets, season with salt and pepper, and serve heaped on cool plates, accompanied with crusty bread.

SALADE COMPOSÉE DE PÂTE DE ROQUEFORT ET DES POMMES

SALAD OF FRISÉE, ROQUEFORT PÂTÉ, AND SAUTÉED APPLES

– Serves 4 –

A handful of vinaigrette-dressed bitter frisée makes a sharp contrast to the richness of the cheese and the sweetness of the sautéed apples in this composed salad from France's southwest.

Serve a nugget of the Roquefort pâté surrounded by sautéed apples and a handful of the bitter little greens and, to drink, perhaps a Côtes-du-Rhone, or a rustic red from the Auvergne.

4 ounces Roquefort cheese

3 tablespoons crème fraîche or sour cream

1 tablespoon Calvados

3 to 4 tablespoons minced shallots

3 unpeeled firm tart green apples, cored and thinly sliced

1 tablespoon butter

½ *teaspoon sugar*

3 cups frisée leaves

2 tablespoons olive oil

2 teaspoons wine or balsamic vinegar, or
*   to taste*
Salt and pepper to taste

✦✦ Mash the cheese and work in the crème fraîche or sour cream, Calvados, and a little minced shallot, if you like. Set aside; this can be done up to 2 days earlier and chilled.

✦✦ In a medium sauté pan or skillet over medium-low heat, sauté the apples in the butter while sprinkling with the sugar, until they are crisp-tender, about 5 minutes. Remove them from the pan.

✦✦ Toss the frisée leaves with the remaining shallots, then dress them with the olive oil, vinegar, salt, and pepper.

✦✦ Arrange the leaves on individual plates around a mound of the cheese mixture. Garnish with sautéed apple and serve right away.

SALADE DE FIGUES, POIRES, NOIX, ET FROMAGE DE BREBIS

MIXED LEAVES AND HERBS WITH FIGS, PEARS, FRESH FENNEL, SHEEP'S MILK CHEESE, AND TOASTED WALNUTS

– Serves 4 –

We ate this salad in the Isère; the walnuts had been grown in the surrounding fields and the greens grown in the little *potager,* a vegetable and herb garden just outside the kitchen door.

If sweet ripe figs are not in season leave them out, or substitute something exotic such as mango. And if a light fresh sheep's milk cheese

La baguette

is unavailable, use a fresh white goat cheese, or even chunks of feta. A Meursault would be lovely with this, or perhaps a Gewürztraminer or a white Côtes-du-Rhône.

4 handfuls mixed baby greens and 1 bunch
*   arugula*
1 to 2 tablespoons walnut oil
1 to 2 tablespoons mild vegetable oil
1 to 2 tablespoons raspberry vinegar
1 fennel bulb, trimmed and cut into
*   julienne*
6 to 8 ripe figs, halved
1 flavorful ripe pear, cut into thin strips
½ cup walnut halves or bits, toasted (see
*   page 211)*
6 ounces brebis (fresh white sheep cheese),
*   fresh white goat cheese, or feta, broken*
*   into bite-sized bits*
1 tablespoon minced fresh chervil
1 tablespoon minced fresh chives
Pepper to taste

✦✦ Place the greens in a salad bowl and dress them with the oils and vinegar.

✦✦ Arrange the fennel, figs, and pear on top, then scatter with the cheese, toasted walnuts, chervil, chives, and pepper. Serve right away.

VARIATION In place of walnuts, use peeled toasted hazelnuts, and in place of walnut oil, a mixture of hazelnut and vegetable oil.

SALADE D'HARICOTS VERTS, FROMAGE DE COMTÉ, CHAMPIGNONS, ET ŒUFS

SALAD OF GREEN BEANS, COMTÉ CHEESE, EGGS, AND MUSHROOMS

– Serves 4 to 6 –

A friend was heading towards Le Havre so, feeling bored, we jumped in his car and went along. The weather was unseasonably hot, so when we sat down in a little bistro for lunch we positioned ourselves out of doors, under the umbrella, in a breezy corner. And when it came time to order we ate this bistro classic: a salad of beans, raw mushrooms, cheese, and hard-cooked eggs, with a few strands of baby frisée lettuce to keep it all together. Each serving came in a big chilled glass bowl, as delicious to press against our flushed skin in the sultry heat as the salad was to eat.

A cool Alsatian Sylvaner would be nice with this.

4 hard-cooked eggs, shelled
4 ounces haricots verts or baby Blue Lake
*   green beans*
8 ounces Comté, Beaufort, Gruyère, or
*   other good-quality Swiss-type cheese,*
*   cut into dice or large julienne*
4 ounces white mushrooms
5 to 8 shallots, minced
1 cup baby frisée leaves, or 1 to 2 handfuls

frisée fronds (1 to 2 small heads)
1 tablespoon Dijon mustard
1 tablespoon red wine vinegar
3 tablespoons vegetable or mixed olive
*   and vegetable oil*
Salt and pepper
1 teaspoon each minced fresh dill, chervil,
*   chives, and parsley (or any combination)*

✦✦ Cut the eggs into wedges and set aside.

✦✦ Cook the green beans until crisp-tender, about 4 minutes, then rinse in cold water and drain.

✦✦ Combine the cheese, mushrooms, shallots, frisée, and cooled drained beans in a bowl.

✦✦ Mix the mustard and vinegar, then whisk in the oil until it emulsifies; season with salt and pepper.

✦✦ Toss the cheese, mushroom, and vegetable mixture with the dressing, then arrange in bowls. Garnish with the egg wedges and sprinkle with the herbs. Serve right away.

POIREAUX EN VINAIGRETTE ET SA SAUCE BETTERAVES

LEEKS VINAIGRETTE IN BEET PURÉE

– Serves 4 –

When I think of leeks in beet vinaigrette I think of the elegant Parisian bistro Chardenoux, where we sat down to a parade of robust dishes one wintry night last year. Chardenoux is evocative and atmospheric, its decor elegant, its customers utterly Parisian, and its food seriously delicious.

This classic pairing is as traditional as it is beautiful, and it tastes as good as it looks. For a more elegant presentation, layer the leeks into a pâté or timbale shape.

2 beets
12 leeks, including tender green tops
3 tablespoons vegetable oil
2 shallots, minced
3 tablespoons red or white wine vinegar
Pinch of sugar
1 teaspoon balsamic vinegar
Salt and pepper to taste
3 tablespoons minced fresh chives

✦✦ Cook the beets by boiling them until they are just tender, about 30 minutes. Drain, let cool to the touch, and peel (their skins will slip off easily). Dice the beets and set aside.

✦✦ Trim the leeks of their tough ends, then clean them of their grit and sand by slicing the green ends lengthwise and rinsing between the leaves under cold running water. For a professional bistro presentation, tie the leek lengths together into bundles using kitchen string, then untie them to serve. For a homey presentation, leave them in 2-inch lengths and steam them loose.

✦✦ Steam the leeks in a covered pot over boiling water until they are just tender, about 8 minutes, then remove them from heat. Drizzle with 2 tablespoons of the oil and ½ tablespoon of the vinegar, then sprinkle with salt and pepper. Set aside.

✦✦ Combine the cooked beets with the remaining 1 tablespoon oil, the shallots, the remaining 2½ tablespoons vinegar, the sugar, balsamic vinegar, salt, and pepper and whirl it in a blender or food processor until smooth. Use at once or cover and refrigerate for up to 2 days.

✦✦ Spoon a puddle of bright pink sauce onto each plate and top with the lightly dressed leeks. Serve sprinkled with chives.

SALADE FORESTIÈRE

RAW CÈPE SALAD

– Serves 4 –

During wild mushroom season, Nice's Cours Saleya marketplace is heaped with a lavish variety, and bistros throughout the town vie with each other in serving dishes based on these delectable fungi. This salad was inspired by one such offering: provocative, dancing with flavors, and glistening, awash with olive oil.

To be at its best, the mushrooms must be exquisitely fresh and firm and should not be soaked, as their gills will absorb water. You can make this salad with portobellos and it will be good, but not as outstanding as it will be with fresh cèpes.

The salad appears simple at first glance, a teepeelike arrangement of shaved Parmesan surrounded by slices of raw cèpes. But when you lift the cheese you unearth a hidden treasure of diced cèpes, scented with shallots and dressed in vinaigrette. Parmesan cheese, by the way, has been used in the French kitchen for centuries, indeed longer than many French cheeses have been.

About 6 very fresh cèpe (porcini) mushrooms
3 to 4 shallots, minced
½ teaspoon strong Dijon mustard
3 tablespoons extra-virgin olive oil
Juice of ½ lemon
1 tablespoon balsamic vinegar
Salt and cayenne pepper to taste
1 garlic clove, minced

1 tablespoon minced fresh chives
1 tablespoon minced fresh parsley
1 tablespoon minced fresh chervil or basil
3 ounces Parmesan or pecorino cheese,
*   shaved*

❖❖ Finely chop a third of the mushrooms and mix them with the shallots, mustard, 1½ tablespoons of the olive oil, the lemon juice, balsamic vinegar, salt, garlic, cayenne, and half of the herbs. Set aside.

❖❖ Thinly slice the remaining mushrooms and toss them with the remaining 1½ tablespoons oil; season with salt.

❖❖ Divide the chopped mushroom mixture among 4 individual plates and surround each with a fan of thinly sliced mushrooms. Sprinkle the mushrooms with the remaining herbs. Garnish with the shavings of cheese, forming little pyramids or teepees to hide the chopped-mushroom salad.

SALADE DE TOMATES ET

FROMAGE FRAIS PROVENÇAL

TOMATOES, BASIL, AND OLIVE

SALAD WITH FRESH CHEESE

– Serves 4 –

We were driving through the backroads of Provence, stopping at vineyards and tasting rosés. At midday, we stopped at a restaurant that looked more like a dive than a lunch destination, but inside it was lively, loud, and smelled fabulous.

This simple summer salad full of Provençal flavors came to the table right away, while we were thinking about what to order. It had dollops of milky goat cheese that day, but I've since made

it with nearly any fresh cheese: sheep, cow, or goat. A chilled Bandol or Tavel rosé, or a light red from the Luberon would be a nice companion.

8 very flavorful ripe tomatoes, thinly sliced
4 to 6 ounces fresh white goat or sheep
*   cheese, sliced into ¼-inch-thick pieces*
*   or crumbled*
Salt to taste
2 garlic cloves, minced
2 tablespoons olive oil or as desired
About 25 niçoise olives
¼ cup fresh basil leaves, torn or thinly sliced

❖❖ Arrange the tomatoes and the cheese on a plate and sprinkle with the salt and garlic. Drizzle olive oil over it all, then garnish the plate with the olives and basil. Serve right away, or refrigerate for up to 2 hours before serving.

SALADE AIXOISE

A PROVENÇAL

VEGETABLE PLATTER

– Serves 4 –

This plateful of garlicky Provençal vegetables served on a bed of crisp green mesclun is often served in the area of Aix-en-Provence.

When artichokes are young and tender, with no choke to make eating a challenge, they are sliced and eaten raw instead of cooked; if the only artichokes you can find are a little old and on the tough side, with a big choke, cut them into hearts and cook them.

For a fine Provençal flavor, be sure to use the most flavorful fruity olive oil you can find.

4 garlic cloves

Pinch of salt, plus salt to taste

¼ cup coarsely chopped fresh parsley

2 red bell peppers, or 1 red and 1 yellow
    bell pepper, roasted, peeled, and sliced
    (see page 210)

1 teaspoon red wine vinegar

4 to 6 small tender artichokes, or 3 large
    artichokes

¼ cup shelled young fava beans

4 tablespoons extra-virgin olive oil

1 pound boiling potatoes

2 tablespoons dry white wine

1 tablespoon fresh lemon juice

4 shallots, minced

¼ to ½ teaspoon herbes de Provence

10 oil-cured black olives, pitted and halved
    or slivered

1 tablespoon minced fresh mint, or ½ to
    1 teaspoon crushed dried mint

2 to 3 handfuls mixed baby greens

✦✦ In a blender or food processor, purée the garlic with a pinch of salt, then add the parsley and continue to purée until it forms a chunky mixture. Set aside.

✦✦ Toss the sliced peppers with 2 teaspoons of the crushed garlic mixture, salt to taste, and vinegar. Set aside.

✦✦ Trim the artichokes of their sharp-pointed leaves down to their tender hearts; if they are large artichokes, remove their chokes with a sharp-edged spoon or paring knife. If they are young, the choke should not need removal. Slice the artichoke hearts thinly and toss them in 2 tablespoons olive oil and 2 teaspoons of the garlic-parsley mixture. Add the fava beans and set aside. (If the fava beans are not young enough to be eaten raw and unpeeled, boil them until

they are just tender, then squeeze them out of their skins. Toss them with the raw artichokes.)

✦✦ Boil the potatoes until they are just tender. Drain and cut into bite-sized pieces, then toss while still warm with the remaining garlic paste, the wine, lemon juice, remaining 2 tablespoons olive oil, shallots, herbes de Provence, olives, and mint.

✦✦ To serve: Toss the greens with a tablespoon or two of the dressing from the potatoes, then arrange the greens on a platter; place a little pile of each of the vegetables on top: roasted peppers, potato-olive salad, and artichoke-fava salad.

SALADES TIÈDES

WARM SALADS

Warm salads are a bistro mainstay, sustaining enough to satisfy the soul, yet light enough to not smother the appetite for the rest of the meal.

Salad ingredients can be tossed together in a pan with hot dressing over heat until they wilt, or they can be set on plates and have a hot dressing or hot ingredients poured over them.

The best warm salads are made with hearty greens; delicate little lettuces would loose their moisture and freshness. Cabbage, frisée, and vegetables such as beets or potatoes are all good; and a vinaigrette-tossed mixture of baby greens is an excellent base for anything hot, such as grilled artichoke hearts or that bistro classic, hot goat cheese.

In fact, warmed salads with any of the wide variety of goat cheeses and blue cheeses are a bistro classic, adding blasts of big flavor in each *tiny nugget that melts delicately when the warm ingredients are added.*

Young asparagus stalks and green beans, bits of sweet juicy cherry tomatoes, and handfuls of herbs are often tossed into warm salads at the last minute for fragrant freshness.

SALADE DE PISSENLIT ET ROQUETTE, ŒUF POCHÉ

SALAD OF WILD ARUGULA AND DANDELION GREENS, WITH A POACHED EGG

– Serves 4 –

When wild arugula, with its ragged-edged leaves and delicate white flowers, covers the hillsides along France's southern coast, you will find it mixed with young dandelion leaves in the region's best mesclun. Poached egg and crisp garlic croutons make a classic bistro *salade tiède,* with a carafe of Beaujolais or Chinon placed on the table to drink.

1½ cups cubed stale coarse country bread
7 tablespoons olive oil
4 garlic cloves, minced
4 handfuls mixed arugula and young dandelion greens, or mixed baby greens
3 tablespoons minced fresh chives
4 eggs
2½ tablespoons red wine vinegar
3 to 4 shallots, minced
Salt and pepper to taste

✦✦ Preheat the oven to 325°F. Put the bread cubes in a baking pan and toss with 2 tablespoons of the olive oil, then bake 30 minutes, or until golden brown and crisp. Toss with half the garlic and set aside.

✦✦ Toss the greens with the remaining garlic, the chives, and 3 tablespoons of the olive oil; arrange the dressed greens on 4 plates.

✦✦ Poach the eggs in simmering water to which you've added ½ tablespoon vinegar. Cook eggs until the whites are just firm and the yolks are still runny. Remove them from their cooking liquid with a slotted spoon and drain off their excess moisture with a paper towel.

✦✦ In a medium sauté pan or skillet over medium heat, lightly sauté the shallots in the remaining 4 tablespoons olive oil until they are softened and lightly browned in places, 5 to 8 minutes, then pour in the remaining 2 tablespoons of vinegar. Bring to a boil, and cook for several minutes until reduced by about half.

✦✦ To serve, place a hot poached egg on each plate of salad, then pour the hot vinegar over all. Sprinkle with salt and pepper. Serve right away.

le cageot de poires

SALADE DE CHOUX, HARICOTS VERTS, ET NOISETTES

WARM SALAD OF CABBAGE, GREEN BEANS, AND HAZELNUTS

– Serves 4 –

Cabbage is delicious in warm salads. It's sturdy enough to stand up to even the most forceful dressing or the heat of a pan, and you'll often find it in warm bistro salads.

A fruity, acidic white Burgundy, such as an Aligoté, would be good with this salad.

> *4 ounces haricots verts or baby Blue Lake green beans*
> *½ cup hazelnuts, toasted and peeled (see page 211)*
> *1 tablespoon hot Dijon mustard*
> *3 to 4 tablespoons chopped shallots*
> *1½ tablespoons white wine vinegar*
> *2 garlic cloves, minced*
> *2 tablespoons walnut or hazelnut oil*
> *2 tablespoons olive oil*
> *Salt and pepper to taste*
> *1 cabbage, thinly sliced*
> *1 tablespoon coarsely chopped fresh tarragon*
> *1 tablespoon coarsely chopped fresh chervil leaves*
> *1 tablespoon coarsely chopped fresh chives*

✦✦ Cook the green beans by boiling them until they are just tender, about 5 minutes. Rinse them in cold water, drain, and set aside.

✦✦ Mix the mustard with the shallots, vinegar, and garlic, then whisk in the oils; season with salt and pepper.

✦✦ In a large sauté pan or skillet over high heat, heat half of the dressing and add the cabbage, letting it cook until just wilted, then add the green beans and hazelnuts, cooking just a minute to warm them through.

✦✦ Spoon onto a plate and sprinkle with the remaining dressing; taste and adjust the seasoning.

✦✦ Serve right away, sprinkled with the herbs.

SALADE TIÈDE AUX HERBES, VINAIGRE DE PRUNES

WARM SALAD OF FRISÉE, SAUTÉED MUSHROOMS, AND PEARS WITH PRUNE VINAIGRETTE

– Serves 4 –

This salad is from the southwest region of Gers, an area known for its warm salads and vinegars made from the local fruits. I might accompany it with crusty bread spread with a robust goat cheese, fresh and milky, but with a rustic fragrance.

Enjoy with a nice robust Cahors or a Gaillac, *rouge* or *blanc*.

> *½ cup red wine vinegar*
> *2 tablespoons sugar*
> *Pinch of ground pepper*
> *Pinch of nutmeg*
> *Pinch of cinnamon*
> *⅓ to ½ cup loosely packed pitted prunes*
> *Leaves from 1 head frisée*
> *3 tablespoons fresh chervil leaves*

2 tablespoons minced fresh chives

3 tablespoons olive oil

Salt and pepper to taste

8 to 12 ounces mixed wild mushrooms
   (girolles, cèpes, chanterelles, oyster
   mushrooms, shiitakes, and so forth),
   cut into bite-sized pieces

2 shallots, minced

2 pears, cored and cut into julienne (peel
   if you like; I prefer to leave the peel on)

1 tablespoon Armagnac or brandy

✦✦ In a small saucepan, combine the vinegar, sugar, pepper, nutmeg, cinnamon, and prunes. Bring to a boil, then let cool; if possible, let sit overnight.

✦✦ Toss the frisée with the chervil and chives and arrange on a platter or on plates. Dress with 2 tablespoons of the olive oil and the salt and pepper.

✦✦ In a large sauté pan or skillet over medium heat, heat the remaining 1 tablespoon olive oil and lightly sauté the mushrooms and shallots, then remove from the pan and sauté the pear slices for a few moments. Add 4 of the soaked prunes and warm through. Pour in the Armagnac or brandy and cook until it nearly all evaporates, then add the wine vinegar and heat through.

✦✦ Spoon some of the mushroom mixture, pear mixture, and prune vinegar over each of the salads and serve right away.

NOTE Leftover vinegar can be used for another salad, such as the one below.

SALADE TIÈDE AU CHÈVRE, AVEC OLIVES ET CRÊPES DE POMMES DE TERRE

WARM SALAD WITH GOAT CHEESE, BLACK OLIVES, AND CRISP POTATO CAKES

– Serves 4 –

The contrast between fresh raw greens, tangy goat cheese, and crisply browned potatoes is marvelous; in recent years I've found variations and variations on this theme in bistros all around France.

A scattering of black olives adds a jaunty accent, and the goat cheese melts seductively on the salad greens when the hot potato cakes are added. Serve with a crisp Sancerre or a Sauvignon Blanc from the Loire.

2 to 3 unpeeled white boiling potatoes,
   halved

Salt and pepper to taste

2 tablespoons butter or more as needed

4 handfuls mixed baby greens

2 tablespoons minced fresh chervil

3 tablespoons minced fresh chives

1 tablespoon minced fresh parsley

1 shallot, minced

2 tablespoons olive oil

1½ tablespoons white wine vinegar

3 ounces fresh white goat or sheep cheese,
   cut or crumbled into pieces

8 to 12 flavorful black Mediterranean
   olives, pitted

✦✦Cook the potatoes in boiling water until they are halfway tender, about 15 minutes. The potatoes should be still slightly crunchy.

✦✦Rinse in cold water, then shred or grate using the large rasps of a grater or in a food processor. Most of the peel should slip off in the process; ignore any that doesn't and discard the peel that does. Season the potato shreds with salt and pepper.

✦✦In a large, heavy cast-iron or nonstick skillet, melt the butter over medium-high heat and spoon in mounds of the potato mixture, pressing them down as they brown, until the bottoms of the pancakes are golden brown, adding more butter if needed. Turn and cook the second side until the cakes are crisp-edged and browned.

✦✦Meanwhile, combine the greens with the chervil, chives, parsley, and shallot, then dress with the olive oil and vinegar.

✦✦Sprinkle the top of the salad with the goat cheese and olives.

✦✦When the potato pancakes are cooked through, place them on the dressed salad leaves. Serve right away.

SALADE VERTE AUX CROÛTES

ET CHÈVRE CHAUD

MIXED GREENS AND HERBS

WITH GARLIC TOASTS

AND WARM GOAT CHEESE

– Serves 4 –

C*hèvre chaud,* or warm goat cheese, just might be served in one of its many guises in every bistro in France.

In this recipe, it is melted onto thick rye toasts redolent with garlic and set on a tangy bed of mixed greens and herbs. Use more goat cheese if you like; in this salad you can either be restrained or greedy and I do both, as my mood and pantry dictate. A light red wine such as a slightly chilled Saumur-Champigny would be nice with this.

4 handfuls mixed baby greens
2 shallots, minced
2 tablespoons minced fresh chervil
2 tablespoons minced fresh chives
2 tablespoons chopped fresh tarragon
2 tablespoons minced fresh parsley
2 garlic cloves, minced
8 small thick slices (about 1 ounce each)
*   country bread, preferably rustic rye or*
*   whole wheat*
3 tablespoons olive oil
4 ounces aged goat cheese with an edible
*   white rind (Bucheron, Lezay, etc.), cut*
*   into slices to fit the bread*
2 to 3 teaspoons white wine vinegar, or to
*   taste*
Salt and pepper to taste

✦✦In a big bowl, combine the greens, shallots, herbs, and half the garlic. Set aside.

✦✦To make the rye toasts: Lightly toast the bread under the broiler on each side, then remove them from the oven and toss them with 1 tablespoon of the olive oil and the remaining garlic. Top each toast with a slice of cheese. Set aside.

✦✦Dress the salad with the remaining 2 tablespoons olive oil, vinegar, salt, and pepper, then arrange on 4 salad plates.

✦✦Broil the cheese-topped toasts until the cheese heats through and just begins to melt.

✦✦Place 2 hot toasts on each plate of salad and serve right away.

SALADE TIÈDE D'AUVERGNE

SALAD WITH HERBS, AVOCADO, BLUE CHEESE, AND SAUTÉED FIELD MUSHROOMS

– Serves 4 –

Though the avocado is not traditional bistro fare, it has long been enjoyed by the salad-loving French. I especially enjoyed its creamy delicacy in this salad, which I sampled in the Auvergne. In my home kitchen I use fresh shiitakes, and they are very good indeed.

Drink a slightly chilled Beaujolais, or a Côtes-du-Rhônes with this dish.

4 handfuls mixed baby greens
2 tablespoons fresh chervil sprigs
2 tablespoons fresh tarragon leaves
1 garlic clove, minced
2 tablespoons olive oil
½ to 1 teaspoon Dijon or whole-grain mustard
1 teaspoon balsamic vinegar, or to taste
4 shallots, minced
1 avocado, peeled, pitted, and diced
3 ounces blue cheese, preferably a bleu d'Auvergne, fourme d'Ambert, Gorgonzola, or Maytag blue, crumbled
1 carrot, peeled and cut into fine julienne

6 to 8 ounces fresh shiitake mushrooms, stemmed and cut into chunks
Salt and pepper to taste
1 tablespoon red wine vinegar

✦✦Combine the greens with the chervil, tarragon, and garlic. Mix 1 tablespoon of the olive oil with the mustard, balsamic vinegar, and half the shallots and toss with the salad. Arrange on plates and top each with one fourth of the avocado, blue cheese, and julienned carrots.

✦✦In a large, heavy sauté pan or skillet over medium heat, sauté the shiitakes in the remaining 1 tablespoon olive oil with the remaining shallots until the mushrooms are just warmed, wilted, and lightly browned, about 3 to 5 minutes. Season with salt and pepper, then pour in the red wine vinegar and bring to a boil.

✦✦Pour the hot mushrooms and vinegar over the salad and serve at once.

I was once told a story about a splendid goat cheese I was eating: In the hills behind Nice there lived a woman who ran a house of ill repute. It was the finest such establishment in the area, but politicians, in an anti-crime effort, closed her business. The local police were, however, very sensitive to her plight because they, too, had visited her place of business. When she cried, "But what will I do for a living now?" they passed the hat and went out and bought her a flock of the loveliest goats imaginable. She now sells her goat cheese at the Sunday market in Nice.

CHÈVRE CHAUD AUX BETTERAVES

WARM GOAT CHEESE AND BEETS IN SUN-DRIED TOMATO VINAIGRETTE

– Serves 4 –

The intense flavor of sun-dried tomatoes is terribly chic in the south of France these days. The chewy little marinated tomatoes taste of the sun, and combine deliciously with the other flavors of the area: olive oil, goat cheese, and in this dish, beets.

6 to 8 unpeeled beets
A 6-ounce aged goat cheese log with rind,
*   cut into 12 bite-sized pieces*
4 tablespoons olive oil
1 tablespoon balsamic vinegar
2 to 3 oil-packed sun-dried tomatoes (from
*   a jar), chopped or cut into strips*
2 garlic cloves, minced
Salt and pepper to taste
2 tablespoons minced fresh chervil
1 tablespoon minced fresh tarragon
1 tablespoon minced chives or shallots

♦♦Bake the beets in a preheated 350°F oven until just tender, about 1 hour, depending on the size of the beets. Let cool until easily handled. Peel, then slice and arrange in a single layer in a baking dish or on a baking sheet. The beets may be prepared to this point up to 2 days ahead.

♦♦Preheat the oven to 375°F or preheat the broiler. Arrange the slices of goat cheese on top of the beets in a line or border and drizzle with 1 tablespoon of the olive oil.

♦♦Make a vinaigrette by combining the remaining 3 tablespoons olive oil, the balsamic vinegar,

sun-dried tomatoes, garlic, salt, and pepper.

♦♦Bake or broil the beets and goat cheese until the cheese is quite hot and lightly browned in spots.

♦♦Quickly arrange the beets and goat cheese on a hot plate. Splash with the vinaigrette, then sprinkle with the chervil, tarragon, and chives or shallots.

♦♦Serve right away, while the cheese is still hot.

SALADE TIÈDE DE POMMES DE TERRE, FÈVES, ET CHÈVRE

WARM SALAD OF NEW POTATOES AND GOAT CHEESE WITH FAVAS

– Serves 4 –

When the first heat wave hit, I found myself sitting in a little bistro at the edge of a village near Avignon, at a table set in a cool, shady garden.

The following dish of warm potatoes and peas, lubricated with olive oil and tossed with goat cheese, was unforgettable, and by the time we had speared the last little potato, an afternoon breeze picked up and the worst of that summer was over.

The combination of fava beans and goat cheese is classic and tastes of the French countryside. To drink, try a Pouilly-Fumé or a dry white Graves.

2 pounds new potatoes (tiny creamers or
*   fingerlings)*
½ cup shelled young fava beans
5 shallots, minced
1 garlic clove, minced
Salt and pepper to taste
3 to 4 tablespoons olive oil

L'artichaut

4 to 6 ounces mild aged goat cheese such
   as Boucheron or Montrachet, cut or
   crumbled
Few drops of balsamic vinegar

✦✦Cook the potatoes in boiling water until just
tender, about 15 to 20 minutes; drain and, when
cool enough to handle, peel.

✦✦Meanwhile, cook the fava beans in boiling
water until just tender, about 5 minutes. Drain
them and, when they are just cool enough to
handle, remove their skins.

✦✦Combine the warm potatoes and fava beans
with the shallots, garlic, salt and pepper, olive oil,
and goat cheese. Season to taste with balsamic
vinegar and enjoy warm or at room temperature.

*Pommes de Terre et Pois au Chèvre (New Potato
and Young Pea Salad with Goat Cheese)* Instead
of fava beans, toss the potatoes with young tender peas, or petits pois.

*Pommes de Terre au Chèvre, Trois Types de Pois
(New Potatoes with Goat Cheese and Three Peas)*
Replace the fava beans with a mixture of tender
petits pois, snow peas, and pea shoots or sugar
snap peas.

ASSIETTES DE CRUDITÉS

—

ASSORTED VEGETABLE SALADS

*A classic beginning to any bistro meal is a se-
lection of raw and lightly cooked vegetables that
have been shredded, sliced, diced, and tossed
into lively little dressings.*

*The assortment usually includes carrots,
beets, potatoes, and celery root, but may vary
with the season. The dressing will vary with the
region: shallots and cream in northern dressings,
nut oils in the southwest, garlic and olive oil as
you head toward Provence.*

*Some specialties consist of a selection of var-
ious salads, such as* salade Tourangelle *from the
northern coast. Asparagus in nut oil; marinated
artichokes, cucumbers, and potatoes; celery in
vinaigrette; green beans tossed with a little
cream—all go into the selection.*

*Starting a meal with a group of little salads
delights the eyes as well as the palate, as you are
faced with the rainbowlike vegetable array, full
of varied flavors and textures.*

*Paris's classic family-owned bistro Chez Eux
is famous for its two large carts, or chariots, each
crammed with heavy casseroles. One cart is de-
voted to a dazzling array of appetizer salads: celery root rémoulade, ratatouille, marinated beets,
mushrooms in mustard-cream dressing, cucumbers, artichokes and roasted peppers, lentils in
vinaigrette, potatoes in oil, and so on. The waiter
spoons modest portions of several salads onto
your plate as an appetizer, or if you like, you can
make a whole meal of the salads and taste your
way through the entire* chariot.

(The second cart? Desserts, of course.)

SALADE DE TOMATES
À L'EAU-DE-VIE

TOMATO SALAD WITH BRANDY AND WALNUT OIL DRESSING

– Serves 4 –

This Quercynoise salad is utterly refreshing on a summer day, when it is likely to make its appearance on a lunch table, set out with a selection of other salads.

A good accompaniment to this salad is toasted baguette slices rubbed with garlic and spread with goat cheese, and a carafe of robust Cahors to drink.

8 sweet ripe tomatoes
1 tablespoon brandy
Salt to taste
Pinch of sugar (optional)
1 to 2 teaspoons raspberry or other fruity, flavorful vinegar
1 to 2 tablespoons walnut oil
1 tablespoon minced fresh chives

✦✦Slice the tomatoes and arrange them, along with any juices that accumulate as you slice them, on a serving plate.

✦✦Sprinkle with brandy, salt, and sugar, if needed, then drizzle with the vinegar, walnut oil, and chives. Refrigerate until ready to serve.

Emincés de Tomates au Chou Rouge **(Sliced Tomato Salad with Red Cabbage)** Serve the salad surrounded by finely shredded red cabbage, dressed with the same dressing or with any vinaigrette. Garnish with minced fresh parsley and chives.

CÉLERI-RAVE
ET CAROTTES RÉMOULADE

CELERIAC AND CARROT IN MUSTARDY DRESSING

– Serves 4 to 6 –

When you order an *assiette de crudités* or *hors d'œuvre variés,* you will almost always find a mound of tangy celery root salad. Sometimes this rustic root is lightly cooked before being tossed with dressing; at other times it is raw.

While classically it is served plain, I like adding the slightly sweet, earthy accent of carrot. You could, of course, omit the carrot and serve it separately, dressed with a little vinaigrette.

Preparing celeriac can be a trial: The big knobby earth-encrusted root can be fibrous, tough, and hard both to peel and shred. Peel carefully so as not to hurt yourself; as for shredding, a food processor is excellent, especially the blade made for fine julienne.

1 cup coarsely shredded, peeled celery root
2 to 3 carrots, peeled and coarsely shredded
3 shallots, minced
2 teaspoons capers, drained
1 garlic clove, minced
3 tablespoons mayonnaise, or 2 tablespoons mayonnaise mixed with 1 tablespoon yogurt
1 tablespoon Dijon mustard
1 tablespoon vegetable oil
1 teaspoon white wine vinegar or fresh lemon juice
Salt and pepper to taste
1 tablespoon minced fresh parsley

55

✦✦Combine the celery root, carrots, shallots, capers, and garlic, then moisten with the mayonnaise or mayonnaise mixture.

✦✦Mix in the mustard, oil, and vinegar or lemon juice, then season with salt and pepper. Chill until ready to serve.

✦✦Serve sprinkled with parsley.

BETTERAVES RAPÉES DIJONNAISE

GRATED BEETS WITH SWEET-

SOUR MUSTARD DRESSING

– Serves 4 –

Order an *assiette de crudités* almost anywhere in France and there will almost always be beets on the plate. You'll find beets sliced, grated, or diced and served with crème fraîche, vinaigrette, or the following mustard dressing, which I sampled in Dijon.

This salad is even better the next day.

3 to 4 unpeeled beets
½ onion, finely chopped
3 to 4 tablespoons vinegar of choice
2 to 3 tablespoons sugar, or to taste
1 teaspoon Dijon mustard, or to taste

✦✦Bake the beets in a preheated 350°F oven until tender, about 1 hour. Let cool to the touch, then shred them on the large rasps of a grater (their skins should come off as you grate them).

✦✦Mix the grated beets with the onion and set aside.

✦✦Combine the vinegar, sugar and mustard, then pour it over the beet and onion mixture; taste and adjust seasoning.

SALADE DE CHOUX

À L'ALSACIENNE

ALSATIAN SALAD OF CABBAGE,

CARROT, AND TURNIP WITH

CUMIN-MUSTARD DRESSING

– Serves 4 –

Cumin and mustard scent this Alsatian dressing for northern winter vegetables. Serve it as part of a first course selection of crudités, along with Salade Tiède de Pommes de Terre, Fèves, et Chèvre (pages 53–54), or Salade de Pommes de Terre et Concombre (page 57).

¼ head red cabbage, thinly sliced
¼ head white cabbage, thinly sliced
2 carrots, peeled and shredded
1 turnip, peeled and shredded
1 tablespoon dry white wine or dash of
*   fresh lemon juice*
½ cucumber, peeled, seeded, and cut
*   into julienne*
3 to 4 tablespoons crème fraîche or
*   sour cream*
2 teaspoons extra-strong Dijon mustard
⅛ to ¼ teaspoon ground cumin
Dash of red or white wine vinegar
Salt, pepper, and cayenne pepper to taste
3 tablespoons minced fresh chervil

✦✦Combine the cabbage, carrots, turnip, and cucumber; toss with the wine or lemon juice.

✦✦Mix the crème fraîche or sour cream with the mustard, cumin, wine vinegar, salt, and black and cayenne pepper.

✦✦Toss the vegetables with the dressing and chill until ready to serve. Pour off any liquid that accumulates at the bottom of the bowl. Serve the salad sprinkled with chervil.

Salade du Céleri au Cerfeuil (**Celery Salad with Chervil**) Replace the cabbage, carrots, turnips, and cucumber with 2 bunches of celery cut into matchsticks (first remove the large strings). Toss in the above mustard-cumin dressing and serve sprinkled with chervil.

SALADE DE FENOUIL ET POIVRONS ROUGES CITRONNÉS

FENNEL AND RED PEPPER SALAD WITH LEMON DRESSING

– Serves 4 as part of a salad selection –

Such a simple salad, utterly refreshing on a summer day! Nibble on inky black olives before the meal, then serve this salad with a selection of other little salads: Salade de Tomates (page 55) and Haricots Blancs aux Olives (page 60). Follow with a dish of vegetables in a puréed vegetable sauce, as pleasing to the eye as to the palate, such as a Méli-Mélo de Légumes Printaniers et Coulis de Légumes Vertes (page 106). Any light Provençal wine–red, white, or rosé– would be nice with this.

> *1 fennel bulb, trimmed and cut into julienne*
> *1 red bell pepper, seeded, deribbed, and cut into julienne*
> *1 to 2 tablespoons olive oil*
> *Juice of ½ lemon*
> *Salt to taste*

✦✦Combine the fennel with the red pepper and dress with the olive oil, lemon juice, and salt. Serve right away.

SALADE DE POMMES DE TERRE ET CONCOMBRE

POTATO AND CUCUMBER SALAD

– Serves 4 to 6 –

The cooling, silken bite of cucumber interspersed with earthy potatoes gives a special quality to this salad from Alsace. Shallots, white wine, and fresh herbs add their savor.

A sizzling casserole of savory crêpes with leeks and Roquefort (pages 98–99) would be nice as a main course.

> *8 boiling potatoes*
> *½ cup dry white wine*
> *2 shallots, minced*
> *Salt and pepper to taste*
> *1 tablespoon minced fresh chervil*
> *1 tablespoon minced fresh tarragon or dill*
> *1 tablespoon minced fresh chives*
> *1 cucumber, peeled, seeded, and cut into ¼-inch dice*
> *1 tablespoon white wine vinegar*
> *2 tablespoons vegetable or olive oil, or a combination*

✦✦Cook the potatoes in boiling water until just tender, about 20 to 25 minutes. Run them under cold water until they are cool enough to handle, then peel and cut into slices.

✦✦Combine the warm cooked potato slices with the wine and let sit for 10 minutes. If the wine is not absorbed completely by the potatoes, cook them on the stove until the wine evaporates. Remove from heat and let cool to warm room temperature.

✦✦Mix the wine-dressed potatoes with the shallots, salt and pepper, chervil, tarragon or dill, chives, and cucumber and toss with the vinegar and oil.

✦✦Cover and refrigerate until ready to serve.

Artichauts Vinaigrette

Artichoke Hearts

in Oil and Vinegar

– Serves 4 as part of a salad selection –

Catherine de' Medici introduced the artichoke to France in 1533 when she married the Dauphin and brought her cooks and gardeners from Italy.

France has since grown and eaten a wide variety of artichokes. This dish can be made using either large or small artichokes, bearing in mind that with the large ones you will need to remove the pesky choke, but with the tiny chokeless ones you can leave them as is.

While artichokes can easily be purchased marinated or bought frozen and ready to be cooked and marinated, this dish is at its best when made with fresh artichokes, as their nutty, earthy character is the main flavor of this simple dish.

4 large or 12 small artichoke hearts,
quartered and blanched (see page 210)
2 lemons
3 tablespoons olive oil, or as desired
Salt to taste

1 garlic clove or shallot, minced
1 tablespoon minced fresh basil, marjoram,
or oregano

✦✦Drain the hot artichokes and toss them with the remaining ingredients. Serve at room temperature.

Pâtés aux Artichauts **(Artichoke Purée)** Purée the cooked artichokes and their marinade into a chunky appetizer spread for bread or pestolike sauce for pasta.

Artichauts et Fèves **(Artichokes and Fava Beans)** Add 1 cup cooked peeled fava beans to the warm artichoke mixture. Serve as part of an appetizer selection, or spoon onto *salade niçoise* or into a *pan bagnat*.

Asperges Vinaigrette

aux Noix

Asparagus in

Nut Oil Vinaigrette

– Serves 4 –

While asparagus is delicious with nearly any vinaigrette, nut oil adds an elusive accent and makes a delightful change from olive oil.

1 bunch asparagus, tough ends trimmed
2 shallots, minced
1 tablespoon white wine
1 tablespoon white wine vinegar
2 tablespoons walnut oil, or 1 table-
spoon hazelnut oil and 1 tablespoon
vegetable oil

1 tablespoon minced fresh parsley or
    chervil, or a combination
Salt and pepper to taste

✦✦ Cook the asparagus in boiling salted water to cover until it is crisp-tender, about 4 to 5 minutes. Drain and toss it with the remaining ingredients. Serve at room temperature.

Asperges et Lentilles aux Noix (Asparagus and Lentils in Nut Oil Vinaigrette) Combine ½ cup green lentils with 2 bay leaves, 3 garlic cloves, and 1 chopped carrot or chunk of celery root, and cold water to cover. Simmer until the lentils are just tender, about 30 minutes. Drain well and season with salt and pepper.

Spoon some of the lentils onto each plate, then top with the asparagus. Drizzle the nut vinaigrette over the asparagus and lentils and serve warm.

SALADE DE CHAMPIGNONS

CRUS À LA MOUTARDE

RAW MUSHROOM SALAD

IN MUSTARD AND

CRÈME FRAÎCHE DRESSING

– Serves 4 –

This little salad of thinly sliced mushrooms dressed in crème fraîche and Dijon mustard is one of the things I imagine eating when I think about winter in Paris. The crème fraîche is light and kind to mushrooms, not weighing them down into a sodden mess as ordinary vinaigrettes can do.

Be sure you use extra strong Dijon for this dressing; it is the only one that imparts the rich, distinctive flavor of authenticity.

1 pound fresh firm mushrooms, thinly
    sliced
Juice of ½ lemon
2 tablespoons minced fresh chervil
2 tablespoons minced fresh chives
1 to 2 tablespoons extra-strong Dijon
    mustard, or to taste
¼ cup crème fraîche or sour cream
Salt and pepper to taste

✦✦ Toss the mushrooms with the lemon juice, chervil, and chives; set aside.

✦✦ Mix the mustard and crème fraîche or sour cream, then toss with the mushrooms and herbs. Season with salt and pepper and serve within 2 hours.

SALADES AUX HARICOTS ET LENTILLES

—

SALADS WITH BEANS AND LENTILS

You'll find a wide array of beans eaten as salads in bistros throughout France. Their earthy fragrance and hearty texture make them a welcome plate-mate with the savory oils and aromatic vinegars that dress the best salads. Beans and legumes are high in protein and fiber–little powerhouses of nutrition. And they satisfy as few other foods do. Even the chic-est of bistros will offer a dish of beans and/or lentils as an appetizer salad–the exact type depending upon your locale and the favor of the chef.

PUY LENTIL AND RICE SALAD

– Serves 4 –

The Auvergnat Puy lentils give their distinctive flavor and appearance to the simple rice salad so adored throughout France's sunny south.

Serve for lunch as a first course, garnished with hard-cooked egg, crisp-tender green beans, a few salty black olives, and a handful of mixed baby greens.

¼ cup green lentils, preferably lentils de Puy
1 cup water
1 bay leaf
½ cup long-grain white rice
1 cup water
Pinch of salt, plus salt to taste
2 shallots, minced
2 teaspoons strong Dijon mustard
1 garlic clove, minced
1 tablespoon red or white wine vinegar
3 tablespoons olive oil
Pepper to taste
4 handfuls mixed baby greens
2 tablespoons minced fresh chives

OPTIONAL GARNISH

4 ounces green beans, cooked until crisp-
*   tender*
2 hard-cooked eggs cut into wedges
15 to 20 black Mediterranean-type olives
*   such as niçoise, Kalamata, or dry-cured*
*   Italian olives*

✦✦ Combine the lentils, water, and bay leaf in a small saucepan and bring to a boil. Immediately reduce heat, cover, and simmer until the lentils are just tender, about 40 minutes, adding more liquid if needed. Set aside.

✦✦ Meanwhile, combine the water, rice, and a pinch of salt in a small saucepan. Bring to a boil, then reduce heat and simmer, covered, until just tender, 5 to 10 minutes.

✦✦ Drain the lentils and gently mix them into the rice along with the shallots.

✦✦ Mix the mustard, garlic, vinegar, and olive oil, then pour two-thirds into the rice and lentils and toss gently; season with salt and pepper.

✦✦ Toss the greens with the remaining dressing and arrange them on plates with the rice-lentil salad alongside. Sprinkle with chives and garnish with green beans, egg wedges, and olives.

GARLICKY WHITE BEANS WITH BLACK OLIVE DRESSING

– Makes 2 cups –

I like to mound these beans on a bed of arugula and dandelion leaves, surrounded by a summery tomato salad and a handful of boiled new potatoes.

1 garlic clove
Pinch of salt
2 tablespoons olive oil
¼ cup pitted black oil-cured olives,
*   coarsely chopped*
1 teaspoon capers, drained
Pinch of herbes de Provence
Black pepper to taste
2 cups drained cooked white beans such
*   as lingots, cocos, or cannellini*
Squeeze of lemon to taste

✦✦Crush the garlic with a pinch of the salt in a mortar or food processor, then add the olive oil, olives, and capers to make a slightly lumpy sauce with uneven bits of black olive scattered throughout. Season with herbes de Provence and pepper. ✦✦Combine with the beans and add lemon juice. Serve at room temperature.

Pois Chiches aux Olives (**Chickpeas with Black Olives**) Substitute chickpeas for the white beans in the above recipe and garnish with fresh rosemary.

Haricots Blancs à la Vinaigrette de Noisette (**White Beans with Garlicky Hazelnut Vinaigrette**) Omit the capers and black olives from the above vinaigrette and use hazelnut oil in place of olive oil.

Le marché

POIS CHICHES AUX CUMIN

CHICKPEAS IN CUMIN-PARSLEY VINAIGRETTE

– Serves 4 –

This is an exciting little dish, all the more so for its simplicity. Its whiff of cumin takes it beyond the expected parsley vinaigrette. Serve as part of a selection of little salads to begin the meal–terrific for a couscous or grilled vegetable feast.

> 1½ to 2 cups drained cooked chickpeas
> 2 tablespoons minced fresh parsley
> 2 garlic cloves, minced
> Several pinches ground cumin
> 2 to 3 tablespoons olive oil
> 1 teaspoon balsamic vinegar
> Juice of ½ lemon
> Salt and pepper to taste

✦✦Combine all the ingredients. Cover and refrigerate until ready to serve.

SALADE D'HARICOTS À LA LANGUEDOCIENNE

WHITE BEAN SALAD WITH SWEET PEPPERS AND TOMATO VINAIGRETTE

– Serves 4 to 6 –

We ate this salad near Perpignan, in a region that is emphatically Catalan both in culture and cuisine. Puréeing the garlic and tomato as a basis for the dressing makes this salad distinctive.

5 garlic cloves

Pinch of salt

4 ripe tomatoes, diced

1 onion, chopped

2 teaspoons sweet paprika

Pepper to taste

1 teaspoon minced fresh thyme, or
    ¼ teaspoon dried thyme

1 teaspoon minced fresh rosemary, or
    ¼ teaspoon dried rosemary

3 tablespoons wine vinegar

¼ cup olive oil, or as desired

3 cups drained cooked white beans

Pinch of sugar (optional)

½ a red bell pepper, seeded, deribbed, and
    chopped

½ a green bell pepper, seeded, deribbed,
    and chopped

¼ fresh hot green or red chili, minced, or
    Tabasco sauce to taste

1 tablespoon minced fresh flat-leaf parsley

Crusty bread for serving

✦✦ In a mortar or food processor, purée the garlic with a pinch of salt, then add half the tomatoes and purée with half the onion, the paprika, pepper, thyme, rosemary, and vinegar. Blend in the olive oil and set aside.

✦✦ Combine the beans with the remaining tomatoes and onion, then add the chopped peppers and toss with the dressing. Season with chili or Tabasco sauce, if desired.

✦✦ Taste and adjust the seasoning. Serve with crusty bread to dunk into the juices.

Entrées aux Légumes

. . .

Vegetable First Courses

Light vegetable dishes are an appealing choice for a first course, especially during the spring or summer when vegetables are particularly bright and vivacious. Following is a selection of dishes to open your meal, all based on seasonal vegetables.

. . . .

ASPERGES AU TRUFFE

ASPARAGUS WITH TRUFFLES

– Serves 3 or 4 –

Summertime in the Vaucluse means summer truffles and tender asparagus. Pale grayish white in their center instead of the inky black of winter truffles, summer truffles are gently scented and should be prepared simply to highlight their delicacy.

In France, asparagus is one of the very few foods eaten with the fingers; licking the foresty-scented olive oil from your fingers is not socially approved but it is almost irresistible. In keeping with the luxury of asparagus and truffles, you might want to sip Champagne or another vivacious bubbly.

> *1 bunch fresh asparagus, trimmed of tough*
> *ends*
> *½ garlic clove, minced*
> *2 tablespoons olive oil*
> *1 truffle, brushed and shaved*
> *Salt and pepper to taste*
> *Crusty bread or fougasse for serving*

✦✦Cook the asparagus in boiling water until crisp-tender, about 4 to 5 minutes. Drain well and arrange on a serving plate or individual plates.

✦✦Combine the garlic and olive oil, then drizzle it over the cooked asparagus and top with shavings of truffle, salt, and pepper.

✦✦Serve at warm room temperature, along with crusty bread or fougasse to dip into the dressing.

THREE ASPARAGUS STARTERS FROM THE SOUTH OF FRANCE

Asperges aux Champignons (Asparagus with Field Mushrooms) In place of the truffle, use several fresh wild mushrooms or dried mushrooms rehydrated in boiling water and squeezed dry (see page 210) and warmed gently in the garlic and oil over a low heat. Offer lemon wedges for those who would like one.

Pâtes aux Asperges (Asparagus with Tomato Pasta) Serve a flowerlike arrangement of steamed asparagus tips under a mound of tender fettuccine, dressed with Coulis de Tomates (page 205) or a light flavorful sauce, all drizzled with olive oil,

sprinkled with garlic, and blanketed with fresh basil leaves and shavings of Parmesan cheese.

Les Trois Asperges à la Tapenade (Three Types of Asparagus with Black Olive Paste) When truffles and mushrooms are both unavailable, or when you crave the sheer strong, salty flavor of black olives, prepare asparagus with the sunny Niçoise taste of tapenade.

In a little village tucked high in the hills behind Nice, I sat down to a plate of three types of asparagus: wild grasslike asparagus, spindly cultivated green asparagus, and juicy fat purple-white asparagus, all steamed until crisp-tender, then dressed while warm in fragrant extra-virgin olive oil, minced garlic, and a squirt of lemon. They were then garnished with a handful of wild leaves–purslane one time, young dandelion another–and topped with a dollop of salty black olive paste. Gorgeous.

ARTICHAUTS, TOMATES, ET POMMES DE TERRE, SAUCE SORGES

ARTICHOKES, RIPE TOMATOES, AND BOILED POTATOES WITH HARD-COOKED EGG AND HERB VINAIGRETTE

– Serves 4 –

Sauce Sorges is a thick sauce of chopped or crushed hard-cooked egg, bound vinaigrette-style with oil and vinegar, and brightened with sweetly perfumed herbs.

Though it is a specialty of Périgord Blanc and traditionally prepared with a bland vegetable oil, I think the fruity flavor of olive oil is even better, and makes a sauce similar to the *vinegretta* adored in Spain.

The selection of cooked and raw vegetables can vary. Here we have artichokes, ripe tomatoes, and tender boiled potatoes, but you could also choose cooked cardoons, a mound of tender leafy cooked chard, asparagus, crisp little haricots verts or heftier Roman beans, zucchini, or crunchy raw peppers and celery.

Be sure to serve a crusty bread to scoop up the sauce.

SAUCE SORGES

3 hard-cooked eggs, peeled and chopped
1 to 1½ teaspoons Dijon mustard
1 to 1½ tablespoons wine vinegar
4 tablespoons olive oil
2 shallots, minced
1 garlic clove, minced
Several tablespoons minced mixed fresh
herbs such as tarragon, parsley, chives,
chervil, dill
Salt and pepper to taste

2 artichokes
4 to 8 boiling potatoes
4 ounces green beans
8 ripe tomatoes, cut into wedges
Handful of frisée for garnish

✦✦ To make the sauce: Combine the chopped eggs with the mustard, vinegar, olive oil, shallots, garlic, and herbs, then season well with salt and pepper. Set the sauce aside or, if you are serving it more than 1 hour later, cover and refrigerate.
✦✦ With their spiky leaves attached, cut each artichoke in half lengthwise. If desired, clip the ends of the spiky leaves. Steam over boiling water in a covered pot until just tender, about 20 minutes. Remove from heat and set aside for a few minutes.
✦✦ Steam or boil the potatoes until tender, about 15 minutes. Let cool slightly and cut into bite-sized pieces.
✦✦ Cook the green beans in boiling water until they are just crisp-tender and bright green, about 4 to 5 minutes. Drain and rinse in cold water. Drain, dry on paper towels, and set aside.
✦✦ On each plate arrange a mound of tomato wedges, potato pieces, green beans, and frisée, then place an artichoke half on each plate. In the center of each plate, place a generous spoonful of sauce Sorges.
✦✦ Serve right away.

MACÉDOINE AUX LÉGUMES,

SAVEURS D'ETÉ

DICED SUMMER VEGETABLES

IN TOMATO VINAIGRETTE

– Serves 4 –

A *macédoine* is a mixture of diced cooked vegetables served as a saladlike first course, perhaps masked with a mayonnaise or moistened with a seasonal vinaigrette like the one below.

Other summer vegetables, such as yellow crookneck squash, zucchini, or tender young haricots verts, can be served in this salad in addition to, or in place of, the other vegetables, and in autumn try woodsy mushrooms, chervil, and chives.

La citrouille

3 shallots, minced

1 teaspoon white wine vinegar

1 teaspoon sherry vinegar

1 teaspoon balsamic vinegar

3 artichoke hearts, blanched and sliced
   (see page 210)

½ to ¾ cup shelled fava beans

1 bunch asparagus, tough ends removed

2 garlic cloves

Salt and pepper to taste

3 tablespoons olive oil

3 to 4 ripe tomatoes, peeled, seeded, and
   diced (see page 211)

About ¼ cup fresh basil leaves, thinly
   sliced

✦✦ Combine the shallots and three vinegars and set aside.

✦✦ Cook the fava beans in boiling water until they are just tender, about 5 minutes, then drain and rinse well in cold water. When they are cool enough to handle, peel off the skins. Set aside.

✦✦ Cut the asparagus into bite-sized lengths, then blanch them in boiling water for a minute or two, or until crisp-tender. Drain, then plunge them into cold water. Leave for 3 to 5 minutes, then drain and set aside.

✦✦ In a mortar, crush the garlic with several pinches of salt, then work in 1 tablespoon of the olive oil. Combine this with the tomatoes, shallots and vinegar, remaining 2 tablespoons olive oil, and half the basil. Season with salt and pepper.

✦✦ Combine the artichokes, favas, and asparagus, and dress with the tomato vinaigrette. Garnish with the remaining basil and serve right away.

AUBERGINES

ET POIVRONS GITANES

GYPSY-STYLE GRILLED

EGGPLANT, PEPPERS, AND

TOMATOES WITH PISTOU

– Serves 4 –

Perhaps this is called "gypsy style" for its lusty flavors, or perhaps because it is cooked out of doors. Regardless of the reasons for its name, this dish of grilled eggplant, peppers, and ripe tomatoes, perfumed with a delicious smudge of garlic-basil paste, is the essence of summertime.

2 to 3 tablespoons olive oil

2 garlic cloves, minced

Juice of ½ lemon

Salt and pepper to taste

1 eggplant, cut lengthwise into ¼-inch
   slices

La bergerie

2 red or 1 yellow and 1 red bell pepper,
    halved, seeded, and deribbed (leave
    stems on)
2 juicy ripe tomatoes, diced and drained
¼ to ½ cup Pistou (pages 208–209)
4 fresh basil sprigs for garnish

✦✦ Combine the olive oil, garlic, and lemon juice; season with salt and pepper.

✦✦ Place the eggplant and peppers in a nonreactive container and pour the dressing over them. Toss gently to coat well.

✦✦ Light a charcoal fire in a grill or preheat a gas grill. Grill the eggplant slices and pepper halves over medium heat until they are tender and lightly browned in places.

✦✦ Arrange the eggplant and peppers on a plate and decorate with the diced tomatoes, pistou, and basil sprigs. Serve warm or at room temperature.

Aubergines et Courgettes Grillées, Coulis de Tomates aux Poivrons Rouges **(Grilled Eggplant and Zucchini in a Sauce of Tomatoes and Red Peppers)** Substitute zucchini, cut into thin lengthwise strips, for the peppers in the above recipe. Ladle a puddle of Coulis de Tomates aux Poivrons Rouges (page 205) onto each plate. Arrange the grilled eggplant and zucchini on top of the coulis, and decorate with dots of pistou or tiny leaves of basil.

SALADE DU BERGER

ROASTED EGGPLANT, PEPPER, AND ARTICHOKE SALAD

– Serves 4 –

Salade du berger, or "shepherd's salad," was named after the shepherd's way of roasting seasonal vegetables over an open fire, then eating them dressed with garlic, olive oil, and vinegar. It makes an appealing start to a summery lunch or supper, as we discovered one midday sitting at a little table nestled under a shade umbrella in a café in a Provençal village square.

It was market day; the stalls were just packing up and the restaurants readying up their tables. A few little dogs were hopefully rummaging through the piles of goodies left behind, but the square was rapidly emptying as workers and visitors alike headed to the pleasures awaiting at lunch.

Such a lusty dish demands an equally lusty wine, perhaps a Gigondas.

2 Asian eggplants, stemmed
2 red bell peppers
2 unpeeled red onions, halved
9 unpeeled garlic cloves
5 large ripe tomatoes

4 to 6 tablespoons olive oil

Salt to taste

5 to 10 blanched fresh artichoke hearts
(see page 210), or 8 to 10 thawed frozen
artichoke hearts

2 tablespoons red wine vinegar, or to taste

1 teaspoon minced fresh rosemary

Pepper to taste

✦✦ Cut each eggplant into 3 or so chunks each and place in an earthenware baking casserole. Add the onion halves, 6 of the garlic cloves, and the tomatoes, then drizzle them with 1 to 2 tablespoons of the olive oil and sprinkle with salt.

✦✦ Place the vegetables in the oven, turn on the heat to 375°F, and bake for 30 minutes, turning once or twice.

✦✦ Add the artichoke hearts, drizzle with 1 tablespoon of the olive oil, and bake for 20 minutes, or until the artichoke hearts are lightly browned.

✦✦ Remove the vegetables from heat and let cool to the touch.

✦✦ Peel the eggplant and cut or tear the flesh into long strips; peel the peppers and cut them into strips as well, then add to the eggplant.

✦✦ Peel the tomatoes and squeeze the tomato skins well to extract all of their flavorful juices; add those juices to the eggplant and peppers, then dice the tomato flesh and add to the eggplant and peppers.

✦✦ Squeeze the baked garlic cloves out of their skins and into the eggplant mixture. Peel the onions and cut the flesh into strips, then add this to the vegetable mixture as well. Finally, cut the artichokes into strips and add them to the vegetables. Discard any leftover skins.

✦✦ Pour any remaining juices from the pan into

the cut-up vegetables. Mince the remaining 3 garlic cloves and add to the vegetables with the remaining 2 to 3 tablespoons olive oil, the vinegar, rosemary, and salt, and pepper to taste.

✦✦ Serve with chunks of country bread.

Croûte à l'Ail, Légumes, et Chèvre (Roasted Vegetables with Garlicky Goat Cheese Toasts) Serve the salad accompanied with baguette slices that have been rubbed with garlic, brushed with olive oil, and spread with goat cheese.

Tarte aux Légumes, Olives, et Herbes (Tart of Roasted Vegetables, Olives, and Herbs) Add an extra ½ to ¾ cup diced tomatoes to the vegetable mixture, along with ½ cup pitted black Mediterranean olives and a few generous sprinklings of minced fresh herbs: marjoram, parsley, oregano, basil. Pile into a 9-inch unbaked tart shell (page 203) and bake in a preheated 350°F oven for about 30 minutes, or until the crust is golden. Serve warm or at room temperature, sprinkled with more chopped herbs to taste.

CASSOLETTE AUX AUBERGINES,

COURGETTES, POIVRONS,

ET TOMATES

CÔTE D'AZUR VEGETABLES,

ROASTED AND

BAKED WITH CHEESES

– Serves 4 –

This ratatouillelike mixture of eggplant, zucchini, peppers, and tomatoes bakes into an intensely flavored mélange, punctuated with the occasional bite of salty fresh cheese.

The topping of crispy melting cheese is enticing, too. And though Parmesan, Gruyère, and Gouda are all imported cheeses, the combination has been a Provençal one since the eighteenth century.

1 large eggplant, cut into bite-sized pieces
Salt for sprinkling
4 tablespoons olive oil
15 to 20 unpeeled garlic cloves, plus 3 to 5
  garlic cloves, minced
1 onion, quartered
3 zucchini
2 red bell peppers, roasted, peeled, and cut
  into strips (see page 210)
8 to 10 tomatoes, diced
1 tablespoon minced fresh rosemary
4 to 6 ounces fresh goat cheese or feta,
  diced or crumbled
1 tablespoon grated Parmesan
1 tablespoon grated Gruyère
1 tablespoon grated Gouda

✦✦Sprinkle the eggplant generously with salt and let sit for 30 minutes. When brown droplets of moisture have appeared on the surface, rinse the eggplant in cold water, then pat dry with paper towels.

✦✦Heat a heavy skillet, preferably a nonstick one, until very hot, then heat 1 tablespoon of the olive oil and add the eggplant cubes, whole unpeeled garlic cloves, and onion quarters. Reduce heat and cook until the vegetables are lightly charred. Remove from heat and let cool to the touch.

✦✦Cook the zucchini in boiling water until tender, about 15 minutes. Drain and let cool.

✦✦Preheat the oven to 375° to 400°F. Peel the

whole garlic cloves and return them to the eggplant mixture; dice the onion quarters and return those, too, to the eggplant mixture.

✦✦Dice the cooked zucchini and add it, along with the red pepper strips, tomatoes, minced raw garlic, rosemary, and cheese, to the eggplant mixture.

✦✦Pour into individual ramekins or a large gratin dish, then sprinkle the top with the grated cheeses.

✦✦Bake until lightly browned and crisped. Serve right away.

ARTICHAUTS À LA BARIGOULE

ARTICHOKES BRAISED

IN WHITE WINE

– Serves 4 –

A *la barigoule* is probably Nice's most famous way with artichokes: baby thistles, edible down to their chokeless heart, simmered in wine and olive oil, perfumed with mountain herbs.

While everyone agrees that it is delicious as a first course either hot or cold, and marvelous for dunking your bread into, no one is quite sure as to how it got its French name. Some say it came about because the artichokes were once cooked with or served grilled along with agaric mushrooms (in Provençal, *barigoule*), while others say the name comes from *farigoule,* the old Provençal name for thyme, which scents the dish.

Artichokes, with their strange chemistry, can alter the taste of the wine you drink, so don't waste a special wine on this meal. But I don't think you can go wrong with a chilled rosé or with the white wine you've cooked the thistles in.

3 onions, chopped

3 carrots, peeled and chopped

5 to 6 garlic cloves, coarsely chopped

3 to 4 tablespoons olive oil

12 to 16 tiny baby artichokes, trimmed,
    or 4 large artichoke hearts, quartered
    (see page 210)

1 tablespoon minced fresh thyme, or
    1 teaspoon dried thyme

1 tablespoon minced fresh parsley

1 cup dry white wine

1 cup water

Salt and pepper to taste

Juice of ¼ lemon, or to taste

✦✦ In a medium-large sauté pan or skillet over medium heat, sauté the onions, carrots, and garlic in the olive oil until softened, about 8 to 10 minutes. Add the artichokes, thyme, parsley, wine, and water. Bring to a boil, then reduce heat and simmer, covered, for 45 minutes, or until the artichokes are quite tender and the liquid has evaporated. Take care that they don't scorch; add extra water if needed.

✦✦ Season with salt, pepper, and lemon juice and serve either hot or at room temperature.

Barbouiado de Favo (Stewed Artichoke Hearts with Fava Beans) Simmer peeled blanched fava beans with the artichokes in the above recipe.

Barigoule d'Artichauts en Terrine, Coulis de Tomates aux Poivrons Rouges (Terrine of Artichokes Barigoule in Tomato–Red Pepper Sauce) In Aix-en-Provence I found artichokes *à la barigoule* jelled into a light terrine, then served on tomato and red pepper coulis.

To prepare it: Dissolve 1 envelope plain gelatin in ¼ cup cold water. Stir into the above recipe for artichokes *à la barigoule,* then pour into a terrine pan or individual molds. Cover and refrigerate for 3 to 4 hours, or until firm. Unmold and serve sliced in a pool of Coulis de Tomates aux Poivrons Rouges (page 205).

Barigoule aux Raviole des Herbes (Ravioli with Ragout of Artichokes and Herbs) Toss artichokes *à la barigoule* with herb- or pesto-filled pasta such as ravioli, tortellini, or agnolotti, and serve topped with shavings of Parmesan cheese.

JEUNES LÉGUMES AU VINAIGRETTE AUX HERBES

BABY VEGETABLES WITH HERB VINAIGRETTE

– Serves 4 –

Ordinary steamed vegetables and vinaigrette become a "bouquet" of spring vegetables, studded with chives and encircled by a ribbon of green vinaigrette. Sherry vinegar, though it is obviously Spanish in origin, has become very popular in France, as its flavor is gentle and slightly nutty, making a subtle vinaigrette.

For the most beautiful arrangement, choose vegetables whose colors delight: tender snow peas or sugar snaps, baby carrots with the tip end of their greens, red and yellow cherry tomatoes or roasted red peppers, tiny edible corn on the cob or kernels of sweet garden corn, a few fronds of celery leaves, and exotic purple potatoes.

2 to 3 purple potatoes, peeled

12 to 15 tiny baby carrots, stubs of green
    ends intact

20 to 25 tiny edible corn on the cob or kernels cut from 1 to 2 fresh ears of corn

3 tiny yellow crookneck squashes

1 red bell pepper, roasted, peeled, and cut into strips (see page 210)

4 ounces sugar snap peas or snow peas

15 or so cherry tomatoes, either red or yellow, or both

1 shallot, minced

⅓ cup vegetable oil, or as needed

2 to 3 tablespoons sherry vinegar, or to taste

3 to 4 tablespoons minced fresh chervil

3 to 4 tablespoons minced fresh chives

3 to 4 tablespoons minced fresh parsley

Salt and pepper to taste

Handful of fresh chive stems for garnish

8 to 12 tufts celery leaves

✦✦Boil the potatoes until they are just tender, about 15 to 20 minutes. Drain and keep warm.

✦✦Meanwhile, steam the carrots over boiling water in a covered pot until they are almost tender, about 5 to 6 minutes. Add the baby corn and squash and cook for 3 to 4 minutes. Add the pepper, peas, and tomatoes and cook for 2 to 3 minutes. Drain and keep warm.

✦✦Cut the potatoes into about ¼-inch slices. Set aside and keep warm.

✦✦In a blender or food processor, whirl the shallot, oil, and vinegar to form a smooth emulsion. Reserve 2 tablespoons, then add all but 2 tablespoons of the minced herbs. Whirl the vinaigrette and herbs together to form a smooth green purée; season with salt and pepper and let sit for a few minutes.

✦✦Arrange the warm vegetables into bouquets on warm plates and splash each with a little of the reserved vinaigrette (without the herbs). Garnish the vegetables with 2 tablespoons chives

and tufts of celery poked in here and there, then circle the vegetables with a ribbon of green vinaigrette. Sprinkle the minced herbs around the edge of the plate. Serve right away.

TOMATES À LA LANGUEDOCIENNE

OLIVE OIL–ROASTED TOMATOES

IN THEIR JUICES

– Serves 6 to 8 –

Peeled and slow roasted in olive oil, tomatoes become concentrated in flavor. In the Languedoc you might find this as a first course during the height of tomato season, with crusty bread to dip into the olive oil–rich juices. This is quintessential Midi fare, the sort of thing brought to your table without your asking, while you decide on what you will order from the ubiquitous wood-burning fire.

Such summery fare slips down deliciously with a chilled Bandol rosé.

20 to 30 tomatoes, peeled (see page 211)

3 to 4 tablespoons olive oil

Salt to taste

2 garlic cloves, minced

1 tablespoon thinly sliced, fresh basil leaves

✦✦Heat the olive oil over medium-low heat in a pan large enough to just hold the tomatoes in one layer (use two pans if necessary). Add the tomatoes, sprinkle lightly with salt, then cover and cook for about 10 minutes. Carefully turn the tomatoes over using a spatula so that you do not break them up.

✦✦Cover and cook 10 to 15 minutes longer or until they shrink to about half their original size.

As the tomatoes cook, the oil will first become cloudy and filled with juices, then it will return to an oil-like state, but with a golden color. Sprinkle the garlic into the hot oil with the tomatoes at the end of the cooking.

✦✦Using a spatula, remove the tomatoes from the pan and place them on a plate. Pour the pan juices over the tomatoes and serve them sprinkled with fresh basil, accompanied with crusty bread to dip into the juices.

PALETS DE POMMES DE TERRE ET GOUSSES D'AIL, BEURRE CITRON

THIN POTATO PANCAKES WITH WHOLE GARLIC CLOVES IN LEMON BUTTER

– Serves 4 –

Little pancakes of grated potato, topped with whole garlic cloves in a lemony butter sauce, are a beguiling way to start a meal.

Aligoté would be a good wine choice, as its acidity balances nicely with the rich sauce.

3 garlic heads
3 to 4 tablespoons butter
Salt and pepper to taste
Juice of ½ lemon
4 baking potatoes
½ onion
2 tablespoons minced fresh parsley

✦✦Separate the garlic into cloves, blanch, drain (reserve the blanching liquid), and let cool to the touch. Peel the cloves.

✦✦Melt 1 tablespoon of the butter in a medium, heavy sauté pan or skillet over medium-low heat. Add the garlic cloves and cook until golden but not dark brown, about 5 to 10 minutes. Season with salt and pepper as they cook.

✦✦When the garlic is lightly browned, add ½ to 1 cup of the blanching liquid and reduce heat. Cook the mixture until the liquid has evaporated. Squeeze in the lemon, cook a few moments, then add ½ to 1 cup more blanching liquid and continue to cook until it reduces to 2 to 3 tablespoons of sauce and the garlic is very tender.

✦✦Remove from heat, swirl in 2 tablespoons of the butter, taste for seasoning, and set aside.

✦✦On the fine rasps of a grater, grate the potato and onion. Melt the remaining 1 tablespoon butter in the pan over medium-high heat. Sprinkle the potato and onion well with salt and pepper, and add the mixture to the pan in ¼-cup tablespoon dollops, flattening them into thin pancakes about 4 to 5 inches in diameter.

✦✦Cook until browned on each side. Transfer to warm serving plates.

✦✦Rewarm the sauce. Spoon the garlic and sauce over the pancakes. Sprinkle with parsley and serve.

les poivrons

71

COURGETTES ET DUXELLES EN COULIS DE CAROTTES

ZUCCHINI AND SAUTÉED MUSHROOMS WITH CARROT PURÉE

– Serves 4 –

This recipe was inspired by an elegant plate set in front of me in the medieval town of Cahors, in a little bistro just around the corner from the marketplace as the market was packing up. The *carte* outside said that everything on the menu was fresh from the market that morning, so I walked in and sat down.

My first course was tiny zucchini with the flowers still attached, and each flower was filled with duxelles (sautéed minced mushrooms). The pale green squash were thinly sliced, fanned, and served on a pool of carrot purée. The dish was beautiful, and it was served with a spoon for scooping up the sauce.

A Beaujolais or a chilled Chinon would be good with this.

4 dried morel mushrooms
½ cup boiling water
4 carrots, peeled and thinly sliced
5 tablespoons minced shallots
4 tablespoons heavy cream
2 tablespoons crème fraîche or sour cream
1 teaspoon sweet paprika
3 tablespoons butter
1 tablespoon Coulis de Tomates (page 205)
   or tomato paste
Salt, sugar, and cayenne pepper to taste
4 ounces fresh mushrooms, finely chopped
2 to 3 zucchini, cut diagonally into thin
   slices, or 8 whole baby zucchini with
   flowers, if possible

1 garlic clove, minced
1 to 2 teaspoons minced fresh chives or
   parsley for garnish (optional)

✦✦Soak the dried morels in the boiling water until cool.

✦✦Meanwhile, cook the carrots in boiling water to cover until just tender, about 8 minutes. In a blender or food processor, purée the carrots with 2 tablespoons of the shallots, then return the mixture to the saucepan. Add the cream and cook over high heat for 5 to 7 minutes, or until the mixture forms a thick sauce. Add the crème fraîche or sour cream, paprika, 1 tablespoon of the butter, tomato coulis or paste, salt, sugar, and cayenne. Taste for seasoning, then remove from the heat and set aside.

✦✦Remove the morels from their liquid (reserve the liquid) and cut them into small pieces. Strain the soaking liquid and discard the grit that remains at the bottom.

✦✦Melt 1 tablespoon of the butter in a medium sauté pan or skillet with 2 tablespoons of the shallots and lightly sauté the fresh mushrooms over medium heat for 5 minutes. Add the morels and their soaking liquid and cook until most of the liquid has evaporated, about 5 to 7 minutes. Remove from heat and add half the garlic. Set aside and keep warm.

✦✦Cook the zucchini in boiling water to cover until just tender, about 5 to 7 minutes, drain. Season with salt. In a large, heavy sauté pan or skillet over medium heat, melt the remaining 1 tablespoon butter and cook the remaining garlic and shallots for 3 to 4 minutes. Add the zucchini and heat through.

✦✦To serve, heat the carrot purée and pour a pool of it onto each plate. Arrange the sliced zucchini (if using young zucchini, cut it into fans) in the center of the purée. Spoon little mounds of the mushrooms around the edge of the plate. Serve hot, garnished with chives or parsley, if desired.

FONDS D'ARTICHAUTS FARCIS AU CHÈVRE CHAUD AVEC VINAIGRETTE BASILIC

ARTICHOKE BOTTOMS STUFFED WITH GOAT CHEESE IN BASIL VINAIGRETTE

– Serves 4 –

Artichokes, with their tender earthy flesh, are delicious filled with tangy goat cheese.

Artichokes are always good as a first course, since they possess a nearly magical chemical quality that makes everything else eaten with them taste slightly sweet and more vibrant. (Unfortunately, this same quality can play havoc with wine. I'd probably choose a flinty white to complement the goat cheese, and hope for the best.)

I recently ate this in a Paris bistro on one of the first bright days of spring. The plate was garnished with nasturtiums, and sitting in the sunshine after the long gray winter, I nearly laughed out loud with happiness when I saw the little yellow flowers.

8 ounces fresh white goat cheese

1 egg, lightly beaten

5 garlic cloves, minced

Large pinch of dried thyme or herbes de Provence

3 tablespoons olive oil

2 tablespoons grated Parmesan cheese

4 large artichoke bottoms, or 12 small to medium ones (see page 210)

3 tablespoons fresh bread crumbs

3 tablespoons minced fresh chives

2 teaspoons white wine vinegar or to taste

2 to 3 tablespoons thinly sliced, fresh basil leaves

✦✦Preheat the oven to 400°F. Mix the goat cheese with the egg, half of the garlic, thyme, 1 teaspoon of the olive oil, and the Parmesan cheese. Spoon this mixture into each artichoke bottom. Press the bread crumbs onto the filling and arrange the artichokes in a baking dish or individual gratin dishes. Drizzle with 2 teaspoons of the remaining olive oil and set aside.

✦✦Combine the remaining garlic with the chives, vinegar, and remaining 2 tablespoons olive oil. Season with salt and pepper.

✦✦Bake the artichokes until the crumbs are golden brown and the artichokes are heated through.

✦✦Serve in a pool of chive vinaigrette, garnished with a sprinkling of basil.

QUENELLES DE PETITS POIS À LA CRÈME AUX HERBES

DUMPLINGS OF GREEN PEAS IN HERBED CREAM

– Serves 4 –

Quenelles are poached dumplings made from a base of choux paste. They are not traditionally vegetarian, but make an excellent vegetarian dish when enriched with puréed vegetables and fresh herbs. These taste like the most delicate gnocchi or matzo balls you could wish for, and, resting in a little puddle of cream or sauce, they look quite chic as well.

¾ cup milk

5 tablespoons butter

¾ cup all-purpose or half all-purpose and half whole-wheat flour

6 eggs

1 cup blanched fresh or thawed frozen petits pois

4 shallots or green onions (white part only), minced

3 garlic cloves, minced

⅛ to ¼ teaspoon dried marjoram or basil, crumbled

2 to 3 teaspoons minced fresh parsley

Several gratings of fresh nutmeg

Small pinch of ground cinnamon

Salt and pepper to taste

1½ cups (6 ounces) mixed grated Parmesan and Gruyère cheese

¾ cup vegetable stock (pages 201–202)

¾ cup heavy cream

½ cup fresh whole-wheat bread crumbs

3 to 4 tablespoons minced, mixed, fresh marjoram, parsley, and thyme

✦✦Heat the milk in a saucepan over medium-high heat until it bubbles around the edges; add 3 tablespoons of the butter, stir to melt, then remove the milk from heat.

✦✦Add the flour all at once, then stir well. If the mixture is not very dry already, return it to medium-low heat and cook, stirring, until it is nearly dry.

✦✦Remove from heat and beat in the eggs one at a time. When the mixture is smooth, add the peas. In a blender or food processor, purée the mixture until it is smooth. Stir in the shallots or green onions, garlic, marjoram or basil, parsley, nutmeg, cinnamon, salt, pepper, and cheese. Cover and refrigerate for 30 minutes.

✦✦Preheat the oven to 450°F. In a small saucepan, combine the stock and cream. Bring to a boil and cook over high heat until reduced by about one third. Remove from heat.

✦✦Fill a large sauté pan or skillet with salted water and bring it to a boil. Reduce heat to a simmer. Using 2 tablespoons, form the chilled mixture into oval dumplings and ease them into the water in batches. They will sink to the bottom of the pan, then as they cook they will rise to the surface. Cook for about 10 minutes, or until tender. Using a slotted spoon, transfer the quenelles to a gratin dish and pour the cream sauce over them. Sprinkle with bread crumbs, then dot with the remaining 2 tablespoons butter.

✦✦Bake the quenelles for about 6 minutes, or until lightly browned.

✦✦Immediately serve each portion of quenelles in a pool of sauce, sprinkled with the fresh herbs.

le panier de pommes

ENDIVE AU FROMAGE

À LA GASCONNE

BELGIAN ENDIVES BAKED

WITH ROQUEFORT CHEESE,

GASCONY STYLE

– Serves 4 –

S izzling endives baked with pungent blue cheese are a simple Gascon starter. Sometimes I serve a few spoonfuls of diced baked beets in the center of the flower shape, as the sweet, earthy beet is a blissful partner to both blue cheese and bitter endives.

8 Belgian endives
2 to 3 garlic cloves, minced
2 tablespoons dry white or red wine
2 tablespoons heavy cream
3 to 4 ounces Roquefort or bleu de Causses
*   cheese, crumbled*
1 tablespoon minced fresh parsley

♦♦Preheat the oven to 425°F.

♦♦Core each endive and pull off the leaves.

♦♦Arrange the endive leaves in 4 individual or gratin dishes with their pointed ends out, forming a flowerlike design. Sprinkle with the garlic, wine, cream, and cheese.

♦♦Bake the endives for about 15 minutes, or until they are lightly browned and the cheese has melted.

♦♦Serve right away, sprinkled with parsley.

BEIGNETS DE LÉGUMES VARIÉS

LITTLE VEGETABLE AND

FRAGRANT HERB FRITTERS

– Serves 4 to 6 –

C risp little fritters, brittle on the outside, filled with tender vegetables inside, make a tempuralike treat to begin a summer meal.

This dish delightfully combines a cooked vegetable (salsify), a shredded vegetable (zucchini), and a raw vegetable (eggplant).

Other vegetables, such as bite-sized pieces of artichoke, green onion, and pumpkin, are delicious as fritter fillings, as are edible flowers such as nasturtiums or zucchini flowers, and cheeses such as sliced Parmesan or mozzarella.

BATTER
1 cup all-purpose flour
2 eggs, separated
1 cup beer or sparkling water
1 teaspoon olive oil
Pinch of paprika
Pinch of black pepper

8 ounces salsify
4 zucchini, coarsely shredded
Salt for sprinkling
10 fresh mint leaves, chopped
1 eggplant
1 to 1½ tablespoons minced, mixed,
*   fresh herbs of choice: thyme, marjoram,*
*   parsley*
Handful of fresh sage leaves
Handful of fresh basil leaves
Flour for coating
Olive oil mixed with vegetable oil for
*   frying*

✦✦To make the batter: Place the flour in a large bowl and make a well. Add the remaining ingredients and stir into the flour to make a smooth batter. Let sit in a cool place for 1 hour.

✦✦Meanwhile, peel the salsify and cut it into 1- to 1½-inch lengths. Blanch until just tender, then drain well and set aside.

✦✦Generously salt the zucchini, then place in a sieve to drain for 30 to 60 minutes. Rinse well with cold water, then dry with paper towels. Combine with the mint and set aside.

✦✦Cut the eggplant into sticks about ½ inch wide and 2 inches long. Generously salt them and let sit for 20 to 30 minutes to exude their brownish juices. Rinse well, then pat dry with paper towels. Toss with the minced herbs and set aside.

✦✦Toss each batch of vegetables and the sage and basil leaves with flour to coat them and help the batter stick, then set aside.

✦✦Beat the egg whites until stiff but not dry, then fold into the batter. Divide the batter among 4 small bowls. Add the grated zucchini and mint to one, the cooked salsify to one, the eggplant to one, and the sage and basil leaves to one.

✦✦In a deep, heavy pot, heat the oil over medium-high heat until it is smoking.

✦✦Drop tablespoons of the zucchini mixture into the hot oil in small batches and cook until crisp and golden brown. Using a slotted spoon, transfer to paper towels to drain. Place in a warm oven. Using a slotted spoon, repeat with small batches of the coated salsify, then the eggplant sticks, then the sage and basil leaves. Serve right away.

FIRST COURSES

BASED ON OTHER RECIPES

Timbales de Céleri et Champignons (Celeriac and Wild Mushroom Timbales) Line buttered timbale or individual soufflé dishes with the blanched leaves of Belgian endive, then fill it half full with celeriac and potato purée (pages 142–143). Using a spoon, hollow out an indentation. Fill this with sauteed wild mushrooms, then top with more celeriac and potato purée. Pat well to even it up, and fold the fronds of endive over the top. Dot with butter and cover with aluminum foil, then bake in a preheated 350°F oven for about 20 minutes, until heated through.

Turn out onto hot plates, then sprinkle the rim of each plate with minced fresh chervil, chives, and tarragon.

La Trouchia aux Deux Sauces (La Trouchia on a Bed of Two Sauces) Prepare *Trouchia*, the Provençal flat omelet of spinach (pages 12–13), and cut it into small pieces. Serve each portion on a plate decorated with 2 or 3 contrasting-color sauces: red Coulis de Tomates aux Poivrons (page 205), yellow Coulis de Tomatoes aux Poivrons (the same recipe, prepared with yellow tomatoes and yellow peppers), and Purée de Pois Verts Cressonnière (a green pea purée) (pages 167–168).

Tomates Farcies (Tiny Green, Orange, and Red Stuffed Tomatoes, with Yellow Sauce) Cut off the tops of the tomatoes and, using a paring knife and/or tiny spoon, hollow them out, saving the flesh for another use. Fill the tomatoes with a selection of pistou, garlic-flavored goat cheese, and tapenade. Serve in a puddle of Coulis de Tomates aux Poivrons Rouges (page 205), prepared with yellow tomatoes and peppers, garnished with leaves of fresh herb and pitted olives.

Pomme de Terre à la Brandade (*Potato Filled with Brandade*) Serve a hot baked potato opened, hollowed out, and filled with Brandade de Légumes (page 17). Serve surrounded by strips of roasted red peppers and julienned artichokes, all dressed in a little vinaigrette with a generous sprinkling of minced fresh marjoram and/or other herbs.

Fleurs de Courgettes au Chèvre (*Goat Cheese-Stuffed Squash Flowers on a Bed of Zucchini-Basil Purée*) Purée steamed zucchini, then season it with a generous amount of pistou (pages 208–209). Fill a few squash flowers with mashed fresh goat cheese, then lightly sauté or steam the flowers until the cheese heats through. Place a few squash flowers in a pool of zucchini purée and garnish each plate with leaves of fresh basil. Serve right away.

Courges et Poivrons Verts au Grillé (*Grilled Yellow Squash and Green Peppers in Tomato and Red Pepper Coulis*) Serve grilled yellow squash and green bell peppers in a pool of Coulis de Tomates aux Poivrons Rouges (page 205), the plate encircled with a necklace of little peas.

Asperges, Champignons, et Ravioles (*Asparagus, Wild Mushrooms, and Herb-Filled Pasta*) Rest steamed asparagus on a bed of sautéed wild mushrooms and their juices, with a handful of tiny herb-filled pasta, such as ravioli, tortellini, or agnolini, scattered here and there.

Tartes, Quiches, et Pizzas

. . .

Savory Tarts, Quiches, and Pizzas

How enticing they are: crisp crusts of pie pastry, puff pastry, or chewy rounds of bread topped with vegetables, cheeses, olives, and herbs.

Savory pastries are eaten throughout France, reflecting the traditional regional flavorings and seasonal produce, from the northern flamiches, *or cheese-filled pastries, and the southern pizzas and* pissaladière, *to the variations of quiche eaten in one guise or another from Lorraine and Alsace to Burgundy, Bordeaux, and Provence.*

Any pastry can be eaten in a small portion for a first course, with a contrasting little vinaigrette-dressed salad, or in heftier servings for the main course.

. . . .

TARTE À L'OIGNON, SALADE DE ROQUETTE

ONION TART WITH ARUGULA SALAD

– Serves 6 –

This quintessential Lyonnaise bistro tart is filled with onions so tender they are nearly melting. The recipe is courtesy of food and wine writer Fiona Beckett, who makes her home in both London and the Languedoc.

A handful of arugula leaves dressed in hazelnut oil makes a fresh accent alongside; dress with red wine vinegar for a tangy flavor or with red wine to complement any wine you are drinking with your meal.

1½ pounds onions, thinly sliced
3 to 5 tablespoons butter
Salt and pepper to taste
Pinch of sugar
1 tablespoon flour
1 egg, lightly beaten
2 egg yolks, lightly beaten
2 cups crème fraîche or sour cream
¼ teaspoon or several gratings of nutmeg
One 9-inch partially baked tart shell
*   (page 203)*
3 handfuls young arugula leaves
1 to 2 tablespoons hazelnut oil
1 to 2 teaspoons red wine or red wine
*   vinegar*

✦✦In a covered heavy skillet or wide saucepan, cook the onions in the butter over a very low heat until they are soft, about 20 minutes. Remove the lid and sprinkle with salt, pepper, and sugar. Slowly cook and stir the onions for 5 to 10 minutes until they are lightly golden, then sprinkle in the flour and cook a few minutes longer. Set aside to cool for 10 minutes or so.

✦✦Preheat the oven to 375°F.

✦✦Beat the egg, egg yolks, and crème fraîche or sour cream together. Season with the nutmeg and add the onions, then spoon into the partially baked pie shell.

✦✦Bake for 30 minutes, or until lightly browned and puffed. Remove from the oven.

✦✦Dress the arugula with hazelnut oil, red wine or red wine vinegar, and salt and pepper to taste. Serve the tart hot, warm, or at room temperature, with the salad alongside.

GALETTES DE POIVRONS ET TOMATES

FLAT TARTS OF ROASTED RED PEPPERS AND TOMATOES

– Serves 4 –

A *galette* means different things in different regions of France. In some places it means a flat sweet or savory cake, in others it means a buckwheat crêpe. Or it just might mean a crisp vegetable tart such as this one.

Adding hazelnut oil to the olive oil gives an elusive flavor that enhances the wheat flour in the crisp pastry, rather than a strong nut flavor.

1⅓ cups all-purpose flour
Generous pinch of salt
¼ cup hazelnut oil
½ cup olive oil
6 tablespoons warm water

*2 red bell peppers, roasted, peeled, and cut
into strips (see page 210)*
3 to 4 ripe tomatoes, diced
3 garlic cloves, minced
*Generous pinch of dried thyme or herbes
de Provence*
Coarse salt for sprinkling

♦♦Combine the flour and salt on a pastry board and make a well in the center.

♦♦Into the well, pour the hazelnut oil, ¼ cup of the olive oil, and the warm water. Using a fork, mix it together, gradually working out to the edges of the flour until it forms a dough, as if you were making pasta.

♦♦When the dough sticks together, roll it into a ball and place it in a plastic bag. Refrigerate for at least 1 hour.

♦♦When ready to make the galettes, preheat the oven to 400°F.

♦♦Remove the dough from the refrigerator and divide it into 4 parts. On a lightly floured surface, roll each into a square or round about ¹/₁₆-inch thick.

♦♦Mix together the red pepper strips, diced tomatoes, garlic, and thyme or herbes de Provence. Top each piece of dough with one fourth of the red pepper mixture and drizzle with 1 tablespoon of the remaining olive oil, leaving a ½-inch border of dough around the edges. Fold the edges of the dough over to form a rectangle or round and sprinkle with coarse salt.

♦♦Bake for about 20 minutes, or until the filling is bubbling and the crust is lightly golden and slightly browned in spots.

♦♦Serve warm.

Galettes de Champignons (Mushroom Tarts) In place of the peppers, fill the pastry with an equal amount of sautéed mushrooms, either one specific type or a variety of types. After baking, sprinkle with minced fresh chives, garlic, and fresh parsley.

QUICHE BRETONNANTE

ARTICHOKE AND SHALLOT TART

WITH BEAUFORT CHEESE

– Serves 4 –

Artichokes and aromatic mountain cheese, punctuated with shallots and bound together in a savory custard, make a lovely quiche-style tart, good eaten warm or at room temperature.

This is a lovely first course, especially when prepared as individual tartlets; a handful of sturdy little greens tossed in a little vinaigrette makes a lively counterpoint. A light, refreshing white wine from the Jura would be good with this.

La vache

1 recipe pastry dough (pages 202–203)

*3 ounces Beaufort Emmentaler or Gruyère
    cheese, thinly sliced*

*4 artichoke hearts, blanched and sliced
    (see page 210)*

5 shallots, minced

3 garlic cloves, minced

3 tablespoons minced fresh chives

3 eggs, lightly beaten

½ cup heavy cream

Salt and pepper to taste

Drop or two of Tabasco sauce

¾ cup (3 ounces) grated Parmesan cheese

✦✦ Preheat the oven to 350°F.

✦✦ Line an 8- or 9-inch tart shell or 3- to 4-inch tartlet shells with the pastry. Trim the edges. Arrange the sliced cheese in the pastry, then top with a layer of sliced artichokes. Sprinkle with the shallots, garlic, and chives.

✦✦ Combine the eggs and cream. Season with the salt, pepper and Tabasco, then pour over the artichokes. Sprinkle with Parmesan cheese.

✦✦ Bake the tart for 20 to 30 minutes and the tartlets for 15 to 20, or until the crust is lightly browned and the savory custard is puffed.

✦✦ Serve hot or at room temperature.

TRUFFAT AU PISTOU

POTATO AND BASIL TART

– Serves 4 to 6 –

While the idea of pastry filled with potatoes might sound, well, a bit stodgy, French cooking abounds with such dishes and they are often wonderful. This one is particularly succulent, with the addition of pistou and creamy white cheese.

More and more chefs in France are unashamedly using Italian cheeses in various cooking. This tart uses Italian fontina, but Cantal or Beaufort would also be good.

Truffat is from southwest France, where potatoes are known as "poor people's truffles." To drink, try a rustic red from the Luberon, or a Côtes-du-Rhône.

4 boiling potatoes

10 to 12 ounces puff pastry

3 shallots, minced

3 garlic cloves, minced

1 tablespoon olive oil

Salt and pepper to taste

¾ cup pistou (pages 208–209)

*1½ to 2 cups (6 to 8 ounces) shredded
    Italian Fontina cheese*

*¼ cup grated Parmesan, pecorino, or aged
    Asiago cheese*

✦✦ Put the potatoes in a saucepan and cover with water. Bring to a boil, then reduce heat and cook the potatoes until they are just firm-tender. Drain and let cool to the touch.

✦✦ Peel and slice the potatoes about ⅛ inch thick.

✦✦ Preheat the oven to 400°F.

✦✦ On a lightly floured surface roll the puff pastry out into a 12-by-18-inch rectangle. Place it on a baking sheet. Sprinkle the shallots and garlic over the top, then arrange the sliced potatoes in a slightly overlapping layer, leaving a ½-inch border around the edge. Brush the potatoes with the oil, sprinkle with salt and pepper, and fold over the edges to form a border of crust enclosing the potatoes.

✦✦ Bake the pastry until the crust and potatoes are lightly golden, about 20 minutes.

✦✦Spread the top generously with the pistou, then sprinkle on a layer of both the cheeses.

✦✦Return the pastry to the oven and bake until the crust is golden brown and the cheese is melted and sizzling.

✦✦Serve right away.

FEUILLETÉE AU CHÈVRE AVEC TOMATES SÈCHES

GOAT CHEESE PASTRIES WITH SUN-DRIED TOMATO VINAIGRETTE

– Serves 4 –

These goat cheese–stuffed pastries are utterly Côte d'Azur food, sweet little nothings to nibble on with a glass of chilled white Côtes-du-Provence as a first course while you await the plat du jour.

> *12 ounces puff pastry*
> *2 to 3 teaspoons coarsely chopped, fresh rosemary*
> *6 to 8 ounces fresh white goat cheese, crumbled*
> *3 garlic cloves, minced*
> *8 marinated sun-dried tomatoes, cut into strips*
> *2 tablespoons olive oil*
> *1 teaspoon balsamic vinegar, or to taste*

✦✦Preheat the oven to 400°F. On a lightly floured board, roll the pastry out and cut into eight 5-inch rounds.

✦✦Arrange 4 of the 8 pastry rounds on a baking sheet, leaving a border of about ½ inch between pastries, and sprinkle them with the rosemary,

goat cheese, and garlic. Wet the pastry edges and top each one with a second pastry round. Press together the edges to seal, using a fork to make an appealing pattern. With a knife, cut several small holes in the tops of the pastries to allow air to escape from the filling.

✦✦Bake for 15 minutes, or until golden brown.

✦✦Serve right away, each pastry in the middle of a plate, with strips of sun-dried tomato arranged in a spoke pattern around the pastry and a drizzle of olive oil and droplets of balsamic vinegar decorating each plate.

FEUILLETÉE AU ROQUEFORT

ROQUEFORT PASTRIES

– Serves 4 –

Crisp turnovers of puff pastry, filled with hot garlic-scented Roquefort cheese, are set atop a handful of vinaigrette-dressed mesclun: a marvelous starter for a Parisian autumn supper, especially when the Beaujolais nouveau has just arrived.

Though a good-quality French blue such as Roquefort, bleu des Causses, or bleu d'Auverne is most delightful and authentic in this little pastry, any strong blue cheese will be very good. Gorgonzola, Stilton, Maytag, or Danish blue will all make delicious pastries.

> *8 ounces blue cheese, crumbled*
> *1 garlic clove, minced*
> *1 tablespoon minced fresh chives*
> *2 tablespoons port or Sauternes*
> *1 drop Tabasco sauce or a few grains cayenne pepper*
> *12 ounces puff pastry*

3 handfuls mixed baby greens
1 shallot, minced
1 tablespoon olive oil
1 teaspoon red wine or balsamic vinegar
Salt and pepper to taste

✦✦Preheat the oven to 425°F.

✦✦Combine the blue cheese, garlic, chives, wine, and Tabasco or cayenne. Mix well to form a paste.

✦✦On a lightly floured board, roll the puff pastry out into four 6-inch squares and place one quarter of the filling diagonally across each. Fold over the corners, leaving the middle slightly open. Make a rim on each side to contain the cheese as it melts.

✦✦Bake the pastries for 15 minutes, or until the crust is golden brown and cheese is melted.

✦✦While the pastries are baking, toss the greens with the shallot, oil, vinegar, salt, and pepper to taste. Divide the salad among 4 plates.

✦✦Serve the pastries hot, each nestled next to a handful of the vinaigrette-dressed greens.

SEVEN SAVORY PASTRIES

Tarte de Ratatouille (Ratatouille Tart) Fill a partially baked 9-inch tart shell (page 203) with 2 cups ratatouille (pages 110–111) and a handful of pitted Mediterranean black olives. Sprinkle with fresh minced thyme and bake in a preheated 375°F oven for 20 minutes, or until the crust is golden and the ratatouille thickened.

Tarte de Courgettes Rapées (Zucchini Tart) Coarsely shred 2 zucchini and drain well. Spread a layer of 1 cup shredded cheese such as Comté, Parmesan, Beaufort, or Gruyère on the bottom of a partially baked 9-inch pie shell (page 203). Top with a layer of the zucchini, a sprinkling of minced garlic, and a scattering of minced fresh basil. Top with 2 to 3 beaten eggs mixed with ½ cup crème fraîche or sour cream. Bake in a preheated 350°F until the crust is golden and the filling is puffy, about 30 minutes. Serve hot or at room temperature.

Galette d'Asperges au Valençay (Asparagus and Goat Cheese Pastry) Valençay frais is a type of goat cheese, richly flavored yet fresh tasting, covered with ash and sold in a pyramid shape. Any slightly aged goat cheese may be used. In a 12-inch square baking pan, place a layer of about 10 ounces puff pastry. Bake in a preheated 350°F oven for 10 minutes, or until slightly colored. Leave the oven on. Spread with 1½ to 2 cups sautéed diced asparagus. Top with dollops of goat cheese. Mix 2 beaten eggs, ½ cup crème fraîche or sour cream, 2 minced shallots, and ¼ to ½ teaspoon minced fresh thyme, then pour it over the asparagus. Cover with a second layer of pastry about the same size as the first, press to seal in the filling, and return to the oven for about 30 minutes, or until the topping is puffed and the crust is golden.

Tartlettes de Vignottes et Mâche (Cheese and Green Tartlets) Press 1 recipe pastry dough (pages 202–203) into four 3- to 4-inch tartlet pans or cut the pastry into four 5- to 6-inch rounds. Bake in a preheated 375°F oven until they are golden and crisp, then fill or top with a layer of Vignottes, Saint-Andre, or another pungent, creamy cheese. Top each tartlet with a handful of vinaigrette-dressed mâche or baby greens and a sprinkling of fresh minced herbs and serve.

Flamiche aux Poireaux (Leek Tart from Flanders and Picardy) Clean and slice 1 pound leeks, including their tender greens. Sauté the leeks and 1 chopped onion in 2 to 3 tablespoons of butter until soft, about 10 minutes. Season generously with salt, pepper, and a tiny pinch of grated nutmeg or ground cinnamon. Spread over the bottom of an 8- or 9-inch partially baked pie pastry (page 203). Whisk 2 eggs with 1½ cups half-and-half and pour it over the vegetables, then bake in a preheated 375°F oven for 20 to 30 minutes, or until slightly browned on top. Let cool for at least 5 minutes, then slice and serve.

Tarte aux Tomates et Romarin (Rosemary- and Garlic-Scented Tomato Tart) Fill a 9-inch partially baked tart shell (page 203) with 4 diced fresh or canned tomatoes, 1 teaspoon minced fresh rosemary, 3 minced garlic cloves, and a sprinkling of salt along with a tiny sprinkling of sugar. Drizzle with olive oil and bake in a preheated 375°F oven for 25 minutes, or until the crust is golden and the tomatoes well cooked. Serve topped with crumbled goat cheese if desired.

Tartes aux Tomates et Basilic (Tomato and Basil Tart) Brush the bottom of partially baked tartlet shells (page 203) with a thick layer of pistou, then top with a thin layer of tomatoes. Sprinkle with minced garlic, salt, and olive oil, then bake in a preheated 350°F oven for 25 minutes, or until the crust is golden and the tomatoes cooked through. Serve warm or cool. (An optional sauce: Combine ½ cup crème fraîche or sour cream thinned with a little milk with 1 minced shallot, salt, and pepper; drizzle it around the little tarts.)

FEUILLETÉE AUX EPINARDS, FROMAGE DE CHÈVRE, ET SAUCES D'OLIVES

SPINACH AND GOAT CHEESE PASTRY WITH TWO OLIVE SAUCES

– Serves 4 –

This is one of the delightful crisp vegetable pastries found throughout France.

The dish is not difficult if you use storebought puff pastry, but it does take a while to prepare the various elements. Once all of the subrecipes are prepared, it takes only a few minutes to assemble them.

The two olive sauces are unusual: Thinned with water instead of oil, and mixed with ground almonds, they are light and delicate.

GREEN OLIVE AND ALMOND SAUCE
25 to 35 green olives, pitted and diced
1 garlic clove, minced
½ teaspoon capers, drained
¼ teaspoon minced fresh rosemary or marjoram
2 tablespoons ground blanched almonds
2 tablespoons water
2 tablespoons olive oil
½ teaspoon fresh lemon juice or to taste

BLACK OLIVE AND ALMOND SAUCE
20 to 25 black olives, preferably oil cured, pitted and diced
2 tablespoons olive oil
2 tablespoons ground blanched almonds
1 to 2 tablespoons water

ONION FILLING
4 onions, thinly sliced
2 tablespoons olive oil
Salt and pepper to taste
A pinch of sugar

16 ounces puff pastry
1 tablespoon milk
1 teaspoon cumin seeds
1 pound fresh spinach, stemmed, or one
10-ounce package frozen spinach
4 ounces fresh white goat cheese or feta
cheese at room temperature
1 garlic clove, minced
1 to 2 tablespoons crème fraîche or sour
cream
1 tablespoon olive oil
2 ripe tomatoes, diced

✦✦ To make the green olive sauce: In a blender or food processor, purée the green olives, then add the remaining ingredients and purée until smooth. Set aside.

✦✦ To make the black olive sauce: In a blender or food processor, purée the black olives, then add the remaining ingredients and purée to a thick sauce. Set aside.

Les fromages

✦✦ To make the onion filling: In a large, heavy sauté or saucepan over medium-low heat, sauté the onions in the olive oil, salt, pepper, and sugar, stirring occasionally, until the onions are soft and golden brown, about 30 minutes. Set aside.

✦✦ Preheat the oven to 425°F.

✦✦ On a lightly floured board, roll the pastry out into a 12-by-18-inch rectangle. Cut the pastry into 8 triangles and arrange on a baking sheet. Brush the triangles with the milk and sprinkle them with the cumin seeds. Bake the pastries until they have puffed and are very lightly golden, about 10 minutes. Let cool to the touch. Slice the pastries in half horizontally.

✦✦ Cook the spinach in 1 inch boiling water until just tender. Drain, then squeeze out the excess liquid and coarsely chop the leaves. Set aside.

✦✦ Mash the cheese and mix well with spinach, garlic, crème fraîche or sour cream, and olive oil. Divide into 4 portions and spoon onto the pastry bottoms. Arrange these cheese-topped pastries on a baking sheet along with the pastry tops.

✦✦ To serve: Preheat the broiler. Onto each plate spoon one fourth of the black olive sauce and one fourth of the green olive sauce in 2 separate pools.

✦✦ Broil the pastries and the pastry tops until the cheese slightly melts and the pastry tops are lightly golden, crisp, and warmed through. Meanwhile, warm the onions in the pan.

✦✦ Place a cheese-and-spinach-topped pastry onto each olive-sauced plate, then garnish with a spoonful of sautéed onions, the pastry tops, and diced tomatoes.

✦✦ Serve right away.

PIZZA AU ROQUEFORT

THIN CRUSTED PIZZA

WITH BLUE CHEESE

– Serves 4 to 6 –

Not long ago in Aix-en-Provence I found myself sitting on a little stool in a bistro on a cobbled side street, eating the most sensational pizza topped with enough garlic to satisfy my passion and keep me safe from vampires, at least for the night.

Though pizza is the gastronomical child of Naples, it was long ago adopted by Provence, no doubt when Nice and its environs were part of the Kingdom of Savoy, which included parts of Italy.

What pizza one eats in Provence! Thin crusted, baked in a wood-burning oven, topped with not only "classic" fillings but also flavors that echo North Africa, or typically French cheeses such as the following Roquefort.

DOUGH

2 packages active dried yeast
1 cup warm (105° to 115°F) water
1 teaspoon sugar
1 teaspoon salt
1 tablespoon olive oil
2½ cups unbleached all-purpose flour,
  more if needed
½ cup semolina, whole-wheat, or rye flour

TOPPING

1 to 1½ cups Coulis de Tomates (page 205)
4 garlic cloves, minced
½ cup diced, fresh or canned tomatoes
6 to 8 ounces blue cheese, sliced ⅛ inch
  thick or crumbled

1 to 2 teaspoons olive oil or as desired
4 to 6 fresh basil leaves
8 to 10 black olives, preferably niçoise
Grated Parmesan cheese for sprinkling
  (optional)

✦✦ To make the dough: Dissolve the yeast in the warm water, then add the sugar and let the mixture stand until foamy, 5 to 10 minutes.

✦✦ Combine the yeast mixture, salt, olive oil, and flours.

✦✦ In a food processor, mix the dough until it forms a ball, then knead it in the machine until shiny, about 5 minutes. To make the dough by hand, combine the ingredients in a large bowl using a wooden spoon. If the mixture is too wet, add more flour; if it is too dry, a little more water. Work the dough until it is smooth and firm.

✦✦ Turn the dough out on a well-floured board and knead until the dough is elastic, about 10 minutes.

✦✦ Oil a large bowl, then place the dough in the bowl and turn it to coat its surface. Cover with a clean cloth and let rise in a warm place until doubled in size, 1 to 1½ hours.

✦✦ Punch the dough down, cover, and let rise for 30 minutes.

✦✦ Preheat the oven to 450°F. If using a pizza stone, preheat it for 15 minutes. If you do not have a pizza stone, fill a ceramic baking dish with hot water and place it on the bottom of the oven. The steam will encourage a crisp crust.

✦✦ Stretch the pizza dough out to make one 24-inch-diameter pizza or four 8- or 9-inch-diameter pizzas. Place on an oiled pizza pan or baking sheets.

✦✦ Smear the top of the dough with the tomato purée, then sprinkle with the garlic, diced tomatoes, and blue cheese. Drizzle with olive oil, and sprinkle with basil leaves, olives, and Parmesan, if you like.

✦✦Bake until golden brown around the edges and slightly puffy here and there, about 15 minutes. Serve right away, sprinkled with Parmesan if desired.

VARIATION For a rustic wood scent, bake the pizza in a kettle grill: Place the pizza pan on the grill over medium coals and close the cover for 15 minutes, or until the dough is cooked through and the cheese topping melted. Check after 10 minutes and from then on every 5 minutes until the pizza is done.

PIZZA AUX LÉGUMES DU SOLEIL

PIZZA TOPPED WITH SUMMER VEGETABLES AND OLIVES

– Serves 4 –

Provençal pizza is wonderful; most of the little villages set in the hillsides behind Nice boast at least one bistro that specializes in the savory dish.

Either leftover ratatouille or grilled vegetables are delicious topping this pizza. And if you've no fresh basil, use any fragrant mountain herb instead: thyme, rosemary, savory, even parsley. A Côtes-du-Rhône or a chilled rosé would be good with this pizza.

1 recipe pizza dough, prepared through the second rise (page 85)
3 garlic cloves
Pinch of saffron
2 tablespoons olive oil

1½ cups Coulis de Tomates (page 205)
3 tablespoons tomato paste
¼ cup coarsely torn, fresh basil leaves
2 cups ratatouille, well drained (pages 110–111), or 2 cups chopped grilled vegetables: eggplant, zucchini, peppers, artichokes, etc.
6 to 8 ounces fresh mozzarella, thinly sliced
3 to 4 tablespoons grated Parmesan cheese
¼ cup flavorful black olives

✦✦Preheat the oven to 450°F. If using a pizza stone, preheat it for 15 minutes. If not, fill a ceramic baking dish with hot water and place it on the bottom of the oven. Stretch the dough out into a 24-inch-diameter circle, or as large as you can roll it, and place it on an oiled pizza pan or baking sheet.

✦✦In a mortar, crush the garlic with the saffron and a pinch of salt, then work in 1 tablespoon of the olive oil; set aside.

✦✦Combine the tomato purée and paste and mix well, then stir in the garlic paste. Spread this mixture over the pizza dough, then scatter with the basil leaves.

✦✦Arrange the ratatouille or vegetables over the top, then the cheese, a sprinkling of Parmesan, and a drizzle of the remaining 1 tablespoon olive oil. Dot with the olives and bake for 15 to 20 minutes, or until the crust is lightly browned around the edges.

VARIATION The pizza may be baked without cheese.

Les brioches et le croissant

FOUÉS

LITTLE WHOLE-WHEAT BREADS

– Serves 4 to 6 –

In a little village in the Loire a café-bistro serves these puffy little focaccialike breads, accompanied with a selection of hors d'oeuvre and a crisp Sancerre. The *hors d'œuvre de la maison* is whatever is in season and on hand: pots of fresh goat cheese, garlicky white beans, ripe tomato salads, and crisp crudités of the season.

> 1 package active dry yeast
> ¼ cup warm (105° to 115°F) water
> 1¼ to 1½ cups unbleached all-purpose
>   or bread flour
> ¾ cup whole-wheat flour
> ½ teaspoon salt
> 2 tablespoons vegetable oil

✦✦ Sprinkle the yeast over the water and let it sit until foamy, about 10 minutes.

✦✦ Meanwhile, combine the flours with the salt and rub in the oil using your fingers or a pastry cutter, mixing until the mixture is the texture of coarse meal.

✦✦ Add the yeast mixture to the flour mixture. Stir to form a soft dough, adding a tablespoon or two of water if dough is too firm.

✦✦ On a lightly floured board, knead the dough until it is smooth and elastic, 5 to 10 minutes, or in a food processor for 3 to 5 minutes. Place it back in an oiled bowl and turn to coat. Cover with a damp cloth and let rise in a warm place until doubled in size, about 35 to 40 minutes.

✦✦ Punch the dough down and pull off walnut-sized pieces. Roll each on a floured board to form little discs about 5 inches in diameter, then arrange on a lightly oiled baking sheet and let rise in a warm place for about 10 minutes.

✦✦ Preheat the oven to 425°F. If you have a pizza stone, preheat it for 15 minutes; otherwise, fill a ceramic baking dish with hot water and preheat it in the oven for 15 minutes. This will encourage a crisp crust.

✦✦ Bake for 4 to 5 minutes, or until the breads have puffed up and are just cooked through but not brown and crisp.

✦✦ Eat right away, for they harden as they cool.

CHOUQUETTES AU FROMAGE

LITTLE BURGUNDIAN

CHEESE PASTRIES

– Serves 4 –

From humble Burgundian bistros to Paris's chic Benôit, these little pastries might appear at your table to nibble on while you look over the menu. They're also good with a bunch of sweet, juicy purple grapes after the meal, as a cheese course.

These are very easy to whip together, and they perfume your kitchen with their buttery scent as they bake. Any red Burgundian wine would be good to sip along.

Though traditionally prepared with nutty Gruyère-type cheeses, I think the pastries would also be lovely with Asiago.

5 tablespoons butter
Large pinch of salt
¾ cup water
1 cup all-purpose flour
3 eggs
1 cup (4 ounces) diced Swiss cheese such
*   as Emmenthal, Gruyère, or Beaufort*
Small pinch of cayenne pepper

✦✦ Preheat the oven to 350°F.

✦✦ In a large saucepan, combine the butter, salt, and water. Bring to a boil over high heat then remove from heat. Immediately add the flour all at once, then mix in well with a wooden spoon.

✦✦ Return to heat and, stirring with the wooden spoon, cook until the ball of dough comes away easily at the sides, 3 to 4 minutes.

✦✦ Beat in the eggs one at a time. Remove from heat and beat in the cheese and cayenne.

✦✦ Arrange spoonfuls on a greased baking sheet. Bake for about 20 to 30 minutes, or until golden and crisp-edged, no longer doughy inside, and hollow-sounding when rapped with a spoon.

Gougère (Cheese Pastry Ring) On a greased baking sheet, spoon the cheese pastry into a ring shape. Bake for 30 to 40 minutes, or until golden and lightly browned and no longer doughy inside.

Œufs, Omelettes, Soufflés, et Crêpes

. . .

Eggs, Omelets, Soufflés, and Crêpes

French eggs can be so delicate, so fresh and rich in eggy taste, that I confess to bringing back little half-dozen containers of eggs in my luggage every so often.

Egg dishes in France are treated with respect, and the repertoire is huge and varied. Boiled in their shells to a soft mollet *stage, they might be tossed into a salad or eaten with just-cooked asparagus; hard cooked, they are stuffed, chopped into salads, sliced into sandwiches, or eaten cut into halves and resting on a delicious smear of homemade mayonnaise.*

Eggs are stirred and scrambled, rolled into omelets, whipped into soufflés, or beaten into a pancake batter for tender crêpes.

Unlike in the United States, however, egg dishes are eaten for lunch or dinner rather than for breakfast.

. . . .

ŒUFS AÏOLI ET TAPENADE

HARD-COOKED EGGS WITH

TAPENADE AND AIOLI

– Serves 4 –

O*eufs mayonnaise* is a ubiquitous starter on set menus of homey cafés, as well as humble bistros and bars. While it can be uninspired, it can also be one of the most satisfying dishes imaginable, with deliciously fresh eggs–cooked until the white has just firmed and the yolk is a tender yellow hue–resting in a puddle of homemade mayonnaise.

One afternoon in a village somewhere in the sunny south we sat down to lunch. *Œufs aïoli* was written on the blackboard, and though it sounded okay, we weren't prepared to get excited about the meal. But when it arrived it was lovely: The eggs were masked with golden aioli, garnished with a dab of black olive paste, and scattered with a handful of pungent greens–almost a mini salade niçoise.

4 eggs
1 handful arugula, mâche, or basil leaves
2 tablespoons tapenade
½ to ¾ cup aioli (pages 18–19)

✦✦Cook the eggs by placing them in a saucepan with cold water to cover. Bring to a boil over high heat, then reduce the heat to medium and cook for 5 to 6 minutes. Let cool in the water for 15 minutes or longer until easily handled.
✦✦Shell the eggs and rinse them of any little bits of shells. Cut the eggs into halves lengthwise. They should be at room temperature.

✦✦Arrange the greens on individual plates, then place 2 egg halves on each plate. Garnish with a dab or two of tapenade and a dollop of aioli.

Œufs aux Trois Aïolis **(Eggs with Three Aiolis)** Serve the hard-cooked eggs on a plate with a dab of 3 highly flavored aiolis: plain aioli, aioli mixed with an equal amount of tapenade, and aioli mixed with pistou. Garnish with strips of roasted red peppers.

ŒUFS CRESSONADE

HARD-COOKED EGGS IN

WATERCRESS SAUCE

– Serves 4 –

A version of the bistro classic, *œufs mayonnaise*, the tangy green mayonnaise is delicious with the bland hard-cooked egg. Garnish the dish with added watercress if you like.

1 garlic clove, minced
½ cup watercress sprigs, plus watercress
sprigs for garnish (optional)
1 tablespoon minced fresh tarragon
½ cup mayonnaise
2 tablespoons unsalted butter, melted
Salt and cayenne pepper to taste
Juice of ½ lemon
4 or 8 eggs

✦✦Purée the garlic and the ½ cup watercress in a mortar or food processor. Add the tarragon and mayonnaise and purée. Gradually blend in the melted butter. Add the salt and cayenne, then blend in the lemon juice. Cover and refrigerate for at least 1 hour to mellow the flavors.

✦✦Cook the eggs by placing them in a saucepan with cold water to cover. Bring to a boil over high heat, then reduce the heat to medium and cook for 5 to 6 minutes. Let cool in the water for 15 minutes or longer until easily handled. Serve by pooling several tablespoons of the watercress sauce on each plate, then top with 1 or 2 halved eggs, resting cut-side down.

OMELETTE AUX

BROUSSE ET MENTHE

CORSICAN GOAT CHEESE

AND MINT OMELET

– Serves 1 –

Each day we sat at the beach along the Promenade des Anglais, and at some point the ferry from Corsica would sail into the harbor. One afternoon, we found ourselves on it.

In Corsica we ate this omelet, perhaps the most famous dish from the island. Such a curious combination: goat cheese and mint, bound up in egg and strikingly delicious.

There is a tiny-leafed, delicately flavored mint that grows throughout the island. It is called, appropriately, Corsican mint. The fresh, creamy sheep's milk cheese, Brousse, is the traditional Corsican cheese to use, but a tangy fresh goat cheese is delicious, too.

1 tablespoon butter
2 tablespoons coarsely chopped fresh mint leaves
2 eggs, lightly beaten
1 tablespoon milk
Salt and white pepper to taste

2 to 3 tablespoons slightly aged goat cheese, such as Chevrette or Montrachet, crumbled or broken into small pieces

✦✦In a 6- to 8-inch omelet pan over a gentle low heat, melt the butter with half of the mint leaves. Raise the heat to medium-high. Combine the eggs with the milk and pour into the pan with the butter and mint.

✦✦As the eggs begin to set, lift the edges and let the liquid egg run under to cook.

✦✦Sprinkle the goat cheese over the eggs, then continue to cook until the egg is half cooked. Roll to enclose the filling, then cook gently on both sides just until golden and lightly browned in places, about 1 to 2 minutes, adding more butter if needed.

✦✦Push any egg that runs out back into the omelet; don't worry that it doesn't look right, because when you roll it out of the pan all imperfections will be hidden.

✦✦Roll the omelet out onto a warm plate and sprinkle with the remaining mint. Serve right away.

Le chou.

OMELETTE DE RATATOUILLE AVEC TAPENADE

RATATOUILLE OMELET SPREAD WITH TAPENADE

– Serves 1 –

Spoonfuls of ratatouille tucked into a classic French rolled omelet, spread with a delicious smear of tapenade and a scattering of fragrant basil, makes a summer supper that tastes of Provence. A Provençal red or a Pinot Noir might be a good wine for this dish.

The omelet may be doubled in size for a 2-person portion.

> *2 teaspoons butter or olive oil*
> *2 eggs, lightly beaten*
> *Salt and pepper to taste*
> *2 to 3 tablespoons ratatouille (pages 110–111)*
> *2 to 3 teaspoons tapenade or black olive paste*
> *1 tablespoon thinly sliced fresh basil leaves*

✦✦In an 6- to 8-inch omelet pan over gentle low heat, melt the butter or heat the olive oil. Raise the heat to medium-high, then pour in the eggs, sprinkling with salt and pepper.

✦✦Cook, pulling up the edges and letting the liquid run under, until the eggs are half cooked. Spoon the ratatouille in a line along the center of the omelet, then fold. Cook a moment, then turn and cook the second side of the folded omelet for 1 to 2 minutes.

✦✦Turn the omelet out of pan and spread the top with tapenade or black olive paste, then sprinkle with the basil. Serve at once.

OMELETTE AUX LÉGUMES DE PRINTEMPS ET AU CHÈVRE FRAIS

FLAT OMELET OF YOUNG SPRING VEGETABLES AND GOAT CHEESE

– Serves 4 –

We arrived late at the village bistro; diners were nibbling the last of their cheeses and draining the bottom of their wineglasses. We had been on the road all day and were hungry to the point of irrationality. And everything smelled so good.

"We can only give you what we have left," the *patron* explained–"maybe a little omelet, some leaves of salad, perhaps some potatoes."

This was the little omelet, cooked flat in a pan like a frittata, and filled with impeccably fresh spring vegetables and dollops of fresh goat cheese. We ate potatoes sautéed with garlic and parsley alongside, and a salad of frisée and herbs. For dessert, the patron cut slices from a huge strawberry and almond tart, and poured us glasses of chilled Beaumes de Venise.

> *2 artichoke hearts, blanched and diced (see page 210)*
> *10 to 15 young green beans, blanched and cut into bite-sized lengths*
> *5 to 10 asparagus spears, trimmed, blanched, and cut into bite-sized pieces*
> *1 to 2 zucchini, diced and blanched*
> *2 garlic cloves, minced*
> *2 tablespoons butter or olive oil*
> *Salt and pepper to taste*
> *8 eggs, lightly beaten*
> *2 ripe tomatoes, diced*

*4 ounces fresh white goat cheese or other
  milky soft cheese*
*2 tablespoons minced mixed fresh herbs:
  chervil, chives, tarragon, basil, marjoram, parsley*

✦✦Preheat the broiler. In a large, heavy sauté pan or skillet over medium-low heat, warm the blanched artichokes, green beans, asparagus, and zucchini with the garlic and 1 tablespoon of the butter or olive oil; season with salt and pepper. Remove the vegetables from the pan and add to the beaten eggs.

✦✦To the same pan over medium-heat, add the remaining 1 tablespoon butter or olive oil. Raise the heat to medium-high, then pour in half of the egg mixture. Scatter the diced tomatoes, goat cheese, and herbs over the top, then pour in the rest of the egg-vegetable mixture.

✦✦Cook until the bottom is just firm, then place under the broiler and cook the top until firm. Serve right away.

BROUILLADE AUX CHAMPIGNONS

WILD MUSHROOMS WITH SOFTLY SCRAMBLED EGGS

– Serves 4 to 6 –

A brouillade is a mass of soft buttery egg curds, stirred up with something delightfully fragrant such as a handful of wild mushrooms or, even better, a truffle or two. I've had *brouillade* with tiny wild asparagus and the first tender peas of spring.

As with all exquisitely simple dishes, the raw ingredients are everything: The mushrooms must be foresty fresh, the butter sweet and milky, the

eggs just laid. A chilled Riesling to drink, and crusty bread to scoop up the creamy mélange, are all you need for a memorable meal.

*12 ounces fresh wild mushrooms, or a mix-
  ture of 8 ounces fresh white mixed with
  ½ ounce rehydrated dried cèpe (porcini)
  or morel mushrooms (see page 210)*
3 tablespoons butter
2 garlic cloves, minced
1 tablespoon minced fresh parsley
1 tablespoon minced fresh chives
Salt and pepper to taste
8 to 10 eggs, lightly beaten

✦✦Slice the fresh mushrooms into bite-sized pieces. In a large, heavy sauté pan or skillet over medium heat, sauté the fresh mushrooms in 1½ tablespoons of the butter until they are lightly golden and browned in places. Stir in the garlic and parsley or chives; season with salt and pepper.

✦✦Add the remaining 1½ tablespooons butter; when melted, add the eggs and scramble softly with the mushrooms, over a low heat, stirring until large creamy curds form.

✦✦When the eggs and mushrooms have formed soft curds, they are done. Serve with crusty bread to eat alongside.

Brouillade de Printemps (Creamy Scrambled Eggs and Springtime Vegetables) Add a handful of blanched baby peas or butter-sautéed thin asparagus to the pan when you add the mushrooms and eggs.

Barbouiado de Rabasso (Creamy Scrambled Eggs with Truffles and Gruyère Cheese) Substitute truffles for the wild mushrooms and toss a generous handful of grated Gruyère cheese into the beaten eggs before adding them to the pan. The addition of the cheese would make Beaujolais or a Brouilly a pleasant drink to accompany this dish.

OMELETTE ROUSSILLON

ROLLED OMELET FILLED WITH GARLICKY GREEN BEANS AND TOMATOES

– Serves 4 –

One summer I rented an old stone farmhouse overlooking a village between Cahors and Roussillon. Nearby was a little bistro-cum-café with a vine-shaded stone terrace and a perpetual clientele of locals filling the café with gossip, chatter, and cigarette smoke.

Madame la patronne made omelets with whatever had popped up in her garden that morning; we had only to walk past it to know what was on the menu that day. This was one that she frequently made: It was the midsummer, and both thin green beans and sweet tomatoes were in abundance.

The eggs were plucked from under the plump squawking chickens that nested in the shade alongside the terrace, and the omelets always tasted fresh and delightfully eggy. Drink a rough Cahors, or a chilled steely rosé from Provence with this dish.

3 to 4 garlic cloves, minced
2 to 3 tablespoons olive oil
12 ounces haricots verts or baby Blue Lake
    beans
1½ cups diced fresh or canned tomatoes

Salt and pepper to taste
Pinch of sugar
Several large pinches herbes de Provence
    or minced fresh thyme, sage, rosemary,
    basil, and savory
3 tablespoons minced fresh parsley
8 eggs
2 tablespoons butter

✦✦In a large, heavy sauté pan or skillet over medium heat, cook half the garlic in 1 tablespoon of the olive oil until it smells fragrant, then add the green beans and cook a few moments. Stir in the tomatoes and season with salt, pepper, sugar, and herbes de Provence or minced herbs. Raise the heat to medium high and cook until green beans are crisp-tender and the tomatoes are thickened, about 5 to 10 minutes. Add 2 tablespoons of the parsley, taste and adjust the seasoning, and set aside.

✦✦Beat 2 of the eggs and season with salt and pepper. Heat 1 teaspoon of the remaining olive oil and 1 teaspoon of the butter in a 6- to 8-inch omelet pan over low heat until the butter melts. Raise the heat to medium-high, pour in the beaten eggs and swirl, then lift the edges of the omelet to let the liquid egg cook. The top should be soft. Sprinkle with one fourth of the remaining garlic, then spoon one fourth of the green bean and tomato mixture down the center.

✦✦Fold the omelet, then turn and cook until the egg is just firm enough to hold together, about 5 minutes, or according to your taste and how firm or runny you prefer. Place on a plate in a low oven.

✦✦Repeat to cook all 4 omelets.

✦✦Serve right away, sprinkled with the remaining parsley.

ŒUFS MARITCHOU

EGGS WITH ARTICHOKES AND

CHUNKY TOMATO SAUCE

– Serves 4 –

Oeufs Maritchou is a dish from the Basque country in which tender artichokes are combined with eggs and served with a spicy tomato sauce. The eggs may be either poached or scrambled, served spooned into whole artichoke bottoms, or piled in a crisp sauté alongside–the variety is endless.

In Roussillon one finds a variation, *œufs Gariole*, which substitutes browned eggplant slices for the artichokes.

3 garlic cloves
Pinch of salt, plus salt to taste
1 onion, chopped
2 tablespoons olive oil
8 fresh or canned tomatoes, diced
Several large pinches herbes de Provence
*   or minced fresh thyme, rosemary, savory,*
*   and/or marjoram*
Pinch of sugar
Pepper to taste
Red pepper sauce such as piment
*   d'Espelette or Tabasco sauce*
4 large artichoke hearts or bottoms,
*   blanched (see page 210)*
4 warm poached eggs (see page 204)
½ to 1 teaspoon vinegar
1 tablespoon minced fresh chives or other
*   herb of choice*

✦✦Purée the garlic and pinch of salt to a paste in a mortar or food processor. Set aside.

✦✦In a large, heavy sauté pan or skillet over medium heat, sauté the onion in 1½ tablespoons of the olive oil until softened, about 5 to 8 minutes. Stir in about one third of the garlic paste along with the tomatoes. Cook over medium-high heat until thickened; add the herbes de Provence or other herbs, sugar, salt, pepper, and hot pepper sauce. Add another third of the garlic paste and keep warm.

✦✦In a medium, heavy sauté pan or skillet over medium-low heat, heat the remaining 1½ tablespoons olive oil and cook the artichokes and remaining garlic paste for about 10 minutes, or until easily pierced with a knife.

✦✦To serve, arrange an artichoke on each plate, top with a poached egg, then surround with tomato sauce.

✦✦Sprinkle the eggs with chives or another herb of choice, and serve right away.

VARIATION For scrambled eggs, beat the eggs together lightly and add 1 or 2 tablespoons of milk. Season with salt and pepper. Heat 1 tablespoon olive oil in a medium, heavy sauté pan or skillet, then pour in the eggs and cook over a low heat, lifting the edges and stirring the eggs gently so that they cook into soft gold curds. Remove from heat when just soft and slightly runnier than you desire, as the heat of the pan will continue to cook them.

PIPÉRADE

EGGS SCRAMBLED WITH PEPPERS,

ONIONS, AND TOMATOES

– Serves 4 to 6 –

Pipérade is a creamy mixture of stewed peppers, onions, and tomatoes bound with just enough egg to hold it together. It is one of the Basque region's most illustrious dishes, in part because of that area's exceptionally flavorful peppers, which are both sweet and picante.

Pipérade was the first course of the first meal I ever ate in a bistro, and I'll never forget the moment. How could something so simple be so very good?

Though that was long ago, and I've sampled many exotic sophisticated dishes since, pipérade has not lost its simple enticing charm. It is at its best sprinkled generously with fresh herbs, such as marjoram or basil, and scooped up with chunks of lovely bread. Though it traditionally includes Serrano ham and/or chorizo alongside, it is equally delicious as a vegetarian dish.

2 onions, sliced lengthwise
3 tablespoons olive oil
Salt, pepper, and cayenne pepper to taste
3 red bell peppers, seeded, deribbed, and
  sliced lengthwise
1 green bell pepper, seeded, deribbed, and
  sliced lengthwise
5 to 8 ripe tomatoes, diced (plus a little
  tomato juice if the ripe tomatoes are on
  the bland side)
5 to 7 garlic cloves, minced
4 eggs, lightly beaten
1 to 2 teaspoons minced fresh marjoram

◆◆In a large, heavy sauté pan or skillet over medium-low heat, sauté the onions in the olive oil until they begin to soften, about 10 to 15 minutes. Sprinkle the onions generously with salt, pepper, and cayenne, then add the peppers. Continue to cook, stirring ever so often, until the mixture is saucelike, about 15 minutes. Add the

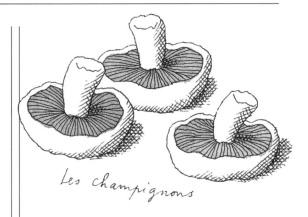

Les champignons

tomatoes and half the garlic and continue to cook until thickened, about 10 minutes.

◆◆Add the remaining garlic and cook 1 to 2 minutes, or to just warm through. Add a few tablespoons of the pepper mixture to the eggs, then pour it all back into the mixture in the pan.

◆◆Stir over low heat until the eggs are slightly set. Taste and adjust the seasoning.

◆◆Serve right away, sprinkled with the marjoram.

FIVE COUNTRY-BISTRO OMELETS

Omelette aux Oignons Nouveaux **(Gascon Green Onion Omelet)** Sauté 5 thinly sliced green onions in 2 tablespoons butter until they wilt. Use as a filling for a rolled omelet.

Omelette aux Asperges à l'Ail Nouveaux **(Young Asparagus and Green Garlic Omelet)** Use the thinnest asparagus stalks you can find; if available, use wild asparagus. If you can't find green garlic stalks, use chopped garlic cloves.

Blanch 3 to 4 chopped asparagus stalks, then heat them over medium-low heat in 1 to 2 tablespoons butter with 3 to 4 chopped green garlic stalks until slightly tender, about 4 to 6 minutes. Pour in 2 beaten eggs mixed with 1 tablespoon milk and seasoned to taste with salt and pepper, then cook until set on the bottom. Serve rolled into an omelet, or broil the top and serve flat. Serves 1.

Omelette aux Herbes Fraîches (Fresh Herb Omelet) Heat 2 tablespoons minced fresh chervil, 2 tablespoons minced fresh parsley, 2 tablespoons minced fresh chives, and 2 tablespoons minced fresh spinach in 1 tablespoon unsalted butter, then add to 2 beaten eggs mixed with a spoonful of milk or cream. Cook as you would for a rolled omelet, then serve sprinkled with additional chopped fresh chervil, parsley, and chives. Serves 1.

Omelette aux Artichauts (Artichoke Omelet from the Southwest) Trim, slice, and dust 4 baby artichokes in flour. Sauté in walnut oil with 1 minced garlic clove or 1 chopped shallot until lightly golden. Pour in 2 beaten eggs mixed with a little milk, salt, and pepper, then cook until set on the bottom. Pop under the broiler to cook the top until it puffs (it will fall when served). Serves 1.

Omelette aux Fruits Flambée (Flamed Fruit Omelet) Beat 8 eggs with 3 to 4 tablespoons sugar and 1 or 2 tablespoons milk or cream. Combine 1½ to 2 cups diced fruit or berries with sugar to taste; heat until the sugar is dissolved. (Apples and cinnamon give a Norman flavor, especially when flambéed with Calvados; blackberries and Armagnac are very Gascon.) Melt 1 to 3 teaspoons unsalted butter in an omelet pan and pour in one fourth of the egg mixture. Cook on the first side until just set on the bottom, then

turn and spoon on ½ cup of the fruit; fold and transfer to a warm platter. Repeat to make 3 more omelets. Garnish them with the remaining fruit mixture. Heat 3 to 4 tablespoons of Armagnac or brandy in a saucepan, taking care that it doesn't flame up on its own accord. Quickly pour over the omelets, light with a match, and let flame. Serve right away with ice cream or lightly whipped cream. Serves 4.

ŒUFS EN MEURETTE

POACHED EGGS IN BURGUNDIAN RED WINE SAUCE

– Serves 4 –

T his is one of the glories of the Burgundian table: rich poached eggs, awash in a sauce of reduced red wine, garnished with mushrooms, shallots, and other savory morsels. When you bite into the yolk of the egg, it runs into the sauce. There are few more delicious dishes.

Œufs en Meurette is a classic on bistro menus, though it is not always vegetarian. I have made the wine sauce more richly flavored by adding browned poached garlic cloves and shiitake mushrooms to the poaching liquid. You can streamline this recipe if you like by omitting the various vegetables, making a simple red wine sauce your sole embellishment.

Often the sauce is further enriched, as it is at Chardenoux, with a lashing of butter whisked into the sauce at the last minute. I have restrained myself in the following recipe, and added a dash of balsamic vinegar instead–the slightly sweet accent sharpens the sauce wonderfully.

Drink any Burgundian wine, preferably the one you've used in making the sauce.

3 to 4 cups warm Sauce Meurette (pages 207–208)

16 to 20 unpeeled garlic cloves

4 to 8 unpeeled shallots

12 dried shiitake mushrooms, broken into small pieces

3 tablespoons butter

4 ounces fresh white mushrooms, quartered

8 warm poached eggs (see page 204)

½ to 1 teaspoon balsamic vinegar

2 tablespoons minced fresh parsley

✦✦ Place the sauce over low heat to simmer. Blanch the whole garlic cloves, then remove them from their cooking liquid with a slotted spoon and place them in a bowl to cool slightly. In the same liquid, blanch the shallots. Remove the shallots as you have the garlic, and to the same cooking water add the shiitakes, simmering them for 5 to 10 minutes, or long enough for them to soften and plump. Remove the shiitakes from their cooking liquid. Strain the cooking liquid into the sauce.

✦✦ Peel the whole garlic cloves and shallots; their skins should slip off easily. Discard the skins and set the garlic and shallots aside with the shiitakes.

✦✦ In a small to medium sauté pan over medium heat, melt 1 tablespoon of the butter and sauté the whole garlic cloves, shallots, and shiitakes for 5 minutes. Add the remaining 2 tablespoons butter and the quartered mushrooms and sauté until lightly browned. Set aside and keep warm.

✦✦ To serve: Stir the balsamic vinegar into the warm sauce. For each portion, ladle a bit of the sauce into a shallow bowl or plate, then add 2 eggs and top with more of the sauce. Scatter the garnish and any juices that have accumulated over the eggs and sauce, then sprinkle with parsley. Serve right away.

ŒUFS À LA PÉRIGORDINE

EGGS POACHED IN CÈPE AND TRUFFLE SAUCE

– Serves 4 –

I ate these luscious poached eggs, cloaked with a creamy sauce of mushrooms and topped with a grating of truffles and a blanket of cheese, in a little Périgordine *ferme-auberge*. These farmhouse inns are a wonderful way to sample the local *cuisine du terroir,* and though many of the specialties are not vegetarian, so many are– truffles and wild mushrooms, for example.

1 onion or 5 shallots, chopped

2 garlic cloves, minced

2 tablespoons butter

1 tablespoon flour

5 to 9 dried cèpe (porcini) mushrooms, broken into tiny pieces

2 dried shiitake mushrooms, broken into tiny pieces

3 tablespoons brandy or Armagnac

½ cup dry white wine

2 cups vegetable stock (pages 201–202)

½ carrot, peeled and finely chopped

¼ teaspoon minced fresh thyme and/or savory, or 1 pinch dried

Grating of nutmeg

⅓ to ½ cup heavy cream

Salt and pepper to taste

8 warm poached eggs (page 204)

I was given a truffle as a gift, wrapped and wrapped and wrapped for keeping until I got home. En route I stopped at a huge agricultural exposition in Paris to sample the wide varieties of regional specialties and to visit the display of farm animals.

Of course, I had forgotten the truffle in my pocket. When I reached the pig enclosure, a class of French twelve-year-olds were having the facts of farm life explained to them. Suddenly the biggest pig of all leapt to his feet and made an agitated lunge for the fence in an effort to reach me. I ran from the pen as quickly and as far as I could. The teacher was pushing the children to safety, a very sexy man next to me was murmuring *ô-là-là*, and

the boar was not to be stopped. The twelve-year-olds were very interested.

Truffles, you see, are said to mimic the scent of the female pig in heat. Eventually, they had to employ a big hoisting machine to get the pig out of the arena, and everyone was looking at me with curiosity and awe. "Why is the pig in love with *l'Américaine?*" I felt flattered and very attractive in a strange way. It wasn't until I reached home that I discovered it wasn't my enormous appeal, rather it was the truffle.

But it was scary. I still have nightmares, late at night when there's a rustling in the quiet house, that the pig is trying to find me.

*1 small to medium fresh truffle, brushed,
    or 1 canned truffle, drained and minced*
*¼ cup grated Beaufort, Comté, or Parmesan
    cheese*

♦♦In a large, heavy sauté pan or skillet over medium heat, sauté the onion or shallots and garlic in the butter until softened, about 5 to 7 minutes. Sprinkle in the flour and stir for 1 or 2 minutes. Stir in the cèpes, shiitakes, and brandy or Armagnac, and cook over high heat until the liquid is almost evaporated (brandy can ignite, so keep your face away from the flames). Stir in the wine, stock, carrot, thyme and/or savory, and nutmeg.

♦♦Cook over medium heat for about 20 minutes, or until the sauce has reduced and coats the back of the spoon.

♦♦Stir in the cream and heat over medium-high heat. Add salt and pepper.

♦♦Ladle the sauce onto individual plates, topping each with 2 eggs and more sauce. Shave the truffle onto the sauce, or sprinkle with the minced truffle, and sprinkle with cheese. Serve right away.

CRÊPES AUX POIREAUX

ET FROMAGE

LEEK AND ROQUEFORT CRÊPES

– Serves 4 –

Not long ago I ate these crêpes in a village bistro in Picardy, where leeks are plentiful and full of flavor. They were served as a first course, sizzling in their little ramekin, rich and enticing.

A Bergerac or Cahors would be a good choice to drink with this, or try a lighter wine, such as a Gamay.

2 leeks, including tender green parts,
  cleaned and thinly sliced
1½ tablespoons butter
8 ounces Roquefort or other blue cheese,
  crumbled
¼ cup shredded Gruyère
2 eggs, lightly beaten
2 tablespoons milk or cream
2 garlic cloves, minced
Salt and pepper to taste
8 crêpes (pages 203–204)

✦✦Preheat the oven to 400°F.

✦✦In a large, heavy sauté pan or skillet over medium-low heat, sauté the leeks in 1 table-spoon of the butter until the leeks are softened but still brightly colored, about 6 to 8 minutes. Remove from heat.

✦✦Combine the leeks with the blue cheese, Gruyère, eggs, milk or cream, and garlic; add salt (if needed–most blue cheeses are salty) and pepper.

✦✦Spoon equal amounts of this mixture into the center of each crêpe and fold each side over, leaving an opening in the center of the now-rectangular parcels.

✦✦Arrange the filled crêpes in a baking pan and dot the top with the remaining ½ tablespoon butter. Bake for 15 to 20 minutes, or until the cheese has melted. Serve very hot.

CRÊPES AU FROMAGE ET CUMIN

CRÊPES FILLED

WITH CHEESE AND CUMIN

– Serves 4 –

Cumin seeds have a real affinity for any rich, pungent cheese; in Alsace, in fact, they are often given as a little gift, twirled into a cone of paper, when one buys the local Muenster cheese.

Cumin was brought to Alsace by Jewish spice merchants fleeing the pogroms of Eastern Europe and Russia. Instead of continuing on to Paris or farther south, many Jews stayed in Alsace, since the local dialect has the same roots in eighth-century German as does Yiddish and they could settle without learning a new language.

2 cups (8 ounces) grated Gruyère
3 to 5 shallots or ½ onion, finely chopped
½ teaspoon cumin seeds
1 egg, lightly beaten
2 tablespoons milk or sour cream
8 crêpes (pages 203–204)
1 tablespoon butter

✦✦Preheat the oven to 400°F.

✦✦Reserve one fourth of the cheese for sprinkling, then combine the rest of the cheese with the shallots or onion, cumin, egg, and milk or sour cream.

✦✦Spoon equal amounts of this mixture into the center of each crêpe, then fold each crêpe into quarters. Arrange the triangle-shaped crêpes in a baking dish just large enough to hold them in one layer.

✦✦Dot with butter and sprinkle with the reserved cheese.

✦✦Bake for 15 to 20 minutes, or just long enough to melt the cheese. Serve right away, sizzling hot.

FILLINGS FOR CRÊPES OR BUCKWHEAT GALETTES

Crêpes aux Herbes (Herbed Butter Crêpes) Mix softened unsalted butter with minced fresh chervil, chives, shallots, and garlic with a little salt and pepper.

Galette à l'Œuf (Egg Crêpes) Break an egg into the center of a hot buckwheat galette, then cover the pan and cook the egg in the pan until the white is set and the yolk is partly cooked. Serve with a nugget or two of the above herbed butter.

Crêpes Farcies Gratinées (Stuffed Crêpes with Cheese) Fill crêpes or galettes with warm Lentilles "Dom Perignon" (pages 114–115), sprinkle with cheese, and brown under a broiler.

Crêpes Farcie Niçoise (Ratatouille Crêpes) Spoon ratatouille (pages 110–111) down the center of each crêpe, then roll up and sprinkle with grated cheese of choice. Bake in a preheated 450°F oven until sizzling hot.

Crêpes au Champignon (Mushroom Crêpes) Serve crêpes or galettes filled with Ragoût de Champignons et du Riz Sauvage (pages 112–113) or sautéed wild mushrooms such as morels, cèpes, chanterelles, or trompettes de la mort.

Crêpes au Fromage de Chèvre à l'Ail et Ciboulette (Crêpes Filled with Goat Cheese, Garlic, and Chives) Fill hot crêpes with crumbled fresh white goat cheese, Boursin, or feta. Add a sprinkling of chopped garlic and chives. Serve hot.

Crêpes aux Broccoli (Broccoli Crêpes) Fill hot crêpes with steamed broccoli, garlic Béchamel (pages 206–207), and a sprinkling of grated cheese. Arrange in a baking pan, sprinkle with a little more cheese, and bake in a preheated 375°F oven until the cheese is melted and the topping lightly browned. Serve right away.

Crêpes aux Epinards au Chèvre (Crêpes with Goat Cheese and Spinach) Fill crêpes with warm Epinards au Chèvre (pages 161–162). Eat right away, or dot with butter and bake until they sizzle.

Crêpes Mediterranées (Mediterranean Crêpes) Cooked spinach or artichokes, mixed with ricotta and Parmesan cheese, then bound together with a little beaten egg, makes a very Mediterranean filling for crêpes. Serve with Coulis de Tomates (page 205) or Coulis de Tomates aux Poivrons Rouges (page 205).

Le jardinier

PÂTÉ AUX LÉGUMES

THREE-COLOR VEGETABLE PÂTÉ

WRAPPED IN CRÊPES

– Serves 6 to 8 –

Though vegetable pâtés were among the discarded darlings of the nouvelle eighties, many deserve a place on our plates. This one is delicious, and its three-color layers are very appealing. It's really a crêpe cake, baked in a loaf, then cut into pâtélike slices.

Serve a slice or two cut into tiny "fingers" as an hors d'oeuvre, or several on individual plates as a first course. They are good cold, with a handful of frisée alongside, and they are equally good hot, sprinkled with a little Parmesan and broiled until slightly glazed.

This pâté has the good manners to be at its best prepared the day ahead. Any vegetables may be used for the layers, as long as the colors contrast and please the eyes. This recipe calls for a layer of orange-hued carrots, dark green spinach, and white cauliflower.

Note that you will need to prepare the béchamel sauce, the crêpes, and the vegetables ahead of time. Once the loaf is constructed and baked, you can chill it for several days before serving, or freeze it for up to 3 months.

3 bunches spinach, stemmed
3 tablespoons water
6 shallots, minced
4 tablespoons butter
3 garlic cloves, minced
1 cauliflower
Grated nutmeg to taste
1 to 2 teaspoons minced fresh tarragon
Salt and pepper to taste

2 pounds carrots, peeled and shredded
*   or coarsely grated*
A pinch of sugar
1 tablespoon minced fresh dill
½ teaspoon minced fresh thyme or
*   marjoram, or pinch of dried*
2 cups (2 recipes) Béchamel Sauce (see
*   page 206)*
3 eggs, lightly beaten
10 crêpes (pages 203–204)
2 cups (8 ounces) shredded Gruyère or
*   Fontina cheese*
Fresh herb sprigs for garnish, or 3 to 4
*   tablespoons grated Parmesan cheese*

✦✦Preheat the oven to 375°F.

✦✦In a covered large saucepan over medium-high heat, cook the spinach in the water until tender and bright green, about 4 minutes. Remove from heat and place the spinach on a plate to cool. Squeeze dry and chop coarsely. Set aside.

✦✦In a small saucepan over medium heat, sauté the shallots in 3 tablespoons of the butter until they are softened and lightly golden, about 5 to 7 minutes. Remove from heat, add the garlic, and set aside.

✦✦Steam the cauliflower over boiling water in a covered pot until it is just tender, about 20 minutes. Drain well. In a blender or food processor, purée the cauliflower until smooth, then place in a pan with one third of the shallot mixture and heat gently. Season with nutmeg, tarragon, salt, and pepper. Set aside.

✦✦Combine the carrots and one third of the shallot mixture in a large, heavy sauté pan or skillet and cook over medium heat until softened, about 5 minutes. Season with sugar, salt, and pepper to taste, and dill. Set aside.

✦✦Combine the spinach and the remaining shallot mixture; season with salt and pepper to taste, and thyme or marjoram.

✦✦Mix the béchamel sauce with the eggs and set aside.

✦✦Line two 8½-by-4½-inch buttered loaf pans with 2 slightly overlapping crêpes, then layer with the spinach. Spread each with one sixth of the béchamel mixture and one sixth of the cheese, then top with a half crêpe. Spread each with half of the cauliflower purée, then one sixth of the béchamel and one sixth cheese, then top with another half crêpe, pressing down firmly so that there are no air bubbles and the whole thing holds together well.

✦✦Layer each with half of the carrots, then with half of the remaining béchamel and cheese. Top with a crêpe, fold over the edges of the crêpes, and top with another crêpe.

✦✦Dot with the remaining 1 tablespoon butter and bake for about 1 hour, or until the crêpes that top the loaves are browned and crisp. The loaves should feel firm to the touch.

✦✦Let cool for about 30 minutes.

✦✦Loosen the sides of each loaf with a blunt knife, then place a plate on top and invert to unmold.

✦✦Wrap in plastic or waxed paper and refrigerate for at least 4 hours or up to 3 or 4 days. To serve: Remove from the refrigerator about 2 hours before serving. Cut into slices while cold, and serve on a pool of coulis. Garnish with herb sprigs. Or, arrange the slices in a baking pan, sprinkle with Parmesan cheese, and bake in a preheated 400°F oven until the cheese lightly browns and the vegetables are heated through. Serve on warm plates.

SOUFFLÉS CHAUDS

—

HOT SOUFFLÉS

Airy billows of egg white studded with savory morsels, soufflés can also be made with cheese, vegetables such as spinach, or a coulis. Sweet soufflés can be mixed with fruit or chocolate. Since the following soufflés are not based on béchamel, they are very delicate and must be eaten right away. Alas, they may be a little temperamental at times too, but if the occasional soufflé does not rise as it should, it will nonetheless taste delicious. Most soufflé recipes call for a béchamel sauce–the flour thickener acts as a stabilizing agent–but I think this interferes with the delicacy of the eggs.

A soufflé might seem mysterious, but there are no mysteries: Put it in the oven and it rises; take it out, and it will, in a matter of minutes or sometimes seconds, deflate.

A soufflé will generally need a collar to rise to its highest height; if you don't care to play around with this sort of thing, however, don't. If you do, simply cut a piece of baking parchment or waxed paper slightly larger than the circumference of the soufflé dish, and about 6 to 8 inches wide. Generously butter the paper and wrap it, buttered side in, tightly around the soufflé dish. Tie it tightly with a string. Pour in the egg mixture and bake as directed; when it has risen, untie the string and present the soufflé.

SOUFFLÉ AU MAÏS, FROMAGE, TOMATES, ET CERFEUIL

CORN, CHEESE, TOMATO, AND CHERVIL SOUFFLÉ

– Serves 4 –

Though the combination of cheese, corn, and tomatoes might seem more New World than Old, corn kernels are showing up more and more in French bistros.

Here, the grassy herb chervil adds a definite French accent to the tomato and corn.

5 egg whites
Pinch of salt
2 tablespoons grated Parmesan
3 egg yolks, beaten
4 ripe tomatoes, diced
2 garlic cloves, minced
1½ cups (6 ounces) shredded Gruyère cheese
Large pinch of cumin seeds
Cayenne pepper or Tabasco sauce to taste
1 to 2 tablespoons minced fresh chervil

✦✦Preheat the oven to 425°F.

✦✦Beat the egg whites and salt until stiff, glossy peaks form.

✦✦Butter a 4-cup soufflé dish or 4 individual 1-cup soufflé dishes and coat the inside with the Parmesan cheese; set aside.

✦✦Mix the egg yolks with the tomatoes, garlic, Gruyère, cumin, cayenne or Tabasco, and half the chervil. Stir in one third of the beaten whites, then fold in the remaining whites.

✦✦Pour into the prepared soufflé dish and bake for 25 minutes, or until soufflé is puffed and golden brown (15 to 20 minutes for the individual soufflés).

✦✦Serve right away, sprinkled with the remaining chervil as a garnish.

SOUFFLÉ AUX TOMATES ET POIVRONS

RED PEPPER AND TOMATO SOUFFLÉ

– Makes 4 individual soufflés –

This tasty soufflé is utterly simple, as the savory coulis serves as both a basis for the soufflé and its sauce, too.

3 to 4 tablespoons grated Parmesan cheese
6 eggs at room temperature, separated
Large pinch of salt
3 cups (2 recipes) Coulis de Tomates aux
  Poivrons Rouges (page 205)

✦✦Preheat the oven to 425°F. Butter the molds generously and coat with the Parmesan. Set aside.

✦✦Beat the egg whites with the salt until they form stiff, glossy peaks. Beat the yolks with half the coulis, then stir in a large spoonful of the whites. Fold this lightened mixture into the whites, then gently pour into the prepared molds.

✦✦Bake for 15 to 20 minutes, or until the soufflés are puffed and slightly golden. If you have a glass window on your oven, look through that. Otherwise, you can open the oven door a tiny bit and quickly peer in. You don't want to lower the heat of the oven, as this can make your soufflé fall. A soufflé rises because the air trapped inside the little pockets of whipped egg whites expands.

✦✦Serve right away, accompanied with the remaining coulis.

Plats du Jour
◆ ◆ ◆
Main Courses

Scrawled onto a blackboard set outside the door or written on the daily menu, the plat du jour is, literally, the plate of the day. Based on whatever is freshest in the market that day, it is the main course. Sometimes it is added to the menu along with the à la carte items; at other times it is the only dish offered, and when it's gone, that's it.

Following is a selection of dishes that make marvelous main courses:

Le jardin potager

vegetables with vegetable sauces, vegetables with rich indulgent sauces, stuffed vegetables, big stewy dishes and casseroles, such as vegetable cassoulet. Many other dishes, not traditionally served as a main course in France, may fill that role: pastas and gratins, egg dishes, savory soufflés, and crêpes.

Try, too, serving a selection of vegetable first courses or side dishes as your main plate. Or, serve a bouquet of vegetables surrounded by risotto, or a big plate of celery root and potato purée surrounded by a carrot and red pepper sauce or roasted root vegetables.

MÉLI-MÉLO DE LÉGUMES PRINTANIERS ET COULIS DE LÉGUMES VERTS

BABY VEGETABLES IN A GARLICKY PURÉE OF PEAS AND SPINACH

– Serves 4 –

A *méli-mélo* is an arrangement of almost anything: Fish or seafood, fruit, or here, an assortment of baby vegetables.

This plate was inspired by a dish I ate one afternoon across the river from Avignon. The tiny vegetables were picked from the garden behind the bistro, and arranged in a pool of exquisite green purée. (If your vegetables are mature rather than baby, cut them into pieces.)

Drink a dry white wine with slightly floral overtones to befriend the peas in the coulis.

GREEN VEGETABLES COULIS

3 garlic cloves

1 cup peas

½ cup water

¼ fennel bulb, trimmed and diced

Pinch of sugar

Pinch of salt

Pinch of black pepper

1 tablespoon minced fresh chervil or parsley

½ teaspoon minced fresh rosemary

½ cup packed chopped spinach leaves or thawed frozen spinach

3 tablespoons butter

12 baby carrots, or 6 regular carrots cut into small pieces

1 small cauliflower, cut into small florets

4 artichoke hearts (see page 210)

4 baby leeks, green onions, or green garlic

4 to 8 baby zucchini, or 3 regular zucchini cut into small pieces

2 ounces haricots verts or baby Blue Lake green beans

4 white mushrooms or shiitakes

✦✦ To make the coulis: Coarsely chop 2 of the garlic cloves. In a small saucepan, combine the chopped garlic, peas, fennel, sugar, salt, pepper, and water to cover. Bring to a boil and cook until the peas and fennel are tender, about 3 to 7 minutes depending upon tenderness of peas.

✦✦ Place the pea mixture in a blender or food processor and purée with the chervil, rosemary, remaining garlic clove, and spinach.

✦✦ Heat over medium heat until it has thickened, then remove from the heat and whisk in the butter. Whirl in a blender or food processor once again.

✦✦ Cook the vegetables in a steamer until they are just tender. They may be cooked separately or together, starting with the vegetables that take the largest to cook. Begin with the carrots and cauliflower. Cook 6 to 8 minutes or until crisp-tender. Add the artichoke hearts, leeks, and zucchini. Cook another 6 to 8 minutes. Add the beans and steam another 3 to 4 minutes. Remove from heat.

✦✦ Serve the warm sauce poured onto a large plate or in a shallow bowl, and arrange the steamed vegetables on top in an appealing way. Serve right away.

Fleurs de Courgette Farcis (**Stuffed Zucchini Blossoms**) If you find squash blossoms, fill them with a savory stuffing: Mashed goat cheese with a little minced garlic, or sautéed finely chopped wild mushrooms. Remove the insides of the flowers, then fill them and hold them together with a toothpick. Sauté as above, then remove the toothpick and serve.

BROCCOLI ET CHOU-FLEUR AVEC PURÉES DE CAROTTES ET POIVRONS DOUX

BROCCOLI AND CAULIFLOWER WITH CARROT AND RED PEPPER PURÉES

– Serves 4 –

Picture the plate: a background of red pepper purée and orange-colored carrot purée, studded with nuggets of green broccoli and white cauliflower. Almost any vegetable could be added to this arrangement: green beans, yellow squash, boiled potatoes, blue potatoes or scarlet beets, a mound of steamed cabbage heated in a little butter.

No matter which vegetables you choose, this dish will taste as beautiful as it looks.

1 bunch broccoli
1 head cauliflower
1 onion, chopped
3 to 4 tablespoons butter
2 carrots, peeled and thinly sliced
Pinch of sugar
Salt and pepper to taste
1 tablespoon flour
1 cup dry white wine

1 cup vegetable stock (pages 201–202)
2 garlic cloves, sliced
1 red bell pepper, roasted, peeled, and
    sliced (see page 210)
Juice of ⅛ to ¼ lemon
Small fresh dill sprigs for garnish

♦♦Trim the broccoli and cauliflower into florets; remove the stems and save for another use.

♦♦Steam the broccoli and cauliflower separately over boiling water in a covered pan until crisp-tender, about 3 minutes for the broccoli, 8 to 10 minutes for the cauliflower. Rinse in cold water and set aside.

♦♦In a heavy, medium saucepan over medium heat, sauté the onion in 1 tablespoon of the butter until the onion is softened, about 5 to 7 minutes. Add the carrots and sprinkle with sugar, salt, and pepper. Sauté for another 5 to 7 minutes, sprinkle with the flour, and cook, stirring for 2 minutes.

♦♦Remove from heat, stir in the wine, stock, and half the garlic, then return to medium heat and

VEGETABLES WITH VEGETABLE SAUCES

Vegetables served in an elegant vegetable coulis are a feast of colors and textures. It is food that delights the eyes as well as the palate, and is rewarding to prepare after a walk through your garden or a visit to your local farmer's market. Use your taste to guide you as the seasons change.

cook until the carrots are very tender and the liquid has reduced to about 1 cup.

♦♦ Place the carrot mixture in a blender or food processor with 1 tablespoon of the butter and purée until smooth. Pour half of this mixture into a small saucepan, then add the roasted red pepper to the blender. Purée until smooth, then pour in a small saucepan. Place both saucepans over very low heat.

♦♦ In a medium saucepan over medium-low heat, melt the remaining 2 tablespoons butter with the remaining garlic and heat the broccoli and cauliflower. Season with salt and pepper to taste and a squeeze of lemon juice.

♦♦ On individual warm plates or 1 large warm platter, pour separate pools of each purée. Top each with one of the vegetables, or place the vegetables in between the sauces.

♦♦ Serve right away, garnished with a few sprigs of feathery dill, if you like.

COURGETTES, ASPERGES,

ET BLETTES À LA SAUCE

HARICOTS ET PISTOU

ZUCCHINI, ASPARAGUS,

AND CHARD IN

BASIL AND WHITE BEAN SAUCE

– Serves 4 –

This lovely, indulgent sauce is thick and creamy with puréed white beans, enriched with a splotch of cream, and given a deliciously fragrant whiff of pistou.

Serve in a shallow soup bowl or on a plate, topped with an assortment of just-tender vegetables–I like to serve all green ones. Other vegetables in season can be happily added: green beans, broccoli florets, artichoke hearts, or sugar snap peas. For a brighter palette, add strips of roasted red or yellow peppers, yellow wax beans, yellow crookneck squash, roasted purple onions, or whatever catches your fancy.

> *2 cups cooked white beans, rinsed and*
>   *drained*
> *1 cup vegetable stock (pages 201–202)*
> *½ cup heavy cream, or as desired*
> *1 bunch Swiss chard, stemmed*
> *3 tablespoons water*
> *2 zucchini, chopped*
> *½ bunch asparagus, trimmed of tough ends*
> *1 to 2 tablespoons butter*
> *½ cup pistou (pages 208–209)*

♦♦ In a blender or food processor, purée the beans and stock until very smooth. Pour the puréed beans into a saucepan with the cream and heat over medium heat until bubbles form around the edges and the mixture is thickened. Stir as you cook so that the purée does not scorch or burn. Remove from heat and keep warm.

♦♦ In a heavy, covered saucepan large enough to hold all the chard, cook the chard over medium heat in the water for about 6 minutes, or until the leaves are bright green and glossy. Remove from heat. Using a slotted spoon, remove the chard and rinse in cold water or just let cool. When cool enough to handle, squeeze the chard dry and roll it into little balls. Set them aside.

✦✦Steam the zucchini over boiling water in a covered pot until crisp-tender, 4 to 5 minutes. Drain and keep warm. Cook the asparagus in boiling water to cover until just crisp-tender, about 3 minutes.

✦✦Melt the butter over medium heat in a large, heavy skillet and heat the vegetables for 5 minutes. Set aside and keep warm.

✦✦Remove the hot bean purée from the stove and stir in the pistou. Pour into shallow soup bowls or plates. Arrange the vegetables on top and serve right away.

BROCCOLI AU SAUCE ROQUEFORT

BROCCOLI IN ROQUEFORT CREAM

– Serves 4 –

Steamed broccoli in rich Roquefort sauce is garnished with crisp nuts in this vegetarian rendition of a classic bistro dish I once ate in Gascony.

Sautéing your own nuts gives a finer dish, I feel, but if you use dry-roasted cashews, be sure that they are not sweetened (i.e., honey-roasted) and, if they are salted, wipe off every grain of salt, as the Roquefort cheese is quite salty on its own.

Begin the meal with a selection of tangy vinaigrette-dressed vegetables: beets, tomatoes, and artichoke hearts for example, or potatoes with cucumbers.

A dish of sizzling endive with garlic and parsley along with the broccoli might be nice, too, with lots of crusty bread and a lusty southwestern wine such as Cahors or, if you're feeling extravagant, maybe a Saint-Emillion.

¾ *cup raw cashew nuts*
3 tablespoons unsalted butter
4 shallots, minced
3 garlic cloves, minced
¾ *cup dry white wine*
Ground nutmeg, pepper and cayenne to taste
¾ *cup crème fraîche or a mixture of sour cream and heavy cream*
2 large bunches broccoli
6 ounces Roquefort cheese, crumbled
Squeeze of fresh lemon juice, if needed

✦✦In a large, heavy sauté pan or skillet over medium heat, sauté the cashew nuts in 1 tablespoon of the butter until they are lightly browned in spots. Set aside.

✦✦In a small to medium saucepan over medium heat, sauté the shallots in the remaining 2 tablespoons butter until softened and slightly golden, about 5 minutes. Stir in the garlic, cook a few moments, then add the wine and raise the heat to high. Cook until it has reduced to about ½ cup. Season with nutmeg, pepper, and cayenne.

✦✦Stir in the crème fraîche or sour cream mixture and heat until it boils. Set aside.

✦✦Steam the broccoli over boiling water in a covered pan until it is just crisp-tender, about 3 to 5 minutes. Drain, set aside, and keep warm.

✦✦Reheat the crème fraîche sauce, then whisk in the crumbled Roquefort. Add a squeeze of lemon juice, to taste.

✦✦Spoon the sauce (which may be a bit chunky) onto a serving plate, then arrange the broccoli on top and scatter the cashew nuts over it. Serve right away.

AIGROISSADE TOULONNAISE

WARM VEGETABLES AND

CHICKPEAS WITH AIOLI

– Serves 4 –

A memorable specialty of the not-too-memorable town of Toulon, about halfway between the chic Côte d'Azur and the decidedly funky, sometimes terrifying, full-of-character Marseilles.

Unlike the more traditionally served aioli, which might be accompanied with whole raw and cooked vegetables for dipping, here the still-warm vegetables are cut into bite-sized pieces and tossed, along with a handful of nutty chickpeas, into the garlicky sauce.

The sauce, too, is special: a saffron-scented, pine nut–enriched aioli known as *agliata*. The resulting mélange is special and satisfying.

Enjoy a cooling Provençal rosé with this dish.

AGLIATA
3 garlic cloves
Large pinch of salt
Several pinches saffron threads
3 to 4 heaping tablespoons pine nuts
2 tablespoons mayonnaise
Squeeze of fresh lemon juice
¼ cup olive oil

8 ounces tiny new potatoes
3 carrots, peeled and cut into ¼-inch dice
4 ounces green beans or Romano beans,
    cut into 1½-inch lengths
3 artichoke hearts (see page 210)
⅔ cup cooked chickpeas, drained

✦✦ To make the *agliata:* In a mortar or food processor, crush the garlic with the salt, then add the saffron and pine nuts. Pound or process the mixture to a paste.

✦✦ Blend in the mayonnaise and lemon juice. Gradually blend in the olive oil. Taste for seasoning, then cover and refrigerate for up to 3 days.

✦✦ Boil the potatoes and carrots until almost tender, about 15 to 20 minutes. Add the green beans and cook 5 minutes, or until the beans are crisp-tender. Add the artichoke hearts and cooked chickpeas and heat through. Drain the vegetables and place them in a serving casserole.

✦✦ Toss the hot vegetables with the reserved *agliata* sauce and serve right away.

RATATOUILLE NIÇOISE

MÉLANGE OF MEDITERRANEAN

VEGETABLES

– Serves 4 to 6 –

Two little bistros–La Merenda and La Pistou–sit side by side near Nice's Old Town and marketplace; each is utterly charming and as full of atmosphere as they are of good food. Anything eaten at those little tables is full of niçoise scents and redolent of sweet basil and garlic. The ratatouille at both is splendid, tasting of sun and earth and summer.

This fine Mediterranean stew depends on quality ingredients and care in preparation. Each vegetable must be cooked separately before they are all simmered or baked together, and you must use plenty of olive oil.

Tossing the finished vegetable mixture with minced parsley, garlic, and olive oil at the end adds a fresh finish.

Ratatouille makes a good lunch or picnic dish, and a good side dish for most any other summer meal, such as pasta with pistou, or zucchini blossoms stuffed with goat cheese.

Salt for sprinkling
1 eggplant, cut into bite-sized pieces
3 zucchini, cut into bite-sized pieces
2 onions, halved lengthwise
5 to 8 garlic cloves, minced
1 red bell pepper, seeded, deribbed, and diced
1 green bell pepper, seeded, deribbed, and diced
5 tablespoons olive oil or as needed
1 fennel bulb, trimmed and cut into bite-sized pieces
2 pounds tomatoes (about 10), or 2 cups canned tomatoes, diced
½ teaspoon wine vinegar or to taste
3 to 4 tablespoons shredded fresh basil, cut into strips or lightly crushed
1 to 2 teaspoons sugar
3 to 4 tablespoons minced, fresh flat-leaf parsley
Salt and cayenne pepper to taste

✦✦Salt the eggplant generously and let it sit until brown droplets form all over the cut sides, about 30 minutes. In a separate bowl, do the same with the zucchini.

✦✦Rinse the vegetables well, pat them dry with paper towels, then set aside while you prepare the rest of the ingredients.

✦✦In a large, heavy sauté pan or skillet over medium heat, lightly sauté the onions, half of the garlic, and the red and green pepper in 1 or 2 tablespoons of the olive oil. Cook until softened, about 10 minutes, then remove mixture from the pan and set aside.

La bergerie

✦✦Sauté the eggplant in 2 tablespoons of the oil, then remove it, using a slotted spoon, from the pan and add it to the onions. Repeat with the zucchini, then the fennel, then the tomatoes.

✦✦Combine the sautéed vegetables and their juices in a heavy saucepan or baking pan and add half the basil. Cover and simmer over low heat, or bake in a preheated 325°F oven for 20 to 30 minutes, or until the flavors have mingled but have not lost their own identity.

✦✦Season the ratatouille with a tiny amount of sugar and vinegar–you only want to enhance the vegetables, not create a sweet-sour flavoring–then simmer a few minutes longer.

✦✦Remove from heat. Stir in the remaining garlic, the remaining basil, and the parsley, then drizzle with 1 or 2 tablespoons olive oil. Add the salt and cayenne.

✦✦Eat warm or at room temperature.

NOTE Ratatouille will keep for up to 1 week well covered and in the refrigerator. As it sits, it will accumulate liquid; simply pour off before you use. Alas, ratatouille does not freeze well.

Ratatouille St. Tropezienne (St. Tropez–style Rata-touille) In Saint-Tropez I tasted a ratatouille that had been seasoned with a few strands of saffron added to the crushed garlic at the end of cooking.

Terrine au Ratatouille (Ratatouille Terrine) Left-over ratatouille is delicious combined with several beaten eggs, poured into a buttered and crumb-lined loaf pan, preferably nonstick, then baked in a preheated 325°F oven until the eggs set, about 40 to 45 minutes. Turn out when cool and serve as an appetizer in slices on a bed of Coulis de To-mates aux Poivrons Rouges (page 205).

Les Œufs au Plat Niçois (Ratatouille with Sun-nyside-Up Eggs) Preheat the oven to 425°F. Heat 1 to 2 cups ratatouille, then spread out in the bot-tom of a large skillet. Make 4 or 8 indentations (depending on whether you serve 1 or 2 eggs per person) and into each indentation slide an egg.

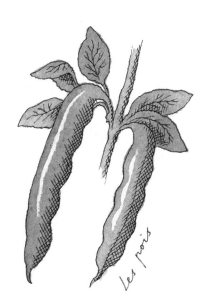

Cook on top of the stove for about 2 minutes, or until the bottoms of the egg are firming up. Bake 2 to 3 minutes longer, or until the whites have firmed but the yolks are still runny. Serve at once, sprinkled with minced fresh parsley.

Ragoût de Champignons et Riz Sauvage

Field Mushroom Stew with Wild and Brown Rices

– Serves 6 –

This lovely, creamy ragout of field mushrooms from Burdundy is scented with nutmeg and the woodsy aroma of the fungi. In asparagus sea-son, add lightly steamed asparagus to the stew to warm through just before serving and, if wild asparagus is available, steam and scatter the stalks atop the mushrooms and their sauce.

A mixture of varied rices, with their brown and rustic hues, continues the foresty theme. Un-til recently, brown rice was not served often in France, but these days there is a great interest in whole foods, and the most *branché* (trendy) restaurants and star chefs include such whole grains as brown rice in their repertoire.

Or you could omit the rice entirely and serve the mushrooms in a casserole with crusty bread for dunking into. A Burgundian white such as a Meursault would be good with this.

¼ ounces dried morel mushrooms
½ ounces dried cèpe (porcini) mushrooms
8 dried shiitake mushrooms
1½ cups hot water
2 onions, chopped

4 garlic cloves, minced

3 tablespoons butter

3 tablespoons brandy

1 cup dry white wine

1 cup vegetable stock (pages 201–202)

1 pound fresh white mushrooms, sliced

Salt and pepper to taste

2 fresh portobello mushrooms

1 tablespoon flour

1½ cups heavy cream

Pinch of grated nutmeg

2 cups hot steamed mixed-grain rice
    (brown, wild, wehani, black, etc.;
    see page 210)

Minced fresh chives for garnish

✦✦Combine the dried morels, cèpes, and shiitakes with the hot water in a saucepan. Simmer for about 5 minutes, then remove from heat and let sit, covered, for 20 to 30 minutes.

✦✦Slice the portobello mushrooms into bite-sized pieces and set aside.

✦✦Drain the dried mushrooms and squeeze them so that the liquid drains back into the pan–this adds extra flavor to your sauce.

✦✦Strain the cooking liquid, discarding the grit left at the bottom, and set aside.

✦✦Cut the drained mushrooms into small pieces. In a large, heavy sauté pan or skillet over medium-high heat, sauté the mushrooms, onions, and half the garlic in 1½ tablespoons of the butter.

✦✦Pour in the brandy and boil the mixture until it has nearly evaporated. It may ignite, so keep it away from your face.

✦✦Add the strained mushroom liquid and boil until it has reduced by about half. Add the wine and stock and cook over high heat until it has reduced to about 1½ cups.

✦✦Pour this mixture into another container and set aside.

✦✦In the same pan over medium heat, melt the remaining 1½ tablespoon butter and lightly sauté the sliced fresh mushrooms for 5 to 7 minutes. Season with salt, pepper, and the remaining garlic, then sprinkle with the flour. Stir and cook for 3 to 4 minutes; do not brown.

✦✦Add the dried mushrooms to the sautéing mushrooms and stir until the sauce thickens. Stir in the cream, then season with nutmeg, salt, and pepper. Set aside and keep warm, or cook up to 2 hours ahead and rewarm just before serving.

✦✦Heat the mushrooms and their sauce, if needed, then serve with the hot rice and garnish with chives.

Ragoût de Champignons et de Blé (*Mixed Mushroom Stew with Whole-Grain Pilaf*) Whole-wheat berries, cooked until tender, make a wonderful accompaniment to the mushrooms in place of wild rice (see page 136). They are nutty tasting, full of B vitamins and fiber, and cost next to nothing.

POTÉE AUX POIS CHICHES
ET AU CHOU
CHICKPEA AND CABBAGE STEW

– Serves 4 –

This Catalan stew tastes best when prepared over a wood fire, as the scent of smoke subtly perfumes the pot.

A rustic red wine and a hunk of slightly sour pain levain bread are superb accompaniments.

1 cup dried chickpeas, soaked overnight in
    cold water to cover

8 cups vegetable stock (pages 201–202)

2 onions, chopped

10 garlic cloves, minced

5 bay leaves

½ celery root, peeled and diced

2 carrots, peeled and sliced

½ red bell pepper, seeded, deribbed, and
    thinly sliced

1 cabbage, cut into wedges

Several fresh rosemary sprigs

Large pinch of paprika

Small piece of ancho chili (in France, nura
    or nora)

Salt and pepper to taste

Olive oil for drizzling

Cooked thin pasta or rice, or thickly sliced
    coarse bread for serving

Minced fresh parsley for garnish

✦✦Drain the soaked chickpeas and put them in a large saucepan. Add enough water to cover them by 1 inch and bring to a boil. Spoon off the white foamy scum that forms on the surface, then lower heat to a simmer, cover, and cook until the chickpeas are tender, from 1 to 3 hours.

✦✦Drain the cooked beans, then return them to the large pot and add the stock, onions, half of the garlic, the bay leaves, and enough water to cover by several inches.

✦✦Cook over medium heat, covered, for about 30 minutes. Add the celery root, carrots, cabbage, half of the rosemary, the paprika and chili. Continue to cook another 30 to 45 minutes, or until the cabbage is quite tender and the soup is richly flavored.

✦✦Add the remaining garlic and rosemary and warm through. Serve ladled into bowls over

pasta or rice, or with chunks of bread for dunking. Let each person drizzle his or her own portion with olive oil to taste.

LENTILS COOKED

WITH CHAMPAGNE

– Serves 4 –

Tart, bubbly Champagne gives earthy lentils a lift of acidic fruitiness. Since the bubbles cook out, any still dry white wine can be used in its place; a spoonful or two of cream added at the end gives the dish a smooth gloss.

For a variation, the lentils can be thinned down with stock and more Champagne or wine, and eaten as soup.

1 cup green lentils (preferably lentils du Puy)

2 bay leaves

3 shallots, chopped

2 tablespoons vegetable oil

2 tablespoons flour

1 cup Champagne or dry white wine

½ cup vegetable stock (pages 201–202)

2 garlic cloves, minced

2 tablespoons minced fresh parsley

3 to 5 tablespoons heavy cream

✦✦Put the lentils in a medium saucepan with the bay leaves and water to cover by about 1 inch. Bring to a boil, then reduce heat to very low and simmer, covered, until the lentils are just tender, 30 to 40 minutes. Remove from heat.

✦✦In a heavy, medium saucepan over medium-low heat, lightly sauté the shallots in the vegetable oil until they are softened, about 5 minutes, then sprinkle in the flour and cook for 2 to 3 minutes, stirring as you cook.

♦♦ Ladle in the lentils with about ½ cup of their cooking liquid, then pour in the wine and stock. Bring to a boil and cook over high heat to reduce to about 3 to 4 tablespoons.

♦♦ Stir in the garlic and 1½ tablespoons of the parsley and taste for seasoning. Stir in the cream and cook a few more moments until the lentils are tender and flavorful and the sauce is nearly nonexistent. Serve with remaining parsley sprinkled over them.

SERVING SUGGESTIONS

Serve a mound of these rich lentils surrounded by roasted carrots and celery root (see page 55).

Spoon warm lentils onto frisée dressed with walnut oil and sherry vinegar, and sprinkle with minced fresh chervil and chives.

Accompany the hot lentils with garlic toasts spread with goat cheese and warmed in a hot oven until they lightly melt.

These are popular winter fare in the Pas de Calais. Use the hot lentils to fill crêpes, then roll them up, place them in a casserole dish, and top with a blanket of grated cheese. Dot with butter, then place under a preheated broiler until they are sizzling.

Toss the creamy lentils with cooked fettuccine, sautéed diced tomatoes, olive oil, Parmesan cheese and minced fresh basil.

Top the creamy lentils with grilled artichoke hearts: Trim chokeless baby artichokes down to their hearts, then marinate them in lemon or white wine, garlic, olive oil, salt, and pepper. Cook over hot coals on each side until they are just tender, about 15 to 20 minutes.

CASSOULET DE LÉGUMES

VEGETARIAN CASSOULET

– Serves 4 to 6 –

This casserole of tender beans, aromatics, vegetables, and an herby crust is baked in a savory sauce. Though cassolet is not traditionally a vegetarian dish, this variation is nonetheless exceedingly good and will charm even carnivores.

I especially like to use the long white cannellinilike beans from France known as lingots. They have a meaty yet delicate flavor. As with any bean, their age is important: Older beans will need a longer cooking time and tender care to see that they don't fall apart during cooking.

A southwestern wine such as Cahors would be good with these crusty beans.

2 cups (1 pound) dried white beans, soaked
overnight in water to cover
1 bay leaf
1 red bell pepper, peeled, seeded, and diced
1 carrot, peeled and diced
cloves from 2 garlic heads
1 potato, peeled and diced
3 tablespoons olive oil
1 teaspoon herbes de Provence, crushed
¼ teaspoon dried thyme leaves, crushed
1½ cups dry red wine

2 cups diced fresh or canned tomatoes
1½ cups vegetable stock (pages 201–202)
Salt and pepper to taste
1 cup fresh bread crumbs
3 tablespoons minced fresh parsley

✦✦ Drain the beans and place them in a saucepan with fresh water to cover by 1 inch. Add the bay leaf, bring to a boil, then reduce heat to a low simmer and cover. Cook for 1½ to 2 hours, or until the beans are tender, adding a little more warm water if needed as they cook. Do not overcook. Drain and set aside.

✦✦ Preheat the oven to 325°F.

✦✦ Reserve 5 of the garlic cloves. In a large, heavy sauté pan over medium-high heat, sauté the pepper, carrot, remaining garlic cloves, and potato in 2 tablespoons of the olive oil until lightly browned, about 5 to 8 minutes.

✦✦ In an earthenware casserole, layer the cooked drained beans, sautéed vegetables, herbes de Provence, thyme, red wine, and stock, sprinkling each layer with salt and pepper.

✦✦ Cover the casserole with a tight-fitting lid and bake for 1 to 1½ hours, adding more liquid if needed to keep beans from burning. The consistency should be slightly soupy.

✦✦ Mince the reserved garlic cloves. Combine the bread crumbs, minced garlic, and parsley with the remaining 1 tablespoon olive oil.

✦✦ Increase the oven heat to 400°F.

✦✦ Remove the casserole from the oven, remove the lid, and spread a third of the crumb mixture over the top. Return the casserole to the oven uncovered and bake for about 15 minutes, or until a golden crust has formed.

✦✦ Break the crust and stir it into the cassoulet, then repeat by spreading the top with another third of the crumb mixture. Bake, then remove from the oven and break the crust, stirring it into the beans.

✦✦ Spread the casserole with the last of the crumbs. Return to oven until this, too, forms a golden crust, then serve right away.

FARCIS DE LÉGUMES NIÇOIS

LITTLE STUFFED VEGETABLES

OF NICE

– Serves 4 –

S tuffed vegetables are as traditional in Nice as they are in the surrounding Mediterranean, Arabic, and Balkan lands.

Any Mediterranean vegetable is delicious stuffed this way: artichokes, tomatoes, peppers, zucchini, patty pan squash, eggplant, onions. The more vegetables you choose, the more flavorful and complex your stuffing will be, as will the pan juices as they mingle during the cooking.

Stuffing the vegetables is time-consuming, but it can also be relaxing, almost meditative. Not long ago I was sitting at a café along the Cours Saleya market, when a chef emerged from his little bistro with a big bowl of vegetables and a tray. He sat down at a table with a small knife and, basking in the springtime sunshine, happily hollowed out, then stuffed each one, as he watched the parade of marketplace life.

1 cup water
Pinch of salt
½ cup long-grain white rice
½ cup cooked green lentils (see page 209)
1 onion, chopped
6 garlic cloves, minced

¼ cup diced fresh or frozen Romano beans

2 tablespoons tomato paste

4 to 6 fresh basil leaves, thinly sliced

2 tablespoons minced fresh parsley

*5 to 6 ounces fresh white sheep or goat
  cheese (such as a Brousse) or feta,
  crumbled*

½ teaspoon herbes de Provence

1 egg, lightly beaten

2 ripe tomatoes

4 small onions

2 zucchini

4 small artichokes

*1 to 2 Asian eggplants about 3 inches in
  diameter*

3 to 4 tablespoons dried bread crumbs

2 tablespoons olive oil

½ lemon, cut into wedges

♦♦In a small saucepan, bring the water to a boil, add the salt, and cook the rice in boiling water until it is just tender, 5 to 10 minutes. Fork lightly to fluff it up, then remove the pan from heat.

♦♦Preheat the oven to 375°F. Combine the cooked rice with the lentils, onion, half the garlic, the Romano beans, tomato paste, basil, parsley, cheese, herbes de Provence, and egg.

♦♦Cut the tomatoes into halves, then scoop out their insides, adding the tomatoey pulp to the rice mixture.

♦♦Peel the onions and hollow out their centers, then coarsely chop the onion centers and add to the rice mixture.

♦♦Cut the zucchini crosswise into 4-inch lengths, then cut each piece lengthwise into 2 halves. Make each half into a boat shape by hollowing out the insides. Take the removed zucchini flesh, chop, and add it to the rice mixture.

♦♦Prepare the artichokes into cuplike bottoms by first slicing off the stems. Peel the stems, chop, and add to the rice mixture. Then trim the artichokes by removing the tough outer leaves until you reach the tender inner leaves. Scoop out each choke, if there is one, using a sharp-edged spoon or paring knife. Blanch the artichoke hearts for 1 minute in water to which you've added a few drops of lemon juice, then drain and set aside.

♦♦Cut the eggplants into 2-inch-thick slices. Carve a hollow in each. Chop the removed flesh and add to the rice and vegetable mixture.

♦♦Arrange the hollowed-out vegetables in a shallow baking pan. Fill each vegetable generously with the chopped mixture, piling it up and pressing it down to firm. Sprinkle the stuffed vegetables with the remaining garlic, then with the crumbs, and finally drizzle with the olive oil.

♦♦Place the vegetables in the oven and bake for 1 hour, or until they are tender and their crumb topping is crisp and golden browned.

♦♦Serve warm or at room temperature, with lemon wedges.

CHOU FARCI

STUFFED SAVOY CABBAGE

– Serves 4 –

A whole stuffed cabbage, poached in white wine and served in big lusty wedges, has gotten many a Parisian through a long cold winter. The slight sweetness of currants and cinnamon adds an unexpected, elusive accent. This dish is best made 1 or 2 days ahead and re-warmed.

An Alsatian white such as a Sylvaner or Traminer would be good with this, or a dry Aligoté.

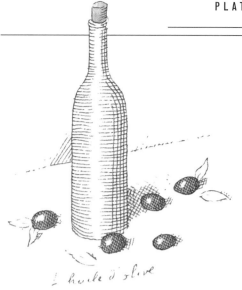

l'huile d'olive

1 cup brown rice (see page 210)

1 cup water

¾ cup cooked drained green lentils (see page 209)

½ onion, chopped

3 garlic cloves, chopped

3 tablespoons tomato paste

2 tablespoons chopped cooked spinach

1 tablespoon minced fresh parsley

1 carrot, peeled and coarsely shredded

Pinch of ground cinnamon

3 tablespoons currants or raisins

1 piece stale bread, soaked in milk and broken into small pieces

1 egg, lightly beaten

Salt and pepper to taste

¼ teaspoon minced fresh thyme, or pinch of dried

About 3¼ cups basic vegetable stock or more as needed (pages 201–202)

1 savoy cabbage

1½ to 2 cups dry white wine

✦✦ Cook the rice (see page 210) in a heavy 3-cup saucepan.

✦✦ Combine the rice, water, lentils, onion, garlic, tomato paste, spinach, parsley, carrot, cinnamon, currants or raisins, crumbled soaked bread, egg, salt, pepper, thyme, and ¼ cup of the vegetable stock. Mix well to form a cohesive mass.

✦✦ Remove all of the cabbage leaves from the core.

✦✦ Blanch the leaves to make them more pliable. Rinse each leaf in cold water, then drain and dry with paper towels. Pile the blanched leaves on a plate beginning with the largest and ending with the smallest.

✦✦ Place about ½ cup of the filling mixture inside one of the smaller cabbage leaves, then spread some filling on another leaf and place the filling-stuffed cabbage leaf, leaf-side down, on top of that. Continue, in effect, rebuilding the cabbage, with stuffing in between the leaves. It is messy, but regardless of how unpromising it looks, will be fine once it is wrapped. And if it falls apart as you put it together, it can easily be rebuilt.

✦✦ Place a large piece of cheesecloth on a plate, then place the stuffed cabbage on top of that. Take 2 opposite corners of the cloth and tie them into a snug knot. Repeat with the other 2 corners. You now have a tightly wrapped cheese-cloth–covered ball of stuffed cabbage.

✦✦ Pour the wine and stock into a saucepan that is just big enough to hold the cabbage. Bring to a boil, then lower heat and add the cabbage. Add more stock as necessary to come two-thirds up the side of the cabbage. Cover with the lid and simmer for about 1 hour.

✦✦ Serve warm, in wedges, in shallow bowls with some of the broth spooned over.

Garnitures

•••

Accompaniments

A savory zucchini gratin, a warm mound of risotto, a sprite sauté of spring vegetables: the variety of side dishes on the French table can be the most exciting part of the menu. Many of these side dishes may also be served as a main course.

Enjoy a bowl of garlicky pasta for a summer lunch; a plate of tender green beans and mushrooms for a light autumnal supper; or a big bowl of mashed potatoes with cheese for a winter feast.

However you decide to serve them, these delicious accompaniments will make every meal a memorable experience.

Le cageot de poires

Pâtes, Riz, et Grains

. . .

Pasta, Rice, and Grains

We might think of pasta as strictly Italian, but France has long been a country of enthusiastic pasta aficionados. Gallic pasta is rich with the flavors and flair that typify French cuisine, including sautéed shallots, wine, herbs, and cream, as well as the cheeses that enrich the bistro kitchen: Roquefort, chèvre, and Gruyère.

Parisian bistros frequently serve pasta as a side dish to accompany the plat du jour. Ravioles, *little goat cheese–filled pastas from northern Provence, are as luscious as they are chic. Thin strands of pasta or a nest of fat noodles might be served sitting with a tomato and pepper coulis to accompany an omelet, an assortment of vegetables, or as its own course.*

Roquefort cheese is a favorite in the south from Gascony to Provence. And in the area around Nice, with its gastronomic ties to Liguria, pasta is truly part of the culinary tradition, especially pâtes au pistou, *a close sibling to* pasta al pesto.

Rice and other grains are often eaten as a side dish with stews and braised casseroles– cooked simply, buttered, and tossed with spices or herbs. In the southern regions toward Italy, rice is stirred into risotto, and in Catalonia, into vegetable paella, perhaps enriched with a poached egg or a splash of spicy sauce.

And chewy grains such as wild rice, wheat berries, rye, and barley are very chic these days.

. . . .

PÂTES AU PISTOU

GREEN PASTA WITH CREAMY SAUCE OF BASIL AND PUNGENT CHEESE

– Serves 4 –

Somewhere in the vicinity of Nice begins the region of aromatic basil sauces cloaking tender pasta, a region that continues along the Ligurian coast through the Italian Riviera and the port city of Genoa.

Though I sampled this in Eze, a tiny neighbor of Monaco, you'll find fragrant versions throughout the area, especially in such Vieux Nice bistros as La Merenda, Tosello, and La Pistou. My version has the addition of tangy fresh chèvre. Once you have the pistou made up, this dish takes about

5 minutes from start to finish. You could, alternatively, use a good-quality storebought pesto.

Pour a glass of Côtes-du-Rhône or a Côtes-du-Provence red and enjoy the fragrant green noodles as a first course, followed by tomatoey *courgettes en gratin*.

> 1 pound fresh spinach fettuccine
> 2 tablespoons olive oil
> 2 garlic cloves, minced
> 4 to 6 ounces fresh white goat cheese,
>   crumbled
> ¼ to ½ cup pistou (pages 208–209)
> ¼ cup shredded fresh basil leaves
> Grated Parmesan cheese as desired

✦✦Cook the fettuccine in a large pot of salted boiling water until al dente, 2 to 3 minutes.

✦✦Drain, then toss with the olive oil, garlic, goat cheese, and pistou.

✦✦Serve right away, garnished with basil leaves scattered over the top and Parmesan as desired.

PÂTES AUX CHAMPIGNONS RÔTIS

FETTUCCINE WITH ROASTED

MUSHROOMS

– Serves 4 –

This exquisite dish of creamy pasta is topped with sizzling, garlicky mushrooms that have been roasted separately, keeping their flavors distinct.

If flavorful mushrooms are available, such as portobellos, cèpes, chanterelles, trompettes de la mort, or shiitakes, choose them, though ordinary white mushrooms will do fine. If the mushrooms are large, slice them before serving.

For white wine, choose a cool, slightly acidic Sancerre; for a red, try an Alsatian Pinot Noir or a chilled Beaujolais.

> 12 ounces large mushrooms
> 5 garlic cloves, minced
> ¼ to ½ teaspoon fresh lemon juice,
>   or 1 tablespoon dry white wine
> 4 tablespoons butter
> Salt and pepper to taste
> 12 ounces fresh fettuccine
> 1½ cups heavy cream
> Grating of fresh nutmeg
> ¾ cup (3 ounces) freshly grated Parmesan
>   cheese

✦✦Preheat the oven to 450°F.

✦✦Arrange the mushrooms caps down in a single layer in a shallow baking pan. Sprinkle with the garlic, lemon juice or white wine, 2 tablespoons of the butter, the salt, and pepper.

✦✦Bake until the mushrooms are sizzling and browned, 10 to 15 minutes.

✦✦Meanwhile, cook the fettuccine in a large pot of salted boiling water until al dente, 2 or 3 minutes. Drain and return it to the hot pan. Add the remaining 2 tablespoons butter and toss the pasta over a low heat, adding the cream, salt and pepper to taste, nutmeg, and half the Parmesan until heated through.

✦✦Place the pasta on a warm platter and top with the hot mushrooms and their juices. Sprinkle with remaining Parmesan and serve right away.

GRATIN DES PÂTES AUX CHAMPIGNONS

WILD MUSHROOM PASTA GRATIN

– Serves 4 to 6 –

Wild mushrooms and pasta is one of the classic combinations, the strong woodsy scent and flavor of the fungi a perfect balance to the tender, bland noodles.

While fresh wild or field mushrooms are extraordinary in this dish, ordinary white mushrooms are quite delicious too when enhanced with the addition of dried cèpes, morels, trompettes de la mort, etc.

The cheese topping can be varied depending on what's on hand; a sprinkling of tangy goat cheese makes a nice addition.

> 1 pound mushrooms, preferably a combination of cèpes, portobellos, shiitakes, chanterelles, or other wild or field mushrooms
>
> 3 tablespoons butter or olive oil
>
> ¼ cup brandy, port, Marsala, or Madeira
>
> 5 shallots, minced
>
> 3 to 5 garlic cloves, minced
>
> ½ cup vegetable stock (pages 201–202)
>
> 1 pound small elbow macaroni
>
> Salt and pepper to taste
>
> 3 to 4 tablespoons minced fresh chives
>
> 1 cup (4 ounces) shredded Gruyère
>
> ½ cup (2 ounces) grated Parmesan cheese

✦✦Preheat the oven to 425°F. In a large sauté pan or skillet over medium heat, sauté the mushrooms in 2 tablespoons of the butter or olive oil until they are lightly browned. Add the spirits, then cook over a high heat for a few moments.

Remove from the heat and add the shallots, garlic, and stock. Set aside.

✦✦Cook the pasta in a large pot of salted boiling water until al dente. Drain well, then toss with the mushroom mixture, salt, pepper, chives, the remaining 1 tablespoon butter or olive oil, and about a third of the Gruyère and Parmesan.

✦✦Spoon into a 12-inch gratin dish, or into individual casseroles. Sprinkle with the remaining cheese and bake until bubbly and golden brown.

✦✦Serve right away.

Macaronis et Champignons au Fromage de Chèvre **(Gratin of Macaroni with Mushrooms and Goat Cheese)** Before topping the casserole with the grated cheeses, add 4 ounces crumbled fresh white goat cheese.

PÂTES À LA MENTON

PASTA WITH ARTICHOKES, LENTILS, CREAM, AND TOMATOES

– Serves 4 –

Just as the little sun-drenched town of Menton straddles the border of Italy and France, so too does its food, with pasta as at home on the table as it is on either side of the border.

This is a vegetarian adaptation of a dish I sampled there not long ago. It is elegant when made with fresh fettuccine, but it's also good with macaroni. If you don't have any cooked lentils on hand or time to cook lentils, the dish is delicious without them as well.

3 shallots, minced

3 garlic cloves, minced

2 tablespoons butter

8 baby artichoke hearts, blanched (see page
210)

½ cup drained cooked lentils (see page
209)

½ cup dry white wine

½ cup vegetable stock (pages 201–202)

1½ cups diced tomatoes

3 bay leaves

Pinch of sugar, salt, and pepper

1 cup heavy cream

3 to 4 tablespoons chopped fresh basil

12 ounces fresh or dried pasta

Grated Parmesan or pecorino cheese

✦✦In a large, heavy sauté or frying pan over medium heat, sauté the shallots and garlic in the butter until they are just softened, about 3 minutes. Add the artichokes and lentils and cook a few moments.

✦✦Raise heat to high and pour in the wine. Bring to a boil and cook until reduced to a syrupy glaze, then do the same thing with the stock.

✦✦Lower heat to medium and add the tomatoes, bay leaves, sugar, salt, and pepper. Cook for 10 to 15 minutes, or until thickened, then add the cream and continue to cook.

✦✦Cook the pasta in a large pot of salted boiling water until al dente, about 10 minutes for dried pasta and 2 to 3 minutes or fresh. Drain and serve blanketed with the sauce, sprinkled generously with the basil and cheese.

PÂTES AU ROQUEFORT

ET PIGNONS

THREE-COLOR PASTA

WITH ROQUEFORT SAUCE

AND TOASTED PINE NUTS

– Serves 4 –

I saw this dish scrawled on a blackboard as a plat du jour in a bistro near Nice's Cours Saleya market and walked in immediately. The pastel-hued strands of fettuccine–spinach green, yellow saffron, and pink tomato–were cloaked with a rich sauce of Roquefort, with pine nuts adding just enough crunch.

As well as being indulgent, it's easily tossed together, making it desirable for last-minute entertaining.

½ cup pine nuts

1 pound fresh fettuccine in a selection of
three flavors: spinach, herb, tomato or
beet, saffron, mushroom, and so forth

12 ounces Roquefort cheese, crumbled

1 to 2 garlic cloves, minced

1 shallot, minced

1½ cups heavy cream

Grated Parmesan to taste

Pepper to taste

✦✦Toast the pine nuts in an ungreased pan until lightly golden. Set aside.

✦✦Cook the fettuccine in a large pot of salted boiling water until al dente. Drain, return to the pot, and toss with the Roquefort, garlic, cream, and Parmesan.

✦✦Season with pepper and sprinkle with the toasted pine nuts; serve right away.

Macaronis au Roquefort et Courgettes (Macaroni and Zucchini in Roquefort Sauce) Cook the macaroni until almost al dente. Add 2 diced zucchini and cook for 1 or 2 minutes, or until al dente. Drain and proceed as above.

le panier de pommes

PÂTES FRAÎCHES SAUCE VIN ROUGE ET ROQUEFORT

FRESH PASTA WITH CREAMY RED WINE AND ROQUEFORT SAUCE

– Serves 4 –

Red wine, reduced to a flavorful essence, is combined with cream and enriched with Roquefort cheese in this distinctive, so very French dish.

I ate this in a little bistro in Cahors, sitting at a table in the shade on a warm summer day. The marketplace had just closed, and we still had our shopping in plastic bags gathered around our feet. The purple sauce mixed with tender pasta was garnished with a delicate mosaic of vegetables.

A robust, slightly spicy red such as a Medoc would be just the wine to use in this sauce, and to drink alongside, too.

> 8 shallots, minced
> 2 unpeeled garlic cloves, sliced
> ½ cup vegetable stock (pages 201–202)
> ¾ cup dry red wine, such as a Cahors
> or a Merlot
> 1 cup heavy cream
> 6 ounces strong blue cheese such as
> Roquefort, crumbled
> Pepper to taste
> 1 pound fresh fettuccine
> 2 tablespoons butter (optional)
> Minced fresh chives (optional)

✦✦In a small saucepan, combine the shallots, garlic, stock, and wine. Bring to a boil and cook over high heat for about 5 minutes, or until reduced to ½ cup.

✦✦Strain, pressing the shallots and garlic with the back of a large spoon to release their flavors into the sauce. Discard the shallots and garlic.

✦✦Combine this mixture with the cream and cook over medium heat until reduced by about one third, then remove from heat.

✦✦Stir the blue cheese into the hot sauce and season with pepper. Set aside and keep warm.

✦✦Cook the pasta in a large pot of salted boiling water until al dente, 2 to 3 minutes. Drain.

✦✦If serving on top of the sauce, gently toss the pasta with the butter, then ladle some of the hot sauce onto hot plates and top with a nest of the pasta. Sprinkle the chives over either the sauce or pasta as a garnish and serve right away. For a simpler though less beautiful presentation, toss the hot drained pasta with the still warm sauce and serve right away, sprinkled with the chives.

PÂTES ET PETITS POIS AU SAFRAN

FRESH PASTA WITH PEAS AND GARLIC-SAFFRON OLIVE OIL

– Serves 4 to 6 –

This dish from a hillside village not far from Grasse combines pasta and peas cloaked in a sauce of garlic, saffron, lemon, and herbes de Provence. It's perfect for a sultry, very hot day when you are too listless to cook anything ambitious, but you crave a big, strong flavor.

Crushing garlic in a mortar gives the strongest, most deliciously garlic flavor–if the garlic you are using is strongly flavored, you might want to use the smaller amount.

3 to 5 garlic cloves
Pinch of salt
2 pinches of saffron threads
Juice of ½ lemon, or more to taste
4 tablespoons olive oil
1 pound farfalle or other dried shaped
   pasta
1 to 1½ cups young peas
¼ teaspoon herbes de Provence
Large pinch of red pepper flakes
Pepper to taste
¼ cup grated Parmesan, Asiago,
   or pecorino cheese

♦♦In a mortar or food processor, crush the garlic with the salt until it forms a paste, then add the saffron and crush it in as well. Stir in the lemon juice and 2 tablespoons of the olive oil, then set aside.

♦♦In a large pot of salted boiling water, cook the pasta until it is almost al dente, but still crunchy inside, then add the peas and continue to cook for 2 to 3 minutes, or until both pasta and peas are al dente. Drain.

♦♦Toss the pasta and peas with the remaining 2 tablespoons olive oil, the garlic sauce, herbes de Provence, pepper flakes, pepper, and cheese. Taste and adjust the seasoning, then serve in shallow soup bowls.

SPAGHETTIS AUX LÉGUMES DU SOLEIL ET FROMAGE DE CHÈVRE

SPAGHETTI WITH GOAT CHEESE AND ROASTED EGGPLANT, ARTICHOKES, AND PEPPERS

– Serves 4 –

Shreds of garlicky roasted vegetables tossed with chewy spaghetti and melting goat cheese is a good reason to make this lusty pasta dish. Drink a big red Gigondas, and enjoy a salad of wild and herby greens, with a handful of olives and a few croutons of pain levain tossed in.

1 pound spaghetti
3 tablespoons olive oil
3 garlic cloves, minced
½ recipe Salade du Berger (pages 66–67)
4 ounces goat cheese, crumbled

Salt and pepper to taste

½ bunch fresh basil, stemmed and thinly sliced

✦✦Cook the spaghetti in a large pot of salted boiling water until al dente, about 10 minutes. Drain. Return the spaghetti to the pan.

✦✦Toss the hot spaghetti with the olive oil, garlic, Salade de Berger, and goat cheese over low heat for 30 to 60 seconds. Add salt and pepper.

✦✦Serve right away, sprinkled generously with basil.

PÂTES AU SAFRAN

AVEC ROUILLE ET BASILIC

SAFFRON PASTA WITH ROUILLE

AND SWEET BASIL

– Serves 4 to 6 –

In Provence we drove far into the hills behind Nice, where, in the middle of a field, was a little country bistro. We ate garlic soup with a crusty cheese topping to start off with and, to finish, fresh peach ice cream with sweet garden cherries.

For our plat du jour we ate this beautiful pasta: yellow saffron-tinted strands topped with a rusty red rouille and a scattering of green basil.

The chili seasoning is not a nouvelle affectation, rather part of the flavor of France's south. In France, you would use a mild dark red chili called nura or nora, an obvious cousin of the ancho.

¼ ancho chili, or ½ to 1 teaspoon ground ancho chili

3 garlic cloves

Pinch of salt

2 generous pinches of saffron threads

½ to 1 red jalapeno or Thai chili

6 tablespoons olive oil

½ red bell pepper, seeded, deribbed, and finely chopped

2 tablespoons tomato paste

1 teaspoon paprika

Juice of ¼ lemon, or to taste

Salt, pepper, and Tabasco or cayenne pepper to taste

1 pound fresh tomato or saffron pasta

¼ to ½ cup fresh basil leaves, thinly sliced

Coarsely grated Parmesan cheese, as desired

✦✦If using the whole chili, place it in a small bowl and cover with boiling water. Leave to soak 30 minutes. Drain, dice, and set aside.

✦✦Crush the garlic with the salt in a blender or food processor. Add the saffron and crush the threads, then add the jalapeno chile and continue to purée. Finally, add the soaked chili or ground chile purée with 1 tablespoon of the olive oil until it forms a smooth paste.

✦✦Add the red bell pepper, tomato paste, paprika, 4 tablespoons of the olive oil, and the lemon juice. Whirl it until it forms a smooth, thick purée.

✦✦Season with salt, pepper, and Tabasco or cayenne and set aside.

✦✦Cook the pasta in a large pot of salted boiling water until al dente, then drain and toss lightly with the remaining 1 tablespoon olive oil. Serve the hot pasta with a dollop of the red sauce in its center, garnished generously with a flurry of the fragrant sweet basil. Offer Parmesan cheese alongside.

NOTE Make a double batch of the rouille; it keeps well for about 1 week in the refrigerator and is sublime to add to a variety of dishes such as the one below.

Aubergine et Figues, Rouille **(Grilled Eggplant with Fig, Port, and Rouille Mayonnaise)** Last spring, in Catalonia, outside Béziers en route to Perpignan, we rented a little cottage on the Canal du Midi, conveniently located about ten steps from an eccentric bistro in an old stone house next to the water. They made the following Catalonian-influenced dish. Simmer a handful of dried figs (either golden or black) in port or a fragrant white wine such as a German one) until the figs are tender. Remove them from their wine bath and dice the fruit, then combine them with equal amount of both the rouille and mayonnaise. (Save the port or sweet wine for another use.)

PÂTES AUX DEUX COURGETTES À LA SAFRAN ET CRÈME

SAFFRON-SCENTED PASTA AND TWO COLORS OF ZUCCHINI

– Serves 4 –

Flat ribbons of delicate pasta are awash in saffron-hued cream, interspersed with slashes of dark and pale green zucchini.

I sampled this rich and succulent dish on the terrace of a chic little bistro in the hills behind Nice. It was a soft spring afternoon when mimosa was in season, and the yellow and green of my plate appeared as sunny and yellow as the mimosa that surrounded us.

2 each green and golden zucchini, cut into
   bite-sized pieces
4 to 5 garlic cloves, coarsely chopped
4 to 6 pinches of saffron threads
3 tablespoons butter
⅔ cup heavy cream
Salt and black or cayenne pepper to taste
12 ounces fresh tagliatelle or fettuccine
3 to 5 tablespoons grated Parmesan cheese,
   plus extra for sprinkling

✦✦Cook the zucchini in boiling water to cover until just tender, about 6 minutes. Drain the zucchini (reserving the liquid for soups), then return it to the pan. Add the garlic to the drained zucchini, cover, and set aside.

✦✦Toast the saffron in a dry heavy pan until it is just fragrant. Remove from heat. When the pan has cooled, add the butter and cream. Set it aside.

✦✦Cook the pasta in a large pot of salted boiling water until al dente, 2 or 3 minutes, then drain. Return to the pan.

✦✦Toss the pasta and still-warm cooked zucchini with the saffron sauce, then with the 3 to 5 tablespoons grated Parmesan.

✦✦Serve right away, with additional Parmesan for sprinkling.

Les pains

PÂTES FRAÎCHES

AUX LENTILLES ET NOIX

FETTUCCINE WITH LENTILS

AND WALNUT-CREAM

– Serves 4 –

Crème fraîche, mascarpone, or sour cream makes a rich walnut sauce, but fromage frais or ricotta cheese is lower in fat with a high-protein heft. The drizzle of walnut oil, however, is what makes this Auvergnat pasta dish special, amplifying its nutty scent.

A light salad of mesclun tossed with strands of blanched young asparagus makes a clean-tasting contrast to the richness of this pasta.

2 garlic cloves
Large pinch of salt, plus salt to taste
¼ cup walnut pieces
½ to ¾ cup crème fraîche, mascarpone, or
  sour cream, or a combination of ½ cup
  sour cream and ½ cup ricotta
1 pound fresh fettuccine
½ cup cooked lentils (see page 209)
2 tablespoons minced fresh chervil
2 tablespoons minced fresh chives
Pepper to taste
1 teaspoon walnut oil
¼ cup grated Parmesan or as desired

✦✦ Crush the garlic with the pinch of salt in a mortar or a food processor. Add the walnuts and crush them into a paste, then add the crème fraîche, mascarpone or sour cream and mix well. Set this sauce aside while you prepare the rest of the dish.

✦✦ Cook the pasta in a large pot of salted boiling water until al dente, 2 or 3 minutes.

✦✦ Meanwhile, heat the lentils.

✦✦ Drain the pasta and lentils and toss with the walnut sauce. Season with salt and pepper, drizzle with walnut oil, and toss with Parmesan. Serve right away.

GRATIN DE PÂTES

À LA MEURETTE

GRATIN OF MACARONI,

RED WINE SAUCE, AND CHEESE

– Serves 4 to 6 –

Layering pasta with cheese and a sauce of reduced wine makes a lusty pasta gratin similar to a vegetarian *macaronade*.

Since Meurette and other wine sauces freeze exceedingly well, I often make a double recipe batch and keep a few cups in the freezer.

1 pound elbow macaroni
1½ to 2 cups Sauce Meurette (pages
  207–208)
½ cup (2 ounces) grated Parmesan
½ cup (2 ounces) grated Asiago or Gruyère

✦✦ Preheat the oven to 450°F.

✦✦ Cook the pasta in a large pot of salted boiling water until al dente, about 10 minutes. Drain well.

✦✦ Spoon half of the pasta into a buttered 8-cup baking dish. Add half the Meurette sauce, toss well, then sprinkle with half of the cheese.

✦✦ Layer with the remaining pasta, spread with the remaining sauce, and sprinkle with the remaining cheese.

✦✦ Bake for 15 to 20 minutes, or just long enough to heat through and to melt and lightly brown the cheese. Serve sizzling hot.

RAVIOLE AU COULIS DE TOMATES AUX POIVRONS ROUGES

TINY CHEESE-FILLED PASTA IN A BED OF CREAMY TOMATO AND PEPPER PURÉE

– Serves 4 –

Serve this delicate Savoy specialty over a bright cream-enriched coulis. The color and flavor of the red pepper and tomato sauce makes a pasta as pretty to look at as it is delicious.

1 recipe Coulis de Tomates aux Poivrons Rouges (page 205)
12 ounces fresh cheese-filled ravioli
½ cup heavy cream
1 cup (4 ounces) shaved Parmesan or aged goat cheese
¼ cup thinly sliced fresh basil leaves

✦✦ Gently heat the coulis; set aside and keep warm.

✦✦ Cook the ravioli in a large pot of salted boiling water until al dente, 2 or 3 minutes. Drain. Set aside and keep warm.

GNOCCHI

Gnocchi are a specialty of Nice and the Côte d'Azur as well as of Liguria. You'll find all sorts of gnocchi in this part of France, often enriched with green spinach, brown mushrooms and fragrant herbs, or combined with vegetables and Mediterranean flavors.

✦✦ Add the cream to the coulis and heat, then toss with the ravioli. Serve right away, topped with the shaved cheese and a generous sprinkling of basil.

GNOCCHI AUX LÉGUMES ET PARFUMS MÉDITERRANÉES

GNOCCHI WITH VEGETABLES AND MEDITERRANEAN FLAVORS

– Serves 4 –

In this dish from Aix-en-Provence, tender potato gnocchi are tossed with sautéed summer vegetables and a garlicky tomato-scented butter. An aged local goat cheese was the topping in Provence, but a flavorful sheep cheese such as pecorino would be fine, too, or the easily available Parmesan or Asiago.

2 small zucchini, thinly sliced
1 tablespoon olive oil
3 garlic cloves, minced
3 to 5 artichoke hearts, halved or quartered and blanched (see page 210)
1 cup sugar snap peas
2 tablespoons tomato paste
12 to 16 ounces potato gnocchi
1 teaspoon minced fresh rosemary
1 teaspoon minced fresh marjoram
2 to 3 tablespoons unsalted butter
Salt and pepper to taste
3 tablespoons coarsely shredded Parmesan, pecorino, or Asiago

✦✦ In a large, heavy sauté pan or skillet over medium heat, sauté the zucchini in the olive oil until it is lightly browned and soft, 5 to 7 minutes.

129

Add the garlic, artichoke hearts, and sugar snap peas. Cook for 2 to 3 minutes. Stir in the tomato paste, cover, and remove from heat.

✦✦Cook the gnocchi in a large pot of salted boiling water until tender, 2 to 3 minutes.

✦✦Drain the gnocchi gently, then toss with the vegetables, rosemary, marjoram, butter, salt, and pepper. Sprinkle with the cheese and serve right away.

RAVIOLE DE MÂCHE ET RICOTTA

PASTA FILLED WITH MÂCHE AND RICOTTA

– Serves 4 –

Italian flavors accent many of the dishes created in modern bistros: pastas, greens, fresh tomato sauces, balsamic vinegar, Parmesan cheese. Here, Italian-inspired filled pasta is stuffed with tender mâche, the little salad green also known as lamb's lettuce. If mâche is unavailable, arugula and/or watercress or even spinach could be used in its place.

Though the Paris bistro where I ate these made their own dough, wonton wrappers are quick and easy, and give a delicate result.

4 handfuls mâche
4 shallots, minced
4 tablespoons butter, melted
1 cup ricotta cheese
1 egg
4 to 6 tablespoons grated Parmesan cheese
Salt and pepper to taste
About 16 to 20 wonton wrappers, or
*   8 ounces sheet fresh pasta cut into*
*   3- to 4-inch squares*
1 garlic clove, minced

✦✦Blanch 3 cups of the mâche until bright green, then plunge it into ice water. Drain well, then dry on paper towels and chop coarsely. In a small sauté pan or skillet, cook the shallots in half the melted butter until softened.

✦✦Combine the blanched mâche with the shallots, ricotta, egg, the remaining 2 tablespoons melted butter, half the Parmesan, the salt, and pepper. Cover and refrigerate for at least 1 hour.

✦✦To make the ravioli, place 1 tablespoon filling in the center wrapper or square, wet the edges, then fold it over into a triangle and seal the edges. Set the ravioli out on a well-floured board to dry until ready to use (check every so often to be sure they are not sticking; add more flour if needed).

✦✦Cook the ravioli in a large pot of salted boiling water until tender, 2 to 3 minutes.

✦✦Meanwhile, in a medium sauté pan or skillet over medium heat, sauté the remaining mâche in the remaining melted butter and 1 or 2 tablespoons of the ravioli cooking liquid. Cook over high heat until the liquid is slightly reduced. Stir in the garlic.

✦✦Drain the ravioli carefully, then toss with the sautéed mâche and the remaining Parmesan. Serve right away.

CANNELLONI CORSE

CHARD- AND MINT-STUFFED CANNELLONI IN TOMATO SAUCE

– Serves 4 to 6 –

From the island of Corsica comes this very Mediterranean pasta dish. Preparing the dish with egg roll wrappers might seem a bit inauthentic, but the result is a very delicate noodle that doesn't need to be precooked. Indeed, throughout France, chefs are using Asian products in traditional dishes.

Herbs are an important feature of Corsican food, especially the tiny fragrant mint that grows wild on the island and is so good with other herbs and greens.

1 pound raw Swiss chard or spinach,
    stemmed and thinly sliced
2 tablespoons minced fresh parsley
1 tablespoon minced fresh mint
1½ cups ricotta or a mixture of half ricotta
    and half fresh white goat cheese
2 eggs, beaten
1½ cups (6 ounces) grated Parmesan or
    pecorino cheese
¼ to ½ teaspoon grated nutmeg, or to taste
Pepper to taste
2 tablespoons olive oil
2 cups tomato sauce
3 garlic cloves, minced
Several pinches of mixed fresh herbs or
    herbes de Provence
8 to 12 egg roll wrappers (about 10 ounces),
    or fresh pasta cut into 6-inch squares
½ cup water

✦✦ Cook the chard or spinach in a large covered saucepan with several tablespoons of water for about 5 minutes. Remove from heat, rinse in cold water, then drain and squeeze dry.

✦✦ Combine the cooked chard or spinach with the parsley, mint, ricotta or ricotta mixture, eggs, ½ cup of the Parmesan or pecorino, the nutmeg, and pepper.

✦✦ Preheat the oven to 375°F.

✦✦ Into the bottom of a medium to large baking dish, spoon 1 tablespoon of the olive oil, 1 or 2 tablespoons of the tomato sauce, half the garlic, and half the herbs or herbes de Provence.

✦✦ Fill each wrapper or square with ¼ cup of the filling, then roll up tightly and lay in a single layer in the dish.

✦✦ Pour the water and the remaining tomato sauce over the rolls, then sprinkle with the remaining 1 tablespoon olive oil, remaining garlic, and remaining herbs. Sprinkle the remaining grated Parmesan or pecorino on top.

✦✦ Bake 20 minutes for egg roll wrappers and 30 to 40 minutes for pasta squares, or until pasta is tender, the liquid is absorbed, and the cheese is melted.

KAESPAETZLE

ALSATIAN DUMPLINGS WITH GARLIC BUTTER

– Serves 4 –

These fine little dumplings are Alsatian first cousins to Germany's spaetzle.

Like spaetzle, they keep their shape and delicate-chewy texture best when prepared ahead of time and warmed with butter just before serving. They are delicious tossed with sautéed mushrooms, especially strongly flavored ones such as shiitakes, chanterelles, cèpes, and so on.

2 cups all-purpose flour
⅓ cup cornmeal
⅓ cup ricotta cheese or puréed cottage
    cheese
3 eggs, lightly beaten
3 tablespoons minced fresh parsley, basil,
    or a combination

2 green onions, including the green part,
 chopped
1 teaspoon salt
¼ teaspoon freshly grated nutmeg
Pepper to taste
¾ to 1 cup water or as needed
3 tablespoons butter
2 to 3 garlic cloves, minced

✦✦In a large bowl, combine the flour, cornmeal, cheese, eggs, half of the parsley and/or basil, green onions, salt, nutmeg, pepper, and water. Mix together to make a smooth batter.

✦✦Using a spaetzle maker or a large-holed colander set over a large pot of boiling water, force the batter through the holes with the back of a spoon.

✦✦The batter will sink, then rise to the surface. Cook the spaetzle 1 minute longer.

✦✦Drain carefully, then rinse in cool water. Drain again.

✦✦To serve, melt the butter in a large sauté pan or skillet over medium-low heat. Add the garlic and cook until translucent, about 3 minutes. Add the spaetzle and cook 3 to 5 minutes, or until heated through. Turn them gently so they do not fall apart.

✦✦Serve right away, sprinkled with the remaining parsley and/or basil.

Les champignons

RISOTTO D'ARTICHAUT, BEURRE DE TOMATE

ARTICHOKE RISOTTO WITH TOMATO BUTTER

– Serves 4 –

This risotto was inspired by one I ate at Nice's Don Camillo's. It is light and savory, with lots of strongly flavored sauce instead of the cheese often found in Italian *risotti*, and tastes quintessentially of the south of France.

1 tablespoon minced garlic or to taste
3 tablespoons butter at room temperature
1 tablespoon tomato paste
2 artichoke hearts, diced and blanched
 (see page 210)
5 to 8 shallots, minced
2 tablespoons olive oil
1½ cups Arborio rice
2½ to 3½ cups hot vegetable stock (pages
 201–202)
1 cup dry white wine
Pinch of herbes de Provence
½ cup (2 ounces) grated Parmesan cheese

✦✦Combine ¼ teaspoon of the garlic with 1½ tablespoons of the butter and the tomato paste. Mix until it forms a smooth mixture. Set aside.

✦✦In a small to medium heavy sauté pan or skillet over medium-low heat, sauté the shallots and half the artichoke pieces in the remaining 1½ tablespoons butter and the olive oil until both are softened, about 5 to 7 minutes. Stir in the rice and cook, stirring, until it colors slightly, about 5 minutes.

✦✦Stir in about ½ cup of the hot stock and a pinch of herbes de Provence and cook over medium heat until the stock is absorbed, then repeat with another ½ cup.

✦✦When about half the stock has been absorbed, begin adding the wine; when that too has been absorbed, add the remaining artichokes and continue adding the remaining stock and, finally, the remaining garlic.

✦✦When the rice is al dente, the risotto is ready. Stir in the cheese and serve each portion with a dab of the tomato butter (stirring first to recombine if needed).

Risotto Catalana (Catalan Risotto) In a large sauté pan or skillet, cook a handful of tender peas, a few strands of roasted pepper strips, and 1 diced zucchini in a little olive oil with a minced garlic clove. Add to the risotto about 3 minutes before the rice is al dente. Serve with a poached egg nestled on top and dab with the tomato butter, and a handful of vinaigrette-dressed mixed baby greens on the side.

Risotto de Courges et Courgettes

Pumpkin and Zucchini Risotto

– *Serves 4* –

Little strands of orange pumpkin and green zucchini melt into this richly flavored risotto. At the very last moment it is perfumed with a spoonful of crushed garlic, giving the dish a provocative, saucy attitude typical of the area–Saint-Tropez–I spooned it up in.

3 garlic cloves
Pinch of salt
3 tablespoons butter
2 tablespoons olive oil
5 to 8 shallots, minced
1½ cups Arborio rice
1 cup dry white wine
*12 ounces pumpkin, peeled and coarsely
    shredded (about 1½ cups)*
Pinch of herbes de Provence
*2½ to 3½ cups hot vegetable stock (pages
    201–202)*
2 to 3 zucchini, coarsely shredded
*½ cup (2 ounces) grated Parmesan cheese,
    plus more for serving (optional)*

✦✦Crush the garlic with the salt in a mortar. Set aside.

✦✦Melt 1 tablespoon of the butter with the olive oil in a large, heavy saucepan over medium-low heat, then sauté the shallots and rice in this mixture until the rice turns golden.

✦✦Stir in the wine, half of the pumpkin, and the herbes de Provence, stirring until the liquid has been absorbed.

✦✦Add ½ cup of the stock, stirring and stirring as it cooks over medium heat until absorbed by the rice. Repeat until the rice is almost al dente, then stir in the remaining pumpkin and zucchini.

✦✦The risotto should be very soupy at this point; if you need extra liquid add more stock or hot water.

✦✦Remove from heat and stir in the crushed garlic mixture, the remaining 2 tablespoons butter, and the Parmesan. Taste and adjust the seasoning and serve right away, with extra cheese if desired.

Risotto d'Orzo aux Asperges et Sauce d'Asperges

Orzo Risotto with Asparagus and Asparagus Sauce

– Serves 4 –

Creamy asparagus purée colors this succulent risotto of tiny grains of pasta. You could use rice in place of the pasta; to do so, follow the directions for cooking the rice in the previous risotto recipes.

1 pound asparagus, trimmed and cut into
*   bite-sized pieces*
2 tablespoons olive oil
4 to 5 garlic cloves, minced
Large pinch of minced fresh savory
3½ to 4 cups vegetable stock (page 201)
½ cup heavy cream
Juice of ½ lemon, or to taste
12 ounces orzo
Salt and pepper to taste
½ cup (2 ounces) grated Parmesan cheese,
*   or as desired*

✦✦ In a large, heavy sauté pan or skillet over medium heat, sauté the asparagus in the olive oil with the garlic until the asparagus is crisp-tender; do not brown. Transfer half of this to another saucepan and set aside.

✦✦ To the remaining asparagus mixture add the savory and ½ cup of the vegetable stock. Bring to a boil and cook until most of the liquid has evaporated, then add the cream. Reduce heat to very low and let simmer while you prepare the risotto. Check ever so often to be sure it is not sticking or burning; if necessary, add a little more stock or water. Season with lemon juice.

✦✦ Heat the remaining asparagus mixture over medium heat, then stir in the orzo and cook until it is lightly gilded.

✦✦ Stir in the remaining hot stock, cover, and cook for 5 to 8 minutes.

✦✦ Meanwhile, in a blender or food processor, purée the asparagus. Add salt and pepper.

✦✦ When the orzo is tender, remove from heat and stir in the Parmesan.

✦✦ Serve in warm shallow soup bowls surrounded by the warm asparagus sauce.

Risotto

In the niçoise dialect, *risotou* refers to the soupy rice mixture known across the border as risotto. Made with medium-grain rice that cooks into a creamy mound, risotto is as much a dish of Nice as it is of Italy.

To turn risotto into a fetching main dish or plat du jour, serve it spread onto a plate much as you would a vegetable purée or sauce, and in the center place a "bouquet" of lightly buttered steamed vegetables to mix or match with the risotto.

Risotto makes a good bed for grilled vegetables, too. Grilled artichokes atop artichoke risotto would be a wonderful way of celebrating the new artichokes of the season. When mushrooms come into season, bake them in a little butter, then serve them atop a simple risotto, letting their juices enrich the saucy rice.

RIZ AU CUMIN

CUMIN-SCENTED RICE MOLDS

– Serves 4 –

Whole cumin seeds have a marvelous affinity with rice, as they do with cheese.

Placing the rice in little molds at first seems like a bit of an affectation, but it is an appealing and nearly effortless way of serving it. Unmolded, it is all over the plate, a messy pile of grains. Molded, it is prim and tidy, as elegant to look at as it is delicious to eat.

1 onion, chopped
2 tablespoons butter
1 teaspoon cumin seeds
1 cup long-grain white rice
2 cups vegetable stock (pages 201–202)
Salt and pepper to taste

✦✦ In a medium saucepan, sauté the onion in the butter over medium-low heat until golden and soft, then stir in the cumin seeds and rice. Cook for a few moments until the rice begins to turn opaque.

✦✦ Stir in the stock, salt, and pepper, then cover tightly. Bring the rice to a boil and immediately reduce the heat to very low. Cook until tender, 10 to 15 minutes.

✦✦ Fluff the rice with a fork.

✦✦ To mold: Spoon the fluffed rice into 4 buttered 1-cup containers such as soufflé dishes or custard cups, or one 4-cup soufflé dish or round bowl. Press lightly and evenly, making a level surface on top.

✦✦ Let the lightly pressed hot rice sit a moment or two, then carefully unmold onto a serving plate or plates. Serve right away.

SERVING SUGGESTIONS

Serve this rice mold with Aubergines et Poivrons Gitanes (pages 65–66) or Œufs Maritchou (page 94).

Serve with sautéed mushrooms or Ragoût de Champignons et Riz Sauvage (pages 112–113), garnished with freshly grated or thinly shaved Parmesan cheese.

Serve the rice at room temperature with the rouille from Pâtes au Safran avec Rouille et Basilic (pages 126–127), surrounded by room-temperature pan-browned slices of eggplant and fennel.

GRATIN DE POLENTA ET CÈPES AUX TROIS FROMAGES

POLENTA WITH CÈPES IN A THREE-CHEESE GRATIN

– Serves 4 –

Beneath the sizzling cheese topping lies a cache of creamy mushroom-studded polenta.

Though we think of polenta as Italian, the region of France that now includes Nice was once part of the kingdom that included Liguria. Pistou, pasta, gnocchi, pizza, and polenta are part of this gastronomical heritage.

This gratin is convenient to make for a large group, as it can be made ahead of time and baked just before serving. There are endless ways of varying this rustic dish, all of them delicious. You could omit the mushrooms completely and let the richness of both cheese and polenta shine through. Or you could add diced tomatoes for a pizzalike topping.

> 2 cups water
> ½ cup polenta
> 5 slices or so dried cèpe (porcini) mush-
>   rooms, broken into small pieces
> Salt to taste
> 2 tablespoons unsalted butter
> 6 ounces blue cheese, thinly sliced
>   or crumbled
> 3 ounces fresh white goat cheese, thinly
>   sliced or crumbled
> ¼ cup grated Parmesan, pecorino,
>   or Asiago

✦✦ Preheat the oven to 375°F.

✦✦ Combine ½ cup of the water with the polenta and let sit for a few minutes for the grains to swell.

✦✦ Put the remaining 1½ cups water in a saucepan and bring to a boil. Stir in the softened polenta, dried mushroom pieces, and salt. Reduce heat to medium low and cook, stirring (preferably with a wooden spoon), until the polenta is thickened and comes away from the sides of the pan, 10 to 15 minutes or longer.

✦✦ Remove the polenta from heat and stir in the butter.

✦✦ Butter a 12-inch gratin dish. Pour the polenta into the dish, dot with the blue cheese and goat cheese, then sprinkle with the Parmesan cheese.

✦✦ Bake for 20 to 30 minutes, or until the cheese topping is melted and lightly golden. Serve hot.

Gratin de Polenta et Tomates au Romarin **(Polenta Gratin with Tomatoes and Rosemary)** Replace the mushrooms with 1 tablespoon minced fresh rosemary. Sprinkle 2 to 3 diced ripe tomatoes over the top of the polenta before adding the cheese topping.

SOUPE D'EPEAUTRE

WHOLE-WHEAT BERRIES

– Makes 2½ to 3 cups –

Wheat berries cook into chewy little nutty-tasting grains, somewhat like barley, and are enormously satisfying. Enjoy them as a side dish with a hearty gravy, such as the Ragoût de Champignons et Riz Sauvage (pages 112–113), or spooned into a wintry soup.

You can also prepare a risottolike mixture by adding cooked wheat berries to sautéed onion and garlic, then simmering them with a little stock and white wine. Cooked whole-wheat berries also make a healthy breakfast or a rustic pudding.

> 1 cup (8 ounces) wheat berries
> 6 cups water
> Pinch of salt

✦✦ Combine the wheat berries and water in a pan and bring to a boil.

✦✦ Reduce the heat and simmer, covered, until the water has been mostly absorbed and the kernels are chewy yet tender, 1 to 1½ hours. Add the salt about 10 minutes before the grains are fully cooked.

✦✦ Drain and serve as above, or add to hearty bean soups or stews.

Pommes de Terre

. . .

Potato Dishes

Nothing epitomizes bistro food so much as rustic potato dishes. Whether baked into a crispy crusty gratin or whirled into a creamy purée, potatoes are on the menu in a myriad of guises in nearly every bistro in France.

Potatoes originated in the Andes of Peru and were brought to Europe in the mid-sixteenth century by the Spanish. The plants were considered poisonous and grown for their ornamentation. It was believed that they caused leprosy (not as fanciful as it sounds: When potatoes are exposed to the light they develop a green tinge; this is a toxic substance called solanine. Potatoes in the Middle Ages contained larger amounts than they do now, and caused a skin rash that could be confused with the early stages of leprosy).

France owes its wealth of delicious potato dishes to the brave epicure Antoine-Auguste Parmentier, a military pharmacist who persuaded King Louis XVI to eat them. Parmentier held a state banquet in which each course, from appetizers, soups, salads, and on through bread and dessert, was made of potatoes. To this day in France, potatoes cut into large dice and sautéed in butter bear the name Parmentier.

The French Revolution brought the potato to the people, but only because of the threat of famine. Once the masses safely ate this earthy tuber, however, culinary passion kept them coming back for more. Today there is no region in France without an array of luscious potato specialties.

. . . .

GÂTEAU DE

POMMES DE TERRE ALAIN

CRISP LAYERED CAKE

OF POTATOES WITH

GARLIC AND PARSLEY

– Serves 4 –

A crisp cake of potatoes with a pungent pommade of crushed garlic and parsley rubbed onto it at the last moment. It is at once rich and buttery, crisp and potatoey, and redolent of strong raw crushed garlic.

The dish is basically a variation on the classic pommes Anna. Though it goes by various names, I've called it "Alain" after the most avid potato eater I know, my husband.

3 pounds potatoes, peeled and thinly sliced
½ cup clarified butter
Salt and pepper to taste
4 to 5 garlic cloves
½ cup minced fresh parsley

✦✦ Soak the potatoes in cold water to cover for 30 to 60 minutes. Drain and dry them well on paper towels.

✦✦ Preheat the oven to 375°F.

✦✦ Reserve 2 tablespoons of the butter. Brush some of the remaining butter on the bottom and sides of a 12-inch earthenware casserole or baking dish, then add a layer of potatoes. Drizzle with some of the butter, sprinkle with salt and pepper. Repeat until all of the potatoes are used.

✦✦ Bake for 35 to 45 minutes, or until the top is golden brown and the potatoes are tender.

✦✦ While the potatoes are baking, crush the garlic in a mortar or a garlic press. Combine the crushed garlic with the reserved butter and the parsley; season with salt and pepper to taste.

I ate *tartiflette* one winter in Grenoble. It was snowy outside and our appetites were huge, thanks to the sheer energy it took to do anything in the brittle cold. The bistro was tiny; *madame la patronne* was filled with the energy of someone who adores entertaining and she was terribly chic, to boot. She was so attentive, so doting, that it was hard to believe we were customers, not her guests.

The potatoes by the way, were as beautiful as poetry.

✦✦ Smear the potatoes with the garlic-parsley butter and serve right away.

Galettes des Pommes de Terre **(Potato Galettes)**
Omit soaking the potatoes and instead overlap them in 4 circles about 4 to 6 inches in diameter on a well-buttered baking sheet, letting the starch in the potato slices hold them together. Season with salt and pepper and brush well with butter, then bake until each circle resembles a crisp golden potato flower.

Serve on a bed of crisp greens, or on top of a pool of vegetable purée.

TARTIFLETTE

CASSEROLE OF POTATOES, ONIONS, AND CHEESE

– Serves 4 –

This rustic casserole of boiled potatoes tossed with browned onions, then topped with chunks of cheese and baked, is a Savoyarde specialty. Its name comes from the local patois: *Tartifle* is the word for potato.

The authentic cheese for this is a Reblochon, creamy and pungent; if it is unavailable, a tomme de Savoie or Epoisses is a good choice; less traditional but delicious is a terroir, a Camembert, or a fresh white goat cheese.

Drink a good Beaujolais, and accompany with a salad of crisp greens, herbs, and minced shallots with a mustardy vinaigrette.

3 pounds white-skinned waxy potatoes
3 to 4 onions, thinly sliced
3 tablespoons vegetable oil or butter
Salt and pepper to taste

*8 to 10 ounces Reblochon or other creamy
    cheese, thickly sliced*
3 to 5 tablespoons minced fresh chives

✦✦ Preheat the oven to 400°F.

✦✦ Peel the potatoes and cut them into chunks. Place in a saucepan with cold water to cover and bring to a boil.

✦✦ Reduce heat to medium and cook until the potatoes are just tender, about 20 minutes. Drain well.

✦✦ Meanwhile, in a large, heavy sauté pan or skillet over medium heat, brown the onions in the oil or butter until they are very soft and lightly browned in places, about 20 minutes.

✦✦ Toss the potatoes with the onions; season with salt and pepper, and pour it all into an 8-cup casserole or baking dish. Top with the cheese.

✦✦ Bake until lightly browned, about 30 to 35 minutes. Serve at once, sprinkled with the chives.

Rösti au Fromage

Potato-Cheese Cakes

– Serves 4 –

Rösti is a cake of grated potatoes with a crisp exterior and a soft interior. A specialty of Switzerland and its neighboring French regions, it's wonderful fare for a cold winter night, especially when paired with a salad of rustic greens, beets, just-tender artichoke hearts or green beans, fresh dill, and chives.

And it is laughingly simple to prepare. Some prepare rösti using raw potatoes, or precook them for a shorter time, but I find a longer pre-cooking gives a lighter, more "potatoey" quality.

4 baking potatoes
*5 shallots or green onions (including the
    green parts), chopped*
3 garlic cloves, minced
2 tablespoons minced fresh parsley
*1 cup (4 ounces) shredded Gruyère,
    Parmesan, or Asiago cheese*
Salt and pepper to taste
*1 to 3 teaspoons olive or vegetable oil
    (optional)*

✦✦ Boil the whole potatoes until they are almost tender, about 15 to 20 minutes. Drain and let cool. (The potatoes must be left to cool. This stabilizes the starch and can be done up to 3 days ahead of time.)

✦✦ Shred the potatoes on the large rasps of a grater. (Don't bother to peel them, as the skins seem to come off in a big piece on their own accord and whatever skin doesn't come off is amalgamated into the dish.)

✦✦ Combine the shredded potatoes with the shallots or green onions, garlic, parsley, cheese, salt, and pepper. Press tightly together to form 4 thick patties.

✦✦ In a large, heavy skillet (preferably nonstick) over medium-high heat, heat the optional oil and cook the patties on both sides until golden brown.

✦✦ Serve right away.

Galettes de Pommes de Terre à la Trappe (Trappist Cheese Potato Cakes) Replace the cheese in the above recipe with Trappist cheese from the southwest or a Port-Salut, and double the amount of garlic.

La citrouille

MEURETTE DE POMMES DE TERRE

BOILED OR STEAMED POTATOES IN RED WINE SAUCE

– Serves 4 to 6 –

Peas, green beans, whole garlic cloves, and shiitake mushrooms, blanched then sautéed, could be used to garnish for this peasant, warm, and comforting dish from Burgundy (see Œufs en Meurette, pages 96–97). Or you could simply ladle it into a warm bowl and spoon it up–delicious.

4 to 6 large baking potatoes
2 cups Sauce Meurette (pages 207–208)
2 tablespoons unsalted butter, cut into
  small pieces
Salt and pepper to taste
3 to 4 tablespoons minced fresh chives

✦✦ Cut the potatoes into chunks and boil them until they are just tender, about 20 minutes.
✦✦ Meanwhile, heat the Meurette sauce.
✦✦ Drain the potatoes, then toss them with the sauce and butter. Season with salt and pepper and serve hot, sprinkled with chives.

TRUFFADE DE POMMES DE TERRE AUX PICODON ET MESCLUN

BROWNED POTATOES WITH GOAT CHEESE AND WALNUT OIL-DRESSED MESCLUN

– Serves 4 –

Rustic simplicity from the Auvergne in France's southwest, this hearty panful consists of browned potatoes mixed with just enough egg to hold them together and nuggets of a firm, fragrant goat cheese known as picodon, all cooked just until the cheese softens. A handful of tangy greens dressed in walnut oil offers the perfect balance to this rich dish. Drink a rustic red wine, also from the southwest.

4 baking potatoes, peeled and thinly sliced
3 tablespoons oil or butter, as desired
A large pinch of herbes de Provence
Salt and pepper to taste
3 garlic cloves, minced
2 picodon goat cheeses, or 4 ounces other
  aged goat cheese, diced
3 eggs, lightly beaten
4 handfuls mixed baby greens or young
  arugula
1 tablespoon walnut oil
1 teaspoon sherry vinegar

✦✦ In a large, heavy sauté pan or skillet over medium heat, sauté the potatoes in the oil or butter until golden brown. Season with the herbes de Provence, salt, and pepper. Stir in the garlic, then add the cheese and eggs. Cook over medium-low heat, letting the eggs run into the potatoes and the cheese slightly melt.

✦✦ Meanwhile, toss the mesclun or arugula with the walnut oil, sherry vinegar, salt, and pepper.

✦✦ Serve the potato mixture very hot, next to a handful of dressed salad leaves.

ALIGOT

PURÉE OF MASHED POTATOES

AND CHEESE

– Serves 4 to 6 –

This dish of hot mashed potatoes and melted cheese is a specialty of the Auvergne. At its best steaming hot and spooned out in delectable cheesey strings, it makes a warming winter meal served in warmed bowls on a frigid night, beside a wood-burning stove or fireplace.

The authentic choice of cheese is Cantal, but other cheeses are good, too. Some recipes add cream to this irresistible purée, but cottage cheese or ricotta has a nice milky quality without the heaviness of cream.

> *2 to 2½ pounds baking potatoes (about 6), peeled and cut into quarters or chunks*
> *4 tablespoons butter*
> *⅔ cup hot milk*
> *Salt and pepper to taste*
> *6 to 7 garlic cloves, minced*
> *14 ounces Cantal cheese, or half mozzarella and half white Cheddar cheese, diced*
> *1 cup cottage cheese or ricotta*

✦✦ Cook the potatoes in rapidly boiling salted water until tender, about 20 minutes. Drain and mash with a fork or potato masher.

✦✦ Over low heat, add the butter, milk, salt, pepper, half the garlic, and the cheeses, beating with a wooden spoon until the mixture turns into a delectable stringy mess.

✦✦ Add the remaining garlic; taste and adjust the seasoning and serve right away, in warm bowls if possible. Eat with a spoon for maximum comfort.

PURÉE DE POMMES DE TERRE

ET TOPINAMBOURS

MASHED POTATOES AND

JERUSALEM ARTICHOKES

– Serves 4 –

Jerusalem artichokes are, in fact, related to neither Jerusalem nor artichokes. The root of a member of the sunflower family, they were once called *girasole,* or sunflower, which was misheard as "Jerusalem."

They are especially good in this recipe, mashed with potatoes, revved up with garlic, smoothed with a bit of cream and butter, flecked with parsley, and served with a drizzle of olive oil.

You could ask for no more comfort than a big bowl and, of course, a spoon.

> *1½ pounds Jerusalem artichokes*
> *Juice from ½ lemon*
> *1½ pounds boiling potatoes*
> *2 garlic cloves*
> *Pinch of salt, plus salt to taste*
> *2 to 3 tablespoons butter*
> *2 to 3 tablespoons milk or cream*
> *Coarsely ground pepper to taste*
> *1 tablespoon minced fresh parsley*
> *1 tablespoon olive oil*

✦✦ Place the Jerusalem artichokes in a saucepan and cover with cold water and lemon juice. Bring to a boil and cook until almost tender, about 15 minutes.

✦✦ Drain and rinse under cold water until cool enough to handle. They should peel easily; discard the peels and cut the flesh into chunks. The vegetable will still be somewhat crisp. Return the chunks to the pan and cover with fresh water.

✦✦ Peel and cut the potatoes into small chunks and place them in the saucepan with the Jerusalem artichokes. Bring to a boil and cook until both the potatoes and Jerusalem artichokes are tender, about 10 to 15 minutes.

✦✦ Meanwhile, crush the garlic with a pinch of salt. Set aside.

✦✦ Drain and mash the potatoes and Jerusalem artichokes, adding the crushed garlic, butter, milk or cream, salt to taste, pepper, and parsley.

✦✦ Serve immediately, drizzled with the olive oil.

PURÉE DE POMMES DE TERRE AU ROQUEFORT

MASHED POTATOES WITH BLUE CHEESE

– Serves 4 to 6 –

I ate this deliciously pungent purée of potatoes and Roquefort cheese in the Auvergne, where it came to the table in a rustic ceramic bowl. Its unashamed richness was lightened with a squeeze of lemon.

It was late spring, and all the accompaniments were in season: a bowl of field greens tossed with tiny young asparagus, and for dessert, a bowl of sweet peaches and a plate of caramelized walnuts.

We drank a rugged red from the Auvergne, but a nice big Côtes-du-Rhône would be good, too.

> *8 to 10 baking potatoes, peeled and cut into bite-sized pieces*
> *6 ounces Roquefort or other sharp blue cheese, crumbled*
> *2 tablespoons minced fresh chives*
> *2 shallots, minced*
> *2 garlic cloves, minced*
> *¼ cup heavy cream*
> *2 tablespoons butter*
> *Juice of ¼ lemon, or to taste*
> *Pepper to taste*

✦✦ Boil the potatoes in salted water to cover until they are just tender, about 15 to 20 minutes.

✦✦ Meanwhile, combine the blue cheese with the chives, shallots, garlic, and cream. Set aside.

✦✦ Drain and mash the potatoes and combine them well with the butter. Stir in the cheese mixture and mix well, then return to heat just long enough to heat through.

✦✦ Season with lemon juice and pepper and serve right away.

PURÉE DE POMMES DE TERRE ET CÉLERI-RAVE LYONNAISE

PURÉE OF POTATOES AND CELERIAC FROM LYONS

– Serves 4 –

C ooking and mashing celeriac with potatoes does a great favor for both vegetables: You end up with a creamy celery-scented purée that tastes of the very earth itself, its potato flavor amplified gracefully.

In addition, I've added quite a good whiff of garlic to this Lyonnaise dish.

2 pounds white boiling potatoes, peeled and cut into bite-sized pieces
2 pounds celeriac, cut into bite-sized pieces
2 garlic cloves, minced
3 to 4 tablespoons butter, or as desired
3 to 4 tablespoons crème fraîche or sour cream
2 tablespoons milk or as desired
Salt and pepper to taste

✦✦ Cook the potatoes and the celery root in boiling water to cover until they are tender, about 30 minutes.
✦✦ Drain the vegetables and mash with a fork or potato masher, then add the garlic, butter, and crème fraîche or sour cream, mashing and stirring until it is blended in, then add just enough milk to achieve a creamy consistency.
✦✦ Season with salt and pepper and serve right away.

> *Pommes purées,* or mashed potatoes, is a comfort food that is so quintessentially French, if you hear someone refer simply to *purée,* it means potatoes.
>
> At bistros this homey mixture of buttered potatoes is exalted and embellished with all manner of delicious fragrant ingredients. Mashed potato dishes are as unique and distinctive as they are delicious.

*Purée de Pommes de Terre et Céleri-rave au Coulis de Tomates aux Poivrons Rouges (**Mashed Potato and Celery Root with Tomato and Red Pepper Coulis**)* As a first or main course, serve a mound of potato and celeriac purée sprinkled with minced fresh herbs such as fennel and chives, surrounded with Coulis de Tomates aux Poivrons Rouges (page 205) and garnished with buttered lightly cooked spinach or chard.

*Purée aux Légumes Rôtis, Sauce Coulis (**Mashed Potatoes and Celery Root with Roasted Carrots and Parsnips, and a Sauce of Puréed Vegetables**)* To turn celery root and potato purée into an elegant main course, serve it as a bed for roasted carrots and parsnips. Cut the carrots and parsnips into long wedges and toss them with salt, olive oil, and a pinch of sugar. Arrange in a shallow baking pan and bake in a preheated 375°F oven for about 40 minutes, or until golden brown. Serve them standing up and leaning against each other pyramid fashion. Spoon a vegetable purée around the edge and dot the edge of the sauce with tiny fava beans, asparagus tips, and a few sautéed morels or sliced cèpes.

*Saucisse de Légumes (**Vegetable Sausages**)* Combine 1½ to 2 cups potato and celery root purée with 2 lightly beaten eggs, then add an assortment of vegetables briefly cooked in vegetable stock: ½ a red pepper, diced, ½ a yellow pepper, diced, ¾ cup diced broccoli, ¾ cup diced cauliflower, ½ cup diced carrots, and ½ cup diced green beans. Pipe this mixture into sausage casings, then twist or tie into sausage shapes. Cook either by lightly poaching or by grilling for a few minutes over hot coals. Serve with a vegetable purée.

les poivrons

POMMES DE TERRE EN GRATIN

POTATO GRATINS

Casseroles of sliced potatoes, baked with a mixture of milk and cream or a savory tomato-based sauce, are one of the glories of the bistro table.

Potato gratins are a favorite throughout France, but especially in the Savoy, and specifically in the town of Grenoble. After eating meal upon meal of these luscious, crusty-edged potato dishes, I wasn't surprised in the least to find that the name Grenoble comes from the Greek word gratinopolis, or "city of gratins," its original name.

Throughout France, potato gratins reflect regional flavors: olive oil, tomatoes, and garlic in the south; cream, onions, and butter in the north. And regional vegetables are likely to find their way into potato gratins.

Like any gratin, the top of a potato gratin should be crisp and browned, the interior delicate and tender. Potato gratins are marvelous for

entertaining since they can be made ahead of time, and in the middle of winter when the weather is icy and winds blow mercilessly, there are few things as enticing as the smell of a gratin baking away in the oven.

GRATIN DE POMMES DE TERRE LYONNAISE AUX BAIES ROUGES

CREAMY POTATO AND ONION GRATIN WITH PINK PEPPERCORNS

– Serves 4 –

Recently in Paris I enjoyed this classic potato and onion gratin garnished with a modern sprinkling of fragrant pink peppercorns and flecks of green parsley.

Begin this meal with a vegetable first course and finish with a plate of cheeses, salad, and an assortment of ripe fruit, with maybe a few chocolates to accompany the coffee. To drink? A bistro classic such as Beaujolais or Brouilly.

3 to 3½ pounds baking potatoes, peeled
   and thinly sliced
2 onions, thinly sliced
3 to 5 garlic cloves, minced
Freshly grated nutmeg to taste
Salt and pepper to taste
3 tablespoons butter
1 cup heavy cream
1 to 2 teaspoons pink peppercorns
2 tablespoons minced fresh parsley

✦✦Preheat the oven to 375°F.
✦✦Butter the bottom and sides of an earthenware gratin or baking dish. Make a layer of pota-

toes, then onions, then potatoes, etc., sprinkling each layer with garlic, nutmeg, salt, pepper, and all but 2 teaspoons of the butter.

✦✦End with a layer of potatoes, pour the cream over the top, then dot with the remaining 2 teaspoons butter and sprinkle with salt and pepper.

✦✦Bake for 1 hour, or until the potatoes and onions are very tender and have absorbed the cream, and the top of the casserole is golden brown.

✦✦Serve right away, sprinkled with the pink peppercorns and parsley.

GRATIN DE POMMES DE TERRE ET CÉLERI-RAVE

RICH POTATO AND CELERY ROOT GRATIN

– Serves 4 –

Celery root (celeriac) is the large, knobby root of the common stalk we know as celery. It has the aroma and flavor of celery, but its texture is starchy and tuberous, rather than crunchy and juicy, as ordinary celery is. A favorite winter vegetable in much of France, it is often served in soups, purées, and the following gratin.

For a classic bistro menu, serve Œufs en Meurette (pages 96–97) as a first course, and finish with salad and Fraises au Citron (page 194) with a scoop of sorbet or Soufflé Glace à l'Anisette (page 199).

2½ pounds potatoes (about 6)
1 large celery root
Juice of ¼ lemon

2 onions, thinly sliced
4 tablespoons butter
5 to 6 garlic cloves, minced
Salt and pepper to taste
1 cup heavy cream

✦✦Peel the potatoes, then cut them into ¼-inch-thick slices and place in cold water to cover. Let soak for 30 minutes, then drain and pat dry with paper towels.

✦✦Peel the celery root and cut it into ¼-inch-thick slices. Place the celery root in cold water to cover and add the lemon juice. Let soak for 30 minutes, then drain and dry with paper towels.

✦✦In a medium, heavy sauté pan or skillet over medium heat, sauté the onions in 2 tablespoons of the butter until lightly browned, about 15 to 20 minutes; as they cook, stir in half the garlic and season with salt and pepper.

✦✦Preheat the oven to 325°F.

✦✦In a 12- to 15-inch gratin dish or ceramic baking pan, spread out the sautéed onions. On top of the onions layer one third of the potato slices, then half of the celery root slices. Repeat with one third of the potatoes, the remaining celery root, and the remaining potatoes. While you are layering, sprinkle with the remaining garlic and the salt and pepper, and dot with 1 tablespoon of the butter.

✦✦Pour the cream over the top of the layered vegetables, dot with the remaining 1 tablespoon butter, and sprinkle with salt and pepper.

✦✦Bake for 1½ hours, or until the potatoes and celery root are quite tender and the top is golden brown. If the potatoes are tender but the top is not brown and crusty, raise the heat to 450°F and bake for about 10 minutes.

✦✦Serve right away.

GRATIN SAVOYARD CHEZ PIERRE

GRATIN OF POTATOES AND WILD MUSHROOMS FROM THE SAVOY

– Serves 4 –

We were snowed in this past winter in a little mountain village in the Jura. Luckily, there was a bistro whose name we never really knew, but as the owner was named Pierre, we called it Chez Pierre. This potato gratin was his specialty, scented with mushrooms he had foraged the previous autumn.

Drink a Macon Blanc with this, and accompany it with an equally rich dish of mushrooms in a creamy mustard sauce, with a crisp salad of frisée at the end.

*1 to 2 ounces dried cèpe (porcini),
    trompette de la mort, chanterelle, or
    morel mushrooms, or a mixture
½ cup boiling vegetable stock (pages
    201–202)
6 to 8 baking potatoes, peeled, thinly sliced,
    and patted dried with paper towels
Salt and pepper to taste
10 shallots, minced
2 garlic cloves, minced
3 to 4 tablespoons butter, melted
½ cup milk
½ cup sour cream
1½ to 2 cups (6 to 8 ounces) shredded jack,
    Asiago, Gruyère, or Comte cheese
1 tablespoon minced fresh parsley*

✦✦ Combine the mushrooms and stock. Let sit for 30 minutes, then remove the mushrooms from the liquid and squeeze them dry, saving the liquid. Dice the mushrooms and set aside.

✦✦ Preheat the oven to 350°F.

✦✦ Butter a baking casserole and make several layers of potatoes and mushrooms, sprinkling the layers with the salt, pepper, shallots, and garlic and drizzling with the melted butter.

✦✦ Combine and warm the milk and sour cream. Pour over the potato mixture and drizzle with the mushroom liquid.

✦✦ Sprinkle with the cheese and bake until the potatoes are tender, the liquid has been absorbed, and the cheese is melted and lightly browned.

✦✦ Serve right away, sprinkled with the parsley.

GRATIN DE POMMES DE TERRE ET AUBERGINES

EGGPLANT AND POTATO GRATIN

– Serves 4 to 6 –

It was late spring in the Languedoc. We fled Northern Europe, which was still shivering in the grip of winter, to a little house on the Canal du Midi where sunshine flooded through the windows.

Often in the afternoon we went to a nearby village bistro with a wood-burning oven, where a variety of casseroles cooked in the glowing embers.

This savory gratin of potatoes and eggplant was one we sampled there. Unlike the potato gratins of the north, this one was filled with sunshine, alternating hefty potatoes with layers of eggplant, red peppers, tomatoes, thyme, and garlic, all bathed in good olive oil.

*1 onion, thinly sliced
1 red bell pepper, seeded, deribbed, and cut
    into strips*

4 tablespoons olive oil

1 cup drained diced tomatoes

3 garlic cloves, minced

Pinch of sugar if needed to balance the
acidity of the tomatoes

Several large pinches of dried thyme

1 eggplant, sliced ⅛ to ¼ inch thick

2½ to 3 pounds white boiling potatoes,
peeled and thinly sliced

Salt and pepper to taste

✦✦Preheat the broiler.

✦✦In a medium, heavy sauté pan or skillet over medium heat, sauté the onion and red pepper in 2 tablespoons of the olive oil until softened, about 5 minutes. Add the tomatoes, two thirds of the garlic, the optional sugar, and the thyme. Cook for a few minutes, then set aside.

✦✦Brush 1 tablespoon of the olive oil over the eggplant slices and arrange them on a baking sheet. Broil until they are lightly browned in spots, then turn and lightly brown the other side.

✦✦Preheat the oven to 375°F. In the bottom of a 4- to 6-inch-deep earthenware casserole, layer one third of the potatoes. Sprinkle them with salt, then a layer of half the eggplant, then another third of the potatoes, then the remaining eggplant.

✦✦Spread the tomato sauce over the eggplant, then combine the remaining potatoes with the remaining garlic and spread over the eggplant and sauce.

✦✦Sprinkle the final potato layer with salt and pepper, and drizzle with the remaining 1 tablespoon olive oil. Bake for 1 hour, or until the top is golden and the potatoes are cooked through. Serve hot or at room temperature.

GRATIN DE POMMES DE TERRE

CÔTE D'AZUR

AVEC FROMAGE DE BREBIS

POTATO GRATIN WITH TOMATOES, SAFFRON, AND SHEEP CHEESE

– Serves 4 –

This gratin with the scent of saffron comes from a bistro in the hills behind Nice. It is an enticing, savory casserole that combines potatoes, tomatoes, and a local sheep cheese. Pecorino is good in this dish, but if you cannot find it, use an aged dry goat cheese or a combination of fresh goat cheese and locatelli romano.

Such sunny strong flavors would be good with a Côtes-du-Rhône Villages.

5 to 6 baking potatoes (2½ to 3 pounds)

2 onions, chopped

3 tablespoons olive oil

5 to 7 garlic cloves, minced

Large pinch of herbes de Provence

1 pound ripe tomatoes, diced, or one
14-ounce can dried tomatoes, including
the juices

Sugar, salt, and pepper to taste

Large pinch of saffron

1½ cups (6 ounces) coarsely grated
pecorino cheese

✦✦Preheat the oven to 375°F.

✦✦Cook the potatoes in boiling water for 15 minutes to stabilize the starch. Drain, then rinse under cold water to help loosen skins. Let cool to the touch.

✦✦Peel the potatoes and cut them into ¼-inch slices.

✦✦ In a large, heavy sauté pan or skillet over medium heat, sauté the onions in 2 tablespoons of the olive oil until they are softened and golden in spots, about 6 to 8 minutes. Remove from heat, add the garlic, and set aside.

✦✦ Into a round earthenware gratin dish, drizzle ½ tablespoon of the oil.

✦✦ Arrange a double layer of sliced potatoes in the dish. Sprinkle with some of the sautéed onions, herbes de Provence, diced tomatoes, sugar, salt, and pepper, then repeat until you have three layers. The top layer should be potatoes; pat them down to firm up the layers.

✦✦ Combine the saffron with the remaining tomatoes and their juices and pour over the potatoes. Drizzle with the remaining ½ tablespoon olive oil and bake for 30 minutes.

✦✦ Remove the casserole from the oven, sprinkle the cheese on top, then return it to the oven and bake for 15 to 20 minutes, or until the potatoes are cooked through and tender and the cheese topping is melted and golden.

✦✦ Serve hot.

GRATIN DE POMMES DE TERRE ET ARTICHAUTS

ARTICHOKE AND POTATO GRATIN

– Serves 4 –

This crusty gratin of potatoes and artichokes is irresistible. Serve at the beginning of artichoke season, preceded by Salade Tiède aux Herbes Vinaigre de Prunes (pages 49–50) or a dish of sliced ripe tomatoes.

2 cups water
Juice of ¼ lemon
2 artichoke hearts, blanched (see page 210)
2½ to 3 pounds baking potatoes, peeled
3 tablespoons butter
5 garlic cloves, minced
Salt and pepper to taste
1½ cups (6 ounces) shredded Gruyère cheese
3 tablespoons crème fraîche or sour cream
3 to 5 tablespoons milk

✦✦ In a medium bowl, combine the water and lemon juice.

✦✦ Cut the artichoke hearts into ¼-inch-thick slices and place them in the lemon water. Set aside.

✦✦ Cut the potatoes into ¼-inch-thick slices and place in a bowl with cold water to cover. Let sit for 30 minutes.

✦✦ Drain and dry the artichokes, then drain and dry the potatoes.

✦✦ Preheat the oven to 375°F.

✦✦ Melt the butter until it foams, then drizzle 1 or 2 tablespoons into the bottom of a 6-cup gratin dish. Arrange a layer of half of the potato slices on the bottom, sprinkle them with half the garlic, salt, and pepper, then make a layer of all the artichoke slices. Sprinkle the artichokes with half the cheese, then layer with the remaining potatoes.

✦✦ Top the potatoes with the remaining garlic, then spoon the crème fraîche or sour cream over the top. Drizzle with the milk and sprinkle with the remaining cheese.

✦✦ Bake for 45 to 60 minutes, or until the topping is golden brown and the potatoes are meltingly tender.

✦✦ Serve right away, hot and sizzling.

Gratins et Tians
. . .
Baked Vegetable Dishes

A gratin is a casserole of layered vegetables baked until the top becomes crusty. Sometimes it is topped with crumbs, other times with cheese, and sometimes it is topped with no more than a glistening of butter or cream to encourage the vegetable juices to caramelize and become a crusty topping.

While most any vegetable is usually amicable to becoming a gratin, potatoes are especially good in this way. For a selection of potato gratins, please refer to the proceeding "Pommes de Terre" section .

A tian *is a Provençal gratin, named for the shallow earthenware pan it is baked in. A* tian *can consist of any sort of layered vegetable mixture, usually with a crumbed or cheese-rich topping—the top is firm and sometimes crisp, the interior soft and tender. These gratins have the flavors and aromas of the south: olive oil and garlic, tomatoes and Parmesan cheese, olives and herbs.* Tians *of delicate summery vegetables with a high water content, such as zucchini or spinach, might have partially cooked rice, beaten egg, and/or grated cheese added.*

Many villages have the tradition of baking a large tian *in the baker's oven to celebrate a feast day. For everyday meals,* tians *have baked in the quiet corner of a kitchen fire for centuries, and indeed, in many homes and rustic bistros they still do.*

. . . .

GRATIN AUX TOPINAMBOURS
GASCON GRATIN
OF JERUSALEM ARTICHOKES
– Serves 4 –

Jerusalem artichokes have been a favorite in French homes (and homey restaurants) since they were first imported to France from North America at the beginning of the seventeenth century.

They are favored in soups, salads, and in gratins such as the following one from Gascony. Here the nutty artichokelike root bakes to a soft, tender consistency, while its splash of cream turns into a custardlike cloak, redolent with garlic and parsley.

A nice full-flavored southwestern wine such as a Cahors would be good with this.

2 pounds Jerusalem artichokes
3 tablespoons butter
3 garlic cloves
Salt and pepper to taste
2 tablespoons minced fresh parsley
¾ to 1 cup heavy cream

✦✦Boil the Jerusalem artichokes in water to cover until almost tender, 15 to 20 minutes. Drain, let cool slightly, and peel; the skin should come off quite easily. Slice the flesh into ⅛- to ¼-inch-thick rounds.

✦✦Preheat the oven to 400°F. Dot a large earthenware gratin casserole with 1½ tablespoons of the butter, then toss in the sliced Jerusalem artichokes and the remaining 1½ tablespoons butter, and sprinkle with the garlic and parsley. Season with salt and pepper.

✦✦Pour in two thirds of the cream, then bake for 20 minutes, or until the top is crusty and the cream has evaporated into a thick custardlike mixture.

✦✦Add the rest of the cream and return the gratin to the oven. Bake until the top is golden brown and crusty, another 15 to 20 minutes. Serve hot.

GRATIN AU COURGE

PUMPKIN GRATIN IN CREAMY TOMATO AND RED PEPPER SAUCE

– Serves 4 –

A crisp topping of crumbs and cheese covers a mélange of tender pumpkin, peppers, and tomatoes with just enough cream to bind it all together. This gratin brings back a recent autumn evening of dining on a stone terrace in the hills behind Nice, with the night sounds of Provence all around. The evening had the slightly surreal touch of waves of perfume swirling through the air, for we were only a few kilometers from the perfume factories of Grasse.

I nearly missed eating this fine gratin because my husband and companions–who had a vested interest in what I ordered (I love to share my dinner)–had decided against it. "How good can it be?" they moaned. "Except for pie and risotto, how good is pumpkin?" they whined. I stood firm and ordered the gratin.

When it arrived, of course, forks flew and I had to spear a hand or two to eat my share. This dish is wonderful.

Serve with a chilled light rosé, or a fruity white with a hint of sweetness.

1½ pounds pumpkin, seeded, peeled, and
   diced
1 leek, cleaned and diced
1 tablespoon butter
1 tablespoon vegetable oil
½ red bell pepper, seeded, deribbed, and
   diced
4 small tomatoes, diced
½ cup dry white wine
½ cup heavy cream
3 garlic cloves, minced
2 tablespoons tomato paste
Several large pinches of herbes de Provence
Salt and pepper to taste
3 tablespoons grated Gruyère, Parmesan,
   pecorino, aged jack, or Asiago cheese
2 tablespoons fresh bread crumbs
1 to 2 teaspoons olive oil

✦✦Preheat the oven to 350°F.

✦✦In a large, heavy sauté pan or skillet over

medium-high heat, sauté the pumpkin and leek in the butter and oil until lightly golden. Add the red pepper and tomatoes, and continue to cook until the tomatoes are saucy, about 15 minutes.

♦♦Add the wine and cook until it is reduced by about half, then stir in the cream, half of the garlic, the tomato paste, herbes de Provence, salt and pepper.

♦♦Pour the pumpkin mixture into a 12- to 15-inch baking dish or gratin dish. Mix the remaining garlic with the cheese, bread crumbs, and oil, then sprinkle over the pumpkin in the casserole.

♦♦Bake just long enough to melt the cheese, lightly brown the top, and finish cooking the pumpkin, 20 to 25 minutes.

♦♦Serve hot.

VARIATION Substitute a fruity, slightly sweet white, such as Riesling or Liebfraumilch, for the dry white wine. The sweetness of the wine brings out the best of the pumpkin and red peppers, leaving no cloying sweetness and enhancing the vegetables' flavor.

GRATIN AU CHOU-FLEUR

CREAMY CAULIFLOWER GRATIN

– Serves 4 to 6 –

Spoon into this crisp gratin and you find a layer of tender cauliflower florets and a creamy purée of cauliflower. It is exquisitely satisfying on a cold day. I like serving individual casseroles, so that each person can enjoy the crisp buttery edges of the gratin.

2 heads cauliflower, broken into florets
2 cups Béchamel Sauce (page 206)

1 to 2 teaspoons minced fresh tarragon,
*   or ¼ to ½ teaspoon dried tarragon*
1½ cups (6 ounces) freshly grated
*   Parmesan cheese*
2 eggs, lightly beaten
3 shallots, minced
2 garlic cloves, minced
Salt and pepper to taste
¼ cup fresh bread crumbs
2 tablespoons butter

♦♦Steam the cauliflower florets over boiling water in a covered pot until they are just tender, about 15 to 20 minutes. Remove from heat and reserve about a quarter of the florets. Coarsely chop the remaining cauliflower; you should have 3½ to 4 cups.

♦♦Purée the chopped cauliflower, then mix well with the béchamel sauce, tarragon, cheese, eggs, shallots, and garlic. Season with salt and pepper.

♦♦Preheat the oven to 425°F.

♦♦Generously butter a 18- to 24-inch gratin dish or individual baking dishes, then spoon in half the purée. Make a layer of the

La table de ferme

reserved florets, then top with the rest of the purée. Sprinkle the surface with bread crumbs, then dot with the butter.

✦✦Bake for 25 to 40 minutes, or until the gratin is golden and crisp and the edges are puffy and bubbling. Serve right away, sizzling hot.

GRATIN DE POIREAUX AUX TROIS FROMAGES ET CIBOULETTE

GRATIN OF LEEKS WITH THREE CHEESES AND CHIVES

– Serves 4 –

This rich Gascon dish of sizzling leeks baked with melting cheeses can be served in small portions as a first course, or as a main course surrounded by unsauced fettuccine.

4 to 6 leeks, including tender green parts, cleaned
½ cup Béchamel Sauce (page 206), crème fraîche, or sour cream
Ground pepper and nutmeg to taste
6 ounces Roquefort or other blue cheese of choice, crumbled
1½ cups (6 ounces) shredded Gruyère, Comté, or Cantal cheese
3 tablespoons grated Parmesan cheese
3 tablespoons minced fresh chives

✦✦Cut the leeks into 2- to 3-inch lengths, then blanch them in salted boiling water until they are brightly colored and just tender. Drain, reserving the cooking liquid for soup. Season the leeks with salt and pepper.

✦✦Preheat the oven to 425°F.

✦✦In an 8-by-12-inch gratin dish, casserole, or individual ramekins, spoon half of the béchamel, crème fraîche, or sour cream and spread it over the bottom.

✦✦Sprinkle with one third of the leeks, cheeses, and chives. Repeat twice, ending with a layer of the cheese and chives.

✦✦Bake for 10 to 15 minutes, or until the top of the gratin is sizzling and lightly browned, the leeks are heated through, and the cheese is melted.

GRATIN AUX OIGNONS

ONION GRATIN

– Serves 4 –

This succulent gratin of browned onions is irresistible. The shallots flavor the cream and enhance the onion flavor of the gratin. I like to make this in individual gratin dishes or casseroles to maximize the amount of crispy brown edges.

Precooking the onions with bay leaves brings out their best. So too does a good jolt of nutmeg.

8 onions, peeled
3 to 5 bay leaves
Salt and pepper to taste
5 to 8 shallots, minced
⅛ teaspoon freshly grated nutmeg
5 to 6 tablespoons heavy cream

✦✦Put the onions and bay leaves in a large saucepan with water to cover. Season with salt and pepper and bring to a boil. Reduce heat to medium and simmer until the onions are just tender but still firm, about 20 minutes. Do not let them fall apart.

✦✦Preheat the oven to 375°F. Drain and let cool. Remove and discard the bay leaves.

✦✦Holding each onion firmly, slice through it crosswise to make ¼-inch slices. If they fall apart, just pat them back together. Layer one third of the onions in an 18-by-24-inch buttered gratin dish or individual dishes. Sprinkle with one third of the shallots and some salt, pepper, and nutmeg. Repeat twice.

✦✦Drizzle with the cream.

✦✦Bake for 30 to 40 minutes, or until golden brown with crisp brown edges.

✦✦Serve hot.

COURGETTES EN GRATIN

ZUCCHINI, TOMATOES, AND ONIONS BAKED WITH CHEESE

– Serves 4 –

All winter long, potato gratins grace the plates of the bistros of Paris. Then come the sweet warm days of spring: Suddenly everything is in bloom, everyone's smiling again after winter's siege, and *gratin de courgettes* is scrawled onto nearly every menu board in town.

Zucchini gratin can be creamy and delicate or, like this one, full of tomatoes and garlic. For a more rustic flavor, use sheep cheeses: a well-aged pecorino in place of the Parmesan and a fresher *brin d'amour* in place of the Gruyère.

To serve cold, omit the cheese and top with garlic-seasoned crumbs and a drizzle of olive oil for the final topping and baking.

4 to 5 onions, thinly sliced
3 tablespoons olive oil
Pinch of sugar
Salt to taste, plus pinch of salt
6 garlic cloves
2½ pounds zucchini or other summer
  squash
5 to 7 ripe tomatoes, diced, or one
  14-ounce can diced tomatoes
Several pinches of herbes de Provence or
  dried thyme
Pepper to taste
1½ cups (6 ounces) shredded Gruyère
  cheese
4 to 5 tablespoons grated Parmesan cheese

✦✦Preheat the oven to 350°F.

✦✦In a large, heavy sauté pan or skillet over medium heat, sauté the onions in 2 tablespoons of the olive oil until they are softened and lightly browned in places, about 15 minutes. As the onions cook, sprinkle them with sugar and salt to encourage caramelization. Set aside.

✦✦In a mortar or food processor, crush the garlic with a large pinch of salt until it forms a paste, then set aside.

✦✦Drizzle ½ tablespoon of the oil in the bottom of an 18-by-24-inch gratin dish or casserole, then arrange a layer of one third of the zucchini.

✦✦Dot with a little of the garlic paste, then layer with half the sautéed onions and one third of the tomatoes and sprinkle with the herbes de Provence or thyme, salt, and pepper.

✦✦Repeat twice.

✦✦Sprinkle with the crumbs, then drizzle with the remaining ½ tablespoon olive oil.

✦✦Bake for 1 hour, or until the zucchini is just tender and the crumbs golden. There should still be quite a bit of liquid in the pan.

✦✦Pour the liquid out of the pan, taking care not to disturb or spill the zucchini. Use the liquid to baste the zucchini as it continues to bake. (I like to turn over the top layer of the zucchini so that the crusty topping becomes part of the casserole and the saucy part becomes the topping, somewhat like turning the crumbs of a cassoulet into itself.)

✦✦ Scatter evenly with the cheeses, then return the casserole to the oven. Bake for another 25 to 30 minutes, basting every so often with the reserved casserole juices, until the cheese is melted and the zucchini are very tender.

✦✦ Serve hot.

TIAN DE COURGETTES

PROVENÇAL CASSEROLE OF

MASHED ZUCCHINI, SPINACH,

EGGS, AND PARMESAN

– Serves 4 –

This quintessential Provençal *tian* is a combination of mashed cooked zucchini, spinach, tender rice, cheese, and eggs. It makes a delicious informal summer supper, preceded by several tangy salads such as Pois Chiches aux Cumin (page 61), sliced tomatoes and fat briny olives, and Salade de Fenouil et Poivrons Rouges, Citronnés, (page 57).

For dessert, enjoy sliced peaches and raspberries splashed with brandy and lightly sweetened, along with a dollop of sorbet.

1½ pounds zucchini
¼ cup Arborio rice
1 large onion, chopped
5 garlic cloves, minced
1½ tablespoons olive oil
6 to 8 leaves Swiss chard or spinach,
* thinly sliced*
3 to 5 tablespoons minced fresh basil
3 tablespoons minced fresh parsley
1 egg, lightly beaten
¾ cup (3 ounces) grated Parmesan cheese
½ teaspoon herbes de Provence
Salt and pepper to taste

✦✦ Put the zucchini and rice in a large, heavy saucepan and add water to cover. Bring to a boil, then reduce heat to medium and cook until the zucchini and rice are tender, 15 to 20 minutes.

✦✦ Drain the excess liquid (save it for making soup), then mash the mixture with a potato masher until it makes a coarse rice-flecked purée. Drain in a sieve for 15 minutes.

✦✦ Preheat the oven to 400°F.

✦✦ In a medium sauté pan or skillet over medium heat, sauté the onion and half the garlic in 1 tablespoon of the olive oil until the onion is softened, about 5 minutes. Add the spinach and cook a few minutes until the spinach is no longer watery. Season with salt and pepper to taste.

✦✦ Mix the basil, parsley, egg, and ½ cup of the Parmesan cheese, then combine with the drained zucchini mixture, the sautéed onion and spinach, the reserved garlic, and the herbes de Provence.

✦✦ Pour the mixture into an 18-by-24-inch gratin dish or casserole and sprinkle the remaining Parmesan and remaining ½ tablespoon olive oil over the top.

✦✦ Bake for 30 minutes, or until the top is lightly browned in places.

✦✦ Serve hot or at room temperature.

Le chou.

TIAN D'AUBERGINE

EGGPLANT AND TOMATO MÉLANGE

– Serves 4 –

I first ate this dish in the hills behind Nice, sitting outside on a summer evening, on a stone terrace overlooking the valley. There were sheep baa-ing in the distance, the scent of late summer in the air, and a bottle of cool rosé on the cloth-topped table.

Though we ordered the *tian* as a side dish, we made a meal of it–it was so delicious and summery we could not stop eating it. Serve with an appetizer such as Trouchia (pages 12–13), or a plate of olives and cucumbers, and accompany the *tian* with Riz au Cumin (page 135).

Drink a lusty Rhône valley red, and follow the *tian* with a plate of cheeses from the south, including one or two superb goat and sheep cheeses. A bowl of peaches makes a sweet ending.

2 eggplants
Salt for sprinkling, plus pinch of salt
3 garlic cloves
1 onion, chopped
4 tablespoons olive oil
2 pounds fresh tomatoes chopped, or
    two 14-ounce cans chopped tomatoes
    including the juices
1 or 2 tablespoons tomato paste (optional)
Large pinch of sugar
Large pinch of herbes de Provence
Pepper to taste

✦✦Cut 1 eggplant in half crosswise and cut one half into ½-inch-thick crosswise slices. Sprinkle the slices generously with salt on both sides, then set them aside on a plate for 30 minutes.

✦✦Dice the remaining eggplant and sprinkle it generously with salt; let drain 30 minutes in a colander.

✦✦Preheat the oven to 350°F.

✦✦In a mortar or with a garlic press, crush the garlic with a pinch of salt. Set aside.

✦✦Rinse the eggplant slices of their salt and exuded liquid. Pat dry with paper towels. In a large, heavy, preferably nonstick sauté pan or skillet over medium heat, brown the eggplant slices in 1 tablespoon of the oil. Remove from the pan and set aside.

✦✦Rinse and dry the diced eggplant on paper towels. In the same pan, over medium-high heat, cook the diced eggplant and the onion in the remaining 3 tablespoons oil until the eggplant is softened and lightly browned in places, about 15 to 20 minutes.

✦✦Add the tomatoes a little at a time, sprinkling them with sugar and herbes de Provence as they cook, until the tomatoes make a thick sauce, about 15 to 20 minutes. To add more flavor, add

1 or 2 tablespoons tomato paste. Season with pepper to taste.

✦✦ Remove from heat and stir in the reserved garlic paste, then pour into a 12-inch gratin dish. Top with the browned eggplant slices and press to make an even surface.

✦✦ Bake for 30 to 40 minutes, or until lightly browned. Serve hot or at room temperature.

AUBERGINES ET FENOUIL

SAINT-LOUP

EGGPLANT AND FENNEL

WITH TOMATOES

IN AN EGG-CHEESE CUSTARD

– Serves 4 –

This *tian* is lusty summery stuff, rich with the perfumes of Provence. The eggplant and fennel bake to a savory crusty gratin, which is topped with beaten egg and cheese to form a rich mélange unique among the eggplant casseroles found throughout France and indeed, the Mediterranean.

2 eggplants
Salt for sprinkling
1 large fennel bulb, coarsely chopped
1 large onion, coarsely chopped
4 to 6 tablespoons olive oil
3 garlic cloves, minced
Pinch of sugar
Pinch of pepper
Pinch of herbes de Provence
2 cups diced fresh or canned tomatoes
4 tablespoons tomato paste or to taste

4 tablespoons minced fresh parsley
1½ cups (6 ounces) diced fresh mozzarella
2 eggs, lightly beaten
½ to ⅔ cup grated Parmesan cheese

✦✦ Cut the eggplants crosswise into ¼-inch slices, then sprinkle the slices on both sides with salt and let sit for 30 minutes.

✦✦ Rinse them well with water, then dry with paper towels.

✦✦ Preheat the oven to 375°F.

✦✦ In a medium, heavy sauté pan or skillet over medium heat, sauté the fennel, onion, and half the garlic in 2 tablespoons of the olive oil until they are softened, about 5 minutes. Sprinkle the mixture with salt, sugar, pepper, and herbes de Provence as it cooks.

✦✦ Remove the mixture from the pan and combine with the diced tomatoes, tomato paste, and parsley. Set aside.

✦✦ In a large, heavy sauté pan or skillet over medium heat, sauté the eggplant in the remaining 2 to 4 tablespoons oil until it is lightly browned on each side, then remove from heat.

✦✦ Layer half of the fennel mixture in the bottom of a 15-inch gratin dish, top with the eggplant slices, then finish with a layer of the fennel mixture.

✦✦ Bake for 30 minutes, or until the top is slightly crusty, then remove from the heat. Leave the oven on. Combine the mozzarella and eggs with half of the Parmesan and pour over the vegetables. Sprinkle the remaining Parmesan over the top and drizzle with a little olive oil.

✦✦ Return to the oven and continue to bake until the eggs set and the cheese melts, 20 to 25 minutes.

✦✦ Serve hot, warm, or at room temperature.

Légumes et Haricots

· · ·

Vegetable and Bean

Side Dishes

A selection of several interesting side dishes can make the simplest main dish seem like a feast. Indeed, they can take the place of the plat du jour and become the feast themselves.

Some of the salads, pastas, potato dishes, gratins, and even plats du jours in this book are delicious in small portions alongside the main course—try ratatouille, for example, or a potato gratin of almost any persuasion.

Then there are foods, requiring no recipe at all, that sit happily alongside your main dish soaking up its juices: boiled potatoes sprinkled with chives. Pencil-thin green beans tossed with a few drops of rich cream. Sliced ripe tomatoes simply sprinkled with salt. (Then there are pommes frites*—sizzling hot and nearly greaseless, with a dusting of fine salt—the most shamelessly irresistible of foods.)*

Many of the following side vegetables could be served as a first course, too: sizzling

endives (Endives à l'Ail), shallots in red wine (Echalotes au Vin Rouge), or mushrooms in mustard sauce (Champignons à la Dijonnaise)—all make a delicious start to dinner.

· ·

COURGETTES ET COURGES, SAUCE AU BEURRE ET PAPRIKA

YOUNG SUMMER SQUASH WITH PAPRIKA BUTTER SAUCE

– Serves 4 –

Here is a selection of various squashes–yellow crookneck, baby zucchini, tiny yellow and green pattypans, and so forth–arranged in a pleasing pattern and served with a drizzle of paprika-tinted butter sauce.

It's an excellent dish to make from the garden or after a tour of your local farmer's market.

6 to 8 summer squash, about 2 pounds total: yellow crookneck, baby zucchini (and their flowers, if possible), golden zucchini, tiny pale green pattypans, round zucchini
1 teaspoon good-quality sweet paprika
3 tablespoons dry white wine
1 shallot, minced
1 clove garlic, minced
3 tablespoons unsalted butter, cut into 6 pieces
Salt and pepper to taste

✦✦Cut large squash into bite-sized pieces; leave tiny squash whole. Steam the vegetables over boiling water in a covered pot until they are crisp-tender, about 4 to 7 minutes; remove from heat and drain. Set aside and keep warm.

✦✦Combine the paprika, wine, shallot, and garlic in a small saucepan, then bring it to a boil. Cook until it reduces in volume to little more than a glaze. Remove from heat immediately to prevent burning.

✦✦Whisk in the butter, a little at a time, to make a smooth sauce. Season with salt and pepper.

✦✦Arrange the hot vegetables in an appealing manner on a platter or on individual plates and drizzle the butter sauce around them on the borders of the plate. Serve right away.

VARIATION Leftover paprika butter sauce, with its piquant, slightly smoky flavor, makes a delicious sauce for boiled potatoes and roasted or grilled tomatoes.

L'artichaud

ENDIVES À L'AIL

BAKED ENDIVES WITH GARLIC

AND PARSLEY

– Serves 4 –

We dragged ourselves over the border from Italy into Nice, exhausted, our joie de vivre seriously in jeopardy. Everything tasted gray, and there seemed little point in going on with life.

Then the waitress brought out a sizzling gratin filled with garlicky endives and my life once again seemed interesting.

Serve this as a side dish with Tian de Courgettes (page 154), following a tangy soup such as Soupe d'Asperges du Languedoc (page 25).

4 Belgian endives, cored and halved
    lengthwise
½ to 1 teaspoon fresh lemon juice
3 garlic cloves
Pinch of salt
4 to 5 tablespoons minced fresh parsley
2 to 3 tablespoons olive oil

✦✦Cook the endives in boiling water for 3 to 4 minutes, or until crisp-tender. Drain well. Sprinkle with the lemon juice and arrange in a gratin dish. Set aside.

✦✦Preheat the oven to 425°F.

✦✦Crush the garlic in a mortar or food processor with the salt. Mix this purée with the parsley, then sprinkle all but 1 tablespoon over the endives.

✦✦Drizzle the endives with the olive oil, then bake for 15 to 20 minutes, or until lightly browned and sizzling. Sprinkle the endives with the remaining garlic mixture and serve right away.

CAROTTES VICHY

GLAZED CARROTS WITH

NORTHERN HERBS

– Serves 4 to 6 –

Carrots have long been a favorite French vegetable, but curiously enough, when they were first brought to France in the Middle Ages the root was tossed out and the wispy leaves were used as hair decorations.

This classic bistro dish is called Vichy because it was originally cooked in Vichy mineral water. It is true that vegetables are their best when cooked in good water. Boiled potatoes are an excellent example; so are these carrots.

*8 to 10 carrots, peeled and cut into ¼-inch
    disks*
*Still mineral water (such as Evian, Vichy,
    or Vittel), or filtered tap water*
Pinch of sugar
2 tablespoons butter
2 tablespoons heavy cream
*Leaves from 1 or 2 fresh tarragon sprigs,
    minced*
*Leaves from 1 or 2 fresh chervil sprigs,
    minced*
Salt and pepper to taste

✦✦ Boil the carrots in the mineral or filtered water until they are just tender, 10 to 15 minutes. Drain (reserve the water for another purpose), then toss the carrots with the sugar and set aside.

✦✦ In a medium saucepan, melt the butter with the cream, then add the carrots, tarragon, and chervil and cook over high heat until the cream reduces and the carrots are coated in a creamy glaze.

✦✦ Season with salt and pepper and serve right away.

CHAMPIGNONS À LA DIJONNAISE

MUSHROOMS IN TARRAGON AND

MUSTARD CREAM

– Serves 4 to 6 –

From Dijon comes this classic dish of mushrooms and onions in a tarragon-scented mustard cream.

Though butter is traditionally used for the initial sautéing, I use vegetable oil: the cream sauce is more than rich enough on its own. The flavor of Tabasco or cayenne should not be overwhelming or even obvious; it takes the place of black pepper, which can be inharmonious with mushrooms.

Enjoy this as a superb side dish, or as a first course, sizzling hot in its own little earthenware casserole, served with crusty bread to dip into it.

2 onions, chopped
3 to 4 garlic cloves, minced
1 to 2 tablespoons vegetable oil
*1 to 1½ pounds firm mushrooms, cut into
    quarters*
Salt to taste
½ to 1 teaspoon fresh lemon juice
*1 tablespoon coarsely chopped fresh tarra-
    gon, or ½ teaspoon dried tarragon*
1 cup heavy cream

Tabasco sauce or cayenne pepper to taste
2 tablespoons Dijon mustard

✦✦In a large, heavy sauté pan or skillet over medium-high heat, sauté the onions and garlic in the oil until they are golden and softened, about 5 to 6 minutes. Add the mushrooms, and cook uncovered until lightly golden in places. Sprinkle with salt and lemon juice, cover, and cook 6 to 8 minutes.

✦✦Sprinkle the mushrooms with the tarragon, then pour in the cream and cook 5 to 8 minutes, or until it thickens into a rich sauce.

✦✦Stir in the Dijon mustard, and Tabasco or cayenne. Taste for salt.

✦✦Serve right away.

Gratin de Céleri-rave et Poireaux à la Moutarde
(Celery Root and Leek Gratin) Serve the mustard sauce from the above recipe on a mixture of blanched diced celery root and sautéed diced leeks. Top with 1 cup shredded Gruyère and 1 cup fresh bread crumbs, then dot with butter, cover, and bake in a preheated 350°F oven for 15 minutes. Uncover and bake for about 20 minutes, or until golden brown. Serve hot.

Chou à l'Huile de Noix

Cabbage in Walnut Oil

– Serves 4 –

This Savoyard dish is at its best with a green cabbage with a good leafy flavor. The combination of walnut oil and cabbage is a particularly happy one; for a simple, satisfying bed of vegetables to serve on any delicate pasta, such as cheese-filled ravioli, omit the blanching step and sauté the cabbage and shallots in the walnut oil as below, then cover and cook until crisp-tender.

1 green cabbage, preferably savoy, coarsely
chopped
4 to 5 shallots, chopped
3 tablespoons walnut oil
1 garlic clove, minced
Salt and pepper to taste

✦✦Blanch the cabbage until bright green and crisp-tender, then drain and rinse well in cold water. Set aside.

✦✦In a large, heavy sauté pan or skillet over medium heat, sauté the shallots in 2 tablespoons of the walnut oil. Add the drained cabbage and sauté for 8 to 10 minutes. Cover and simmer for 5 to 10 minutes, then add the garlic and season with salt and pepper. Drizzle with the remaining 1 tablespoon walnut oil.

✦✦Serve hot.

Choucroute Alsacienne

Sauerkraut Simmered in

Spiced White Wine

– Serves 4 –

Throughout France you find brasseries and bistros serving *choucroute garnie* as the plat du jour, even in areas that have never pickled a cabbage in their history. I've had memorable choucroute in the industrial north when the weather outside was sleety. And I've eaten choucroute at a little table set in the sun next to the boules court in Saint-Paul-de-Vence, next to a chic little art gallery, with great gallumphing dogs gathered at my feet, hopeful of whatever might drop their way.

Choucroute garnie might be translated as simply garnished sauerkraut, but the sauerkraut is rinsed of excess salt and brine, then simmered with white wine and various spices. Authentically, the garni for the choucroute is a variety of nonvegetarian ingredients, but the true delight of the dish is the choucroute itself. I've also added a variation for a garnish of root vegetables.

> *3 to 4 cups sauerkraut*
> *½ cup dry white wine*
> *5 to 8 juniper berries, plus an additional few berries if serving with vegetables*
> *½ teaspoon mustard seeds, either yellow or black*
> *½ teaspoon caraway seeds*
> *½ teaspoon whole-grain mustard*

✦✦ Wash the sauerkraut well in running water in a colander or strainer, then place it in a saucepan with the wine, juniper berries, mustard seeds, and caraway or cumin seeds.

✦✦ Cook over a medium heat, stirring occasionally, until it is heated through. Cover it, lower heat, and simmer until the wine has been nearly all absorbed by the cabbage.

✦✦ If serving now, stir in the whole-grain mustard. If not, rewarm when serving and stir in the mustard. Serve right away.

VARIATION Cook 8 peeled whole boiling potatoes, 4 halved carrots and 2 quartered onions in a mixture of ½ cup water, ½ cup vegetable stock, and ½ cup dry white wine with a pinch of mustard seeds, juniper berries, and caraway seeds added.

Bring to a boil, then cook, covered, over medium heat until vegetables are tender, adding more water or stock as needed.

Remove the vegetables from their cooking liquid and serve them scattered over the hot sauerkraut.

Choucroute aux Pommes **(Classic Apple Choucroute)** Add 1 or 2 sliced unpeeled tart green apples to the wine-simmered sauerkraut.

EPINARDS AUX CHÈVRE

GOAT CHEESE–CREAMED SPINACH

– Serves 4 –

Leafy green fresh spinach, cooked to just tender and awash in a luscious goat cheese sauce, makes a delectably rich creamed side dish.

You could also serve creamed spinach anywhere a coulis would be good, say surrounding a lovely mound of puréed celery root and potatoes (pages 142–143). It's good too as a filling for crêpes (pages 203–204), or as a bed for poached eggs.

> *2 pounds fresh spinach, stemmed, or two 10-ounce packages thawed frozen spinach*
> *3 garlic cloves, thinly sliced or chopped*
> *2 tablespoons olive oil*
> *2 green onions, thinly sliced*
> *3 tablespoons heavy cream or sour cream*
> *6 ounces fresh white goat cheese, crumbled*

✦✦ Cook the fresh spinach in boiling water until just tender. Drain, reserving the spinach water for soups or sauces. (If using frozen, do not cook.) Squeeze the spinach to extract the excess liquid; save this, as well.

✦✦ In a heavy, nonreactive saucepan over medium-high heat, heat the garlic in the olive oil until it just begins to turn golden, about 1 minute. Add the spinach and cook for 3 to 5 minutes, then stir in the green onions and the cream.

✦✦ Cook over high heat for about 5 to 10 minutes to thicken the cream. You do not want to overcook the spinach, so if it remains very liquidy, pour off the liquid, boil to reduce it, then recombine with the spinach.

✦✦ Stir in the goat cheese and heat through. Taste for seasoning and serve right away.

EPINARDS AUX POIRES

SPINACH PURÉED WITH PEARS

– Serves 4 to 6 –

The curious combination of spinach and pears startled me at first bite, but the slightly sweet, slightly tart accent of the fruit is surprisingly nice with the tender cooked greens.

Serve this light, provocative vegetable purée in small portions as a side dish.

2 pears, peeled, cored, and halved
1 pound fresh spinach, stemmed
1 to 2 tablespoons butter or as desired
Dash of balsamic vinegar
Dash of fresh lemon juice
Salt and pepper to taste

✦✦ Poach the pears in simmering water to cover until they are tender, about 7 to 10 minutes. Remove them from their liquid and mash. Set aside, saving the poaching liquid for the spinach.

✦✦ Cook the spinach leaves in the pear poaching liquid until bright green and tender.

✦✦ Drain the spinach in a colander, saving the liquid, and squeeze out the excess liquid with the back of a heavy spoon (save the liquid for soup or stew).

✦✦ In a medium saucepan, melt the butter over medium heat, then add the spinach and pears and cook until the excess liquid has been absorbed.

✦✦ Season the spinach mixture with balsamic vinegar and lemon juice and add salt and pepper.

✦✦ Serve right away.

EPINARDS OU BLETTES À LA NIÇOISE

NIÇOISE-STYLE SPINACH OR CHARD WITH PINE NUTS AND RAISINS

– Serves 4 –

The curious combination of spinach or chard and the sweet flavors of raisins and orange is a distinctive Niçoise specialty; in the Niçoise dialect it is known as *espinousos à l'aiga-passera e ai pignoun*. While the combination might sound strange to the uninitiated, the sweet fruity flavors strike a lyrical balance with the leafy greens and reflect an Arabic influence.

For a tidier, more elegant presentation, serve the spinach leaves rolled around little balls of rice (see variation).

2 pounds fresh spinach or 2½ pounds fresh
    chard, stemmed, or two 10-ounce pack-
    ages frozen spinach
3 tablespoons pine nuts

3 garlic cloves, thinly sliced
2 tablespoons olive oil
5 tablespoons golden raisins
⅛ teaspoon grated orange zest
Dash of orange flower water
Juice of ¼ lemon, if needed
Salt and cayenne pepper to taste

✦✦If using fresh spinach or chard, cook in rapidly boiling water until just wilted. If using frozen spinach, cook in a small amount of boiling water until the spinach has thawed and heated through. Drain well and squeeze dry, saving all liquid for other purposes.

✦✦Lightly toast the pine nuts in an ungreased heavy skillet over medium heat, stirring until they are lightly golden and browned in spots. Remove from the heat and set aside.

✦✦In a heavy sauté pan or skillet over medium-high heat, heat the garlic in the olive oil until the garlic lightly colors. Add the spinach, raisins, and orange zest and heat through.

✦✦Season with orange flower water, lemon juice, salt, and cayenne. Taste for seasoning and serve right away or at room temperature.

Boulettes des Blettes (Packets of Aromatic Chard and Rice) Prepare the above mixture. Add ½ cup cooked plain rice (page 210) or cumin rice (page 135); this is a great way to use leftovers. Taste and adjust the seasoning.

Stem 16 to 20 chard leaves, then blanch the leaves and rinse in cold water. Dry the leaves on paper towels, then place 3 to 4 tablespoons of the filling on each leaf. Roll each leaf one turn, then fold in the sides and roll into a cylinder.

Arrange the packets in a baking pan, just touching each other. Drizzle with olive oil and fresh lemon juice. Tuck slivers of garlic in between the packets. Cover and bake in a preheated 350°F oven for 20 minutes.

Serve at room temperature.

ECHALOTES AU VIN ROUGE

SHALLOTS IN RED WINE SAUCE

– Serves 4 –

Boiling red wine with a shallot-flavored stock creates a rich sauce of good, strong character. A robust wine such as a Cahors, Merlot, or a Côtes-du-Rhône is great for this dish, though I've made it with a light and lyrical Beaujolais and it was fine, too.

Serve the sizzling purple shallots in their own ramekins, with chunks of bread to scoop up the sauce. These morsels are so delicious, I think they merit their own course on the menu.

A rustic potato gratin would be good with this. Drink whichever wine you've used for the shallots, and follow with a salad dressed in walnut oil and several delightfully ripe cheeses.

1 pound shallots
4 tablespoons unsalted butter
1 to 2 teaspoons sugar
1 cup vegetable stock (pages 201–202)
1 or 2 generous pinches of herbes de
    Provence or minced fresh or dried thyme
1 cup dry red wine
¼ to ½ teaspoon fresh lemon juice, or to taste
Salt and pepper to taste
1 to 2 tablespoons fresh chervil leaves for
    garnish
Crusty bread for serving

✦✦Peel the shallots but leave them whole.

✦✦Melt 2 tablespoons of the butter in a skillet over medium heat, then add the shallots and cook, stirring gently. As they cook, sprinkle them with the sugar to encourage caramelization.

✦✦When the shallots are lightly golden, after about 6 to 8 minutes, pour in the stock and herbes de Provence or thyme and simmer for about 10 minutes, or until the shallots are almost tender.

✦✦Pour in the red wine, raise heat to medium-high, and cook until the shallots are very tender but whole and the red wine-broth has reduced to an almost syrupy glaze, about 10 to 15 minutes.

✦✦Stir the lemon juice into the sauce, then remove from heat and stir in the remaining butter. The sauce should be just thick enough to coat the back of a spoon. Add salt and pepper, then serve the shallots in their sauce, sprinkled with chervil and accompanied with crusty bread for dipping.

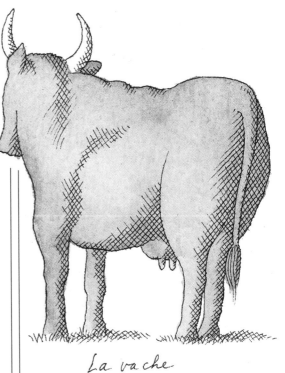

La vache

LES PETITS OIGNONS ET GROUSSES DE L'AIL EN CONFIT PROVENÇAL

ONIONS AND GARLIC SIMMERED IN SWEET AND SOUR PRESERVES

– Serves 4 –

Confit is a way of preserving foods by salting, slow-cooking, then storing them submerged in fat. Traditionally confit was made with poultry or different types of meats, but it can also refer to cooking whole garlic cloves, onions, and other vegetables in olive oil and/or vinegar to make a savory chutneylike preserve. *(Confitures are sweet fruit jams and preserves.)*

This sweet and sour Provençal mixture reflects the flavors of neighboring Italy. It is very good as a side dish for grilled or roasted vegetables with spicy cumin rice alongside, or as part of an appetizer selection with roasted peppers, fat juicy olives, and sliced cucumbers and tomatoes.

1 pound baby onions or shallots
2 garlic heads, separated into cloves
1 cup water
6 garlic cloves, coarsely chopped
3 tablespoons olive oil
¼ cup red wine or fruit vinegar

3 tablespoons packed brown sugar

¼ cup tomato purée or paste

⅓ cup raisins

Pinch of dried thyme

Pinch of ground cinnamon

Salt and pepper to taste

✦✦ Blanch the onions and garlic. Drain and rinse in cold water. Slip off the peels.

✦✦ Combine the peeled onions and garlic cloves with the remaining ingredients in a saucepan and simmer over low heat, covered, for about 1 hour.

✦✦ Uncover and cook slowly, another 30 to 45 minutes, or until the liquid has formed a glaze and the vegetables are very tender. Taste and adjust the seasoning.

✦✦ Serve the mixture hot or at room temperature. To store, cover and refrigerate for up to 1 week.

POIREAUX BRAISÉS AUX TRUFFES

LEEKS BRAISED WITH TRUFFLES OR WILD MUSHROOMS

– Serves 4 –

Breathtakingly elegant, yet rustic and simple, this dish combines tender young leeks, cream, and lots of fragrant truffles–as many as you can afford! If truffles are beyond your means or impossible to find, this dish is lovely made with wild mushrooms, even dried ones.

A white Burgundian wine such as Saint-Véran or Aligote would be very nice with this, or try a Sancerre from the Loire.

8 to 10 young leeks, including tender green part, cleaned

2 tablespoons butter

¼ cup heavy cream

1 fresh or canned truffle (about 2 ounces), minced, or 8 ounces cèpe (porcini) or field mushrooms of choice, cut into bite-sized pieces

1 garlic clove, minced

1½ cups vegetable stock (pages 201–202)

✦✦ Cut the leeks into bite-sized lengths. In a medium saucepan over low heat, melt the butter. Add the leeks, cover, and cook until just tender, about 15 to 20 minutes.

✦✦ Meanwhile, if using the truffle, add half of it to the cream.

✦✦ Transfer the leeks to a bowl and keep warm. Add the stock to the pan, bring to a boil, and cook over medium heat until reduced by about half.

✦✦ If using mushrooms, melt the remaining butter in a small to medium sauté pan or skillet over medium-low heat. Add the mushrooms and garlic and cook for 5 to 8 minutes, or until gently stewed and limp. If using truffles, melt the remaining butter in a small saucepan over low heat. Add the garlic and cook about 30 seconds. Add the remaining half of the truffle. Remove from heat.

✦✦ Add the cream (or cream and truffle) and cook for about 5 minutes. Taste and adjust the seasoning, then pour over the leeks. Add the mushrooms, if using. Serve right away.

HARICOTS VERTS AUX CHAMPIGNONS

THIN GREEN BEANS WITH FIELD MUSHROOMS IN OLIVE OIL

– Serves 4 –

Only the thinnest, tenderest, most flavorful green beans will do here; any others will let you down.

If you cannot find haricots verts or baby Blue Lakes, prepare the dish using the tender young asparagus of spring.

> *4 to 6 ounces fresh field mushrooms, or*
> *½ ounce dried wild mushrooms such*
> *as cèpes (porcini), morels, chanterelles*
> *1 pound young haricots verts or baby Blue*
> *Lake green beans*
> *3 tablespoons olive oil*
> *1 to 2 garlic cloves, coarsely chopped*
> *Salt and pepper to taste*
> *Lemon wedges (optional)*

✦✦If using fresh mushrooms, wipe or lightly rinse them to rid them of their bits of grit and sand. Dice and set aside.

✦✦If using dried mushrooms, rehydrate by placing them in a bowl with 1 cup hot water. Cover and let soak for at least 30 minutes, or until the mushrooms have softened. Squeeze dry, letting the liquid drip back into the soaking water (save for another use). Dice the mushrooms and set aside.

✦✦Cook the beans in boiling water until crisp-tender, about 3 minutes. Drain the beans and rinse in cold water to stop the cooking. Set aside.

✦✦Combine the mushrooms, olive oil, and garlic in a saucepan over medium-low heat and cook just long enough to wilt the mushrooms.

✦✦Spoon the warm mushrooms over the cooked beans, then add salt and pepper.

✦✦Serve at room temperature, with lemon wedges if desired.

HARICOTS VERTS À L'HUILE DE NOIX

THIN GREEN BEANS WITH GARLIC AND WALNUT OIL

– Serves 4 –

Thin green beans are one of the glories of the French garden. Cooked until just crisp-tender, then tossed with a simple dressing of walnut oil, garlic and chervil, they taste of summer in the southwest.

Serve as part of a selection of dishes for a plat du jour: Gâteau de Pommes de Terre Alain (pages 137–138), and either roasted tomatoes or a juicy tomato salad. Finish the meal with a particularly luscious cheese course.

> *1 pound haricots verts or baby Blue Lake*
> *green beans*
> *1 tablespoon walnut oil*
> *1 garlic clove, minced*
> *Salt and pepper to taste*
> *1 to 2 teaspoons minced fresh chervil*

✦✦Cook the beans in boiling water until crisp-tender, about 5 minutes. Drain well.

✦✦Return the beans to the warm pan with the walnut oil, garlic, salt, and pepper. Cover and let set for a few minutes, then serve right away, sprinkled with chervil.

Haricots Verts au Crème et Noisettes (Green Beans with Cream and Hazelnuts) Add a tablespoon or two of heavy cream to the green beans, and garnish the dish with a handful of coarsely chopped peeled toasted hazelnuts.

Haricots Verts aux Tomates et Coriandre Frais (Green Beans with Tomatoes and Cilantro) Replace the walnut oil with olive oil and add 4 diced seeded tomatoes and a pinch of cayenne pepper. Increase the amount of garlic to 3 cloves, and serve sprinkled with minced fresh cilantro.

FLAGEOLETS AUX BEURRE DE L'AIL

FLAGEOLET BEANS WITH GARLIC AND PARSLEY

– Serves 6 –

Flageolets are little pale green dried beans that are delicate and light when cooked, yet just starchy enough to satisfy. The following dish is simple, but the garlic and parsley butter show off the best of the little beans.

Serve as a side dish with any simple roasted or grilled vegetables, along with Carottes Vichy (page 159) and Chou à L'Huile de Noix (page 160).

1½ cups dried flageolet beans (or 3 cups fresh flageolets or shell beans)
3 tablespoons butter at room temperature
2 garlic cloves, minced
1 to 2 tablespoons minced fresh parsley
Salt and pepper to taste

✦✦If using dried flageolets, either soak overnight or place in a saucepan with cold water to cover and bring to a boil. Cook over medium-high heat for 10 minutes, then remove from heat and let sit, covered, for 1 hour. If using fresh beans, place in a saucepan with cold water to cover by about 2 inches, and bring to a boil. Reduce the heat to low, and simmer the beans until very tender, about 35 to 40 minutes. After either method, drain the beans, then add fresh water to cover by 2 inches. Cover and bring to a boil, then reduce the heat to low and simmer for 1 hour, or until tender.

✦✦Combine the butter, garlic, and parsley; season with salt and pepper and set aside.

✦✦Heat the beans until warmed through, if necessary. Drain, reserving a little of the cooking water.

✦✦Toss the warmed beans with the garlic butter, mashing a few of the beans with a spoonful or two of the cooking water to help thicken the beans and hold them together. Taste and adjust the seasoning. Serve right away.

PURÉE DE POIS VERTS CRESSONNIÈRE

PURÉE OF GREEN SPLIT PEAS WITH MARJORAM AND WATERCRESS

– Serves 4 –

This dish of cooked green split peas puréed with watercress comes from France's northern coast, between Boulogne and Montreuil, an area known for this peppery herb.

3 shallots, minced
½ carrot, peeled and diced
½ celery stalk or ¼ celery root, peeled and
diced
2 tablespoons butter
2 cups water
½ cup green split peas
1 teaspoon minced fresh marjoram or
a pinch of dried marjoram
Salt and pepper to taste
½ bunch watercress, stemmed and
chopped (about ½ cup)

✦✦In a medium saucepan over medium heat, sauté the shallots, carrot, and celery or celery root in 1 tablespoon of the butter until the vegetables have softened, about 5 minutes.

✦✦Add the water and split peas, bring them to a boil, then reduce heat, cover, and simmer until the split peas are very tender and the liquid has almost completely been absorbed, about 40 minutes.

✦✦Season with marjoram, salt, and pepper, then purée the mixture in a blender or food processor until smooth.

Le jardinier

✦✦Just before serving, heat the purée, adding a little water if needed to form a thick, creamy mixture.

✦✦In a small saucepan over medium heat, melt the remaining 1 tablespoon butter and heat the watercress. Stir it into the pea purée and serve right away.

HARICOTS ROUGES
BOURGUIGNONNE

RED BEANS, BURGUNDY STYLE

– Serves 4 to 6 –

R ed beans and red wine are two ingredients that seem made for each other, especially in areas that produce both: I've tasted the dish in Burgundy and Gascony.

2 cups dry red wine
1 cup vegetable stock (page 201–202)
1 bouquet garni: 1 bay leaf, 1 fresh thyme
sprig, 1 fresh rosemary sprig, and 1 fresh
parsley sprig, tied in a cheesecloth bag
5 to 8 shallots, diced
2 to 3 garlic cloves, minced
1 carrot, diced
2 tablespoons butter
1 tablespoon flour
3 cups drained cooked red kidney beans
½ teaspoon minced fresh thyme,
or ¼ teaspoon dried thyme
Salt and pepper to taste

✦✦In a medium saucepan, combine the wine, stock, and bouquet garni. Bring it to a boil over medium-high heat and cook until reduced to about 1 cup.

✦✦Meanwhile, in a medium sauté pan or skillet over medium heat, sauté the shallots, garlic, and carrot in the butter until softened, about 5 to 8 minutes. Sprinkle in the flour and cook, stirring, for 2 or 3 minutes. Stir in the beans and cook for 15 minutes.

✦✦Discard the bouquet garni, then stir in the wine and stock. Simmer for about 20 minutes, stirring occasionally and mashing some of the beans with a fork or masher. Season with thyme, salt, and pepper.

✦✦Serve right away.

Purée d'Haricots Rouges **(Red Bean Purée)** Purée the stew in a blender or food processor. Cook until heated through and serve hot.

Lentilles en Vin Rouge **(Lentils in Red Wine)** Substitute drained cooked lentils for the kidney beans.

HARICOTS BLANCS AUX CRÈME

WHITE BEANS WITH WHITE WINE, AROMATICS, AND CREAM

– Serves 6 to 8 –

This dish is at its most delicious when made with French lingots or tiny cocos. If you are using canned beans such as cannellini, rinse them well to rid them of their salty taste.

½ cup dried white beans, cooked (see page 209) or 4 cups drained canned white beans

2 carrots, peeled and diced

1 celery stalk, including the leaves, chopped

4 garlic cloves, half coarsely chopped and the other half minced

1 bay leaf

1 cup water (optional)

5 shallots or 1 onion, chopped

2 tablespoons butter

Ground nutmeg to taste

½ cup dry white wine

¾ cup heavy cream

Salt and pepper to taste

✦✦Add the carrots, celery, coarsely chopped garlic, and bay leaf to the cooked beans and cook over medium-low heat for 20 to 30 minutes, or until the carrots are tender. Drain, reserving the liquid for soup. If using canned beans, cook the carrot and celery with the bay leaf in the water in a large saucepan; when the carrot is tender, add the beans and heat through. Drain.

✦✦Remove the bay leaf and discard it. Mash the beans and set aside.

✦✦In a heavy, large saucepan over medium heat, sauté the shallots or onion with the minced garlic in the butter until softened and golden, about 5 to 8 minutes. Add the nutmeg, mashed beans, and white wine, then bring to a boil. Cook over high heat until the liquid evaporates, 5 to 8 minutes, then add the cream and mix well. Cook over medium heat until heated through; if the mixture is too thick, add a little of the bean-vegetable cooking liquid.

✦✦Season with salt and pepper and serve hot.

Fromage

♦ ♦ ♦

Cheese

Nowhere else on earth is cheese held in such high esteem as it is in France. There, eating cheese is an adventure of flavors, textures, and smells reflecting the characteristics of the animal who made the milk, the flavor of the herbs and greens the animal fed on, and the quality of life that went into the work of making the cheese. Cheese is an integral part of the culture and regional variation of the country.

Cheese made from raw, unpasteurized milk gives the fullest flavor. Unfortunately, raw-milk cheeses cannot be imported into the United States unless they are subjected to a special procedure. When you are able to sample true handcrafted cheeses made from unpasteurized milk, savor the moment. Let the nubbins warm on your tongue and revel in the sensuality of the experience.

France's history is intertwined with the history of cheese, from the Romans, who brought the ancient art of cheese making northward, to Charlemagne, who ordered that local tithes be paid in Roquefort; to General de

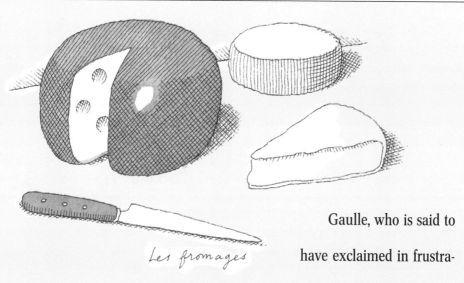

Les fromages

Gaulle, who is said to have exclaimed in frustration: "How can anyone govern a country that produces 324 different types of cheese?"

In fact, 324 is a very modest number. The truth is that the number of cheese varieties made in France is nearly incalculable, as a visit to any good cheese seller and *affineur* will confirm. Besides the most popular cheeses, such as Roquefort, goat cheeses, Gruyère, and Camembert, there are cheeses from regional farms, made in a very personal manner, that perhaps no one else has heard of. (Italian cheeses, too, have been held in great esteem in recent years in France, and even Greek feta is appearing more and more.)

The nearly endless variety of cheeses do, however, fall into a handful of "families," so the selection is not as confusing as it might seem.

SOFT WHITE-BLOOM RIND CHEESES These are delicate, creamy cheeses with a white or slightly golden soft rind. Camembert, Brie, Neufchâtel, Chaource, Carré de l'Est, and Coulommiers are the most popular. When to eat these cheeses depends quite a bit on your personal taste: In Normandy, Camembert's home, it's served ripe but still firm; in Paris it's aged longer to a state of pungent runniness. A good cheese shop will help you find a cheese to suit your preference.

WASHED-RIND CHEESES These strongly flavored cheeses are washed with beer, cider, brandy, wine, or saltwater intermittently as they mature. Washed-rind cheeses include Livarot, Maroilles, Pont l'Evêque, Munster, Epoisses, and the Vacherin Mont-d'Or, so unctuous you need to eat it with a spoon.

GOAT CHEESES There are hundreds and hundreds of types of goat cheeses, made in Picardy, Burgundy, Lyonnais, the Loire Valley, Provence, and the southwest. They come in a dazzling variety of shapes and sizes, textures and flavors. Sold fresh as fromage frais, aged and soft like Camembert, dry and crumbly or very hard for grating, they are also coated with a selection of ingredients such as ashes, herbs, spices, white wine, olive oil, and brandy, or wrapped in edible leaves such as grape or chestnut. Interestingly, several French names for goat cheese, such as Chabichou and Chavignol come from the Arab word *chabli*, meaning goats, as the Arab invasions of France during the eighth century introduced the skill of goat breeding.

Chevrotin (de Valençay and de Moulins being the most famous), Chavignol, Cabécou, Picodon,

Pouligny-Saint-Pierre, Sainte-Maure, Selles-sur-Cher, Pelardon, the pungent bouton-de-culotte, and leaf-wrapped Banon are the chèvres you are most likely to find in France, in addition to the more readily available logs such as Montrachet, Lezay, and Bucheron, which are all available in the United States. You can tell a fresh from an aged goat cheese by its appearance: Fresh cheeses are white and soft; they darken and firm up as they age. Older, firmer, drier goat cheeses are best for grating.

BLUE CHEESES Though most are made with sheep's milk, quite a few blue cheeses are made from cow's milk, and there are some blue chèvres as well. Roquefort has been made since around the year A.D. 800 and is aged in special caves after being sprinkled with powdered moldy rye bread containing the penicillium spores that give the cheese its distinctive pungent blue veins.

Fourme d'Ambert, bleu d'Auvergne, and bleu de Causses are some of France's other blues, and a creamy Brie-style bleu de Bresse is quite popular as well.

Blues must be stored well wrapped so they don't dry out; the temperature should be cool but not icy cold. Store them in the warmest part of your refrigerator.

FROMAGE FRAIS Literally "fresh cheese," also known as *fromage blanc*, or "white cheese," this cheese consists of simple mild curds, somewhat in between ricotta and sour cream in taste and consistency. It can be made from cow's or goat's milk, and less often, but deliciously, with sheep's milk.

Fromage frais is low in fat yet rich in flavor,

cheap, and easily available throughout France. Children eat it sweet, for dessert; adults do too, often with a compote of fruit in liqueur or a drizzle of lavender honey. Fontainebleu is a mixture of fromage frais and whipped cream left to drain in a cheesecloth.

Petit-Suisse, Neufchâtel frais, and Boursin, as well as regional cheeses such as the ricottalike brousse and cremet, are all aged just slightly and can be served with a variety of flavorings.

Fromage frais has a fat content that ranges from 40 percent down to 0 percent, and can be used in cooking in place of cream.

MONASTERY CHEESES Made from either sheep's or cow's milk, monastery cheeses are actually made in monasteries, or *abbayes,* as they have been for centuries, since the Romans taught the French the craft. They include Cantal, Laguiolie, Ossau-Iraty-Brebis Pyrénées, Alpine Reblochon, Sainte-Nectaire, Mimolette, Morbier from the Jura (with a thin layer of ash in its center) and various types of tommes from the Savoy.

HARD CHEESES The great rounds of hard cheeses belong to the Gruyère family. The finest is Beaufort, another legacy from the Romans. Comté, from the Jura, is also wonderful, nutty flavored and delicate, with tiny holes, while Emmental has larger holes and is most often used for cooking.

AGING AND STORAGE Except for small cheeses, buy cheese that is already aged to the state you desire it. In France, some cheese shops, called *affineurs,* specialize in aging cheeses.

Once an aged cheese is cut, it will start to dry out. Aged cheeses can be kept loosely wrapped

CHEESE AS A FIRST COURSE

Don't serve a lavish cheese board before dinner; cheese on its own is just too rich and will blunt appetites before the meal has a chance to begin.

In judicious amounts, however, cheese can be a bright part of the beginning of a meal, especially a light and vivacious goat or sheep cheese. Peruse the salad chapter for dishes featuring goat and sheep cheeses, Roquefort cheese, and Comté and similar cheeses.

at a cool room temperature for a few days, but should be well wrapped and refrigerated after that. Fresh cheeses, however, should always be tightly wrapped and kept in the refrigerator. For the best-quality cheese, buy small amounts and eat within a day or two.

Be sure to remove cheese from cool storage about 2 hours before serving; it should be eaten at room temperature.

FONDUE COMTOISE

CHEESE FONDUE

WITH TOMATOES AND GARLIC

– *Serves 4* –

We ate this one winter when we were snowed in in a French Alpine village known for its Gruyère-type mountain cheeses.

This concoction of cheese, wine, and tomatoes simmered with wine is spooned onto slabs of rustic bread and eaten as a first course, unlike the one-pot fondue of Switzerland.

8 slices stale country bread
3 canned whole tomatoes, diced
1½ cups dry white wine
1½ cups (6 ounces) diced Comté, Gruyère,
    or Asiago
¾ cup (3 ounces) grated Parmesan cheese
2 teaspoons flour
3 garlic cloves, minced
1 green onion (including green part), finely
    chopped
Ground nutmeg and pepper to taste

♦♦Arrange the bread on plates.

♦♦Combine the tomatoes and wine in a medium, heavy saucepan and bring to a boil. Reduce heat and let simmer over low heat.

♦♦Toss the cheeses with the flour to coat them, then stir into the simmering wine and tomatoes. Increase heat to medium and cook, stirring, until the cheese melts. Stir in the garlic, green onion, nutmeg, and pepper.

♦♦Serve right away, spooned onto the sliced bread.

CROÛTES AU FROMAGE

BURGUNDIAN CHEESE TOASTS

– Serves 4 –

Pungent blue and nutty mountain cheese, a few drops of white wine, a grating of nutmeg, and a good dose of garlic–melted onto a crisp chunk of baguette, this makes a lusty hors d'oeuvre or first course, Burgundian style. Enjoy with a glass of chilled white wine or a kir.

A little chopped ripe tomato is nice tucked into the hot cheese mixture; if you can't decide whether to make the toasts with or without, make half with tomatoes and half without.

8 baguette slices, cut on the diagonal
1 tablespoon butter at room temperature
1 tablespoon dry white wine
3 garlic cloves, minced
Grating of nutmeg
4 to 6 ounces blue cheese, sliced or crumbled
2 tablespoons diced tomatoes (optional)
4 to 6 ounces Gruyère, Emmental,
    or Beaufort cheese, sliced

♦♦Spread the baguette slices lightly with a thin layer of the butter. Place the slices on a broiling pan, then sprinkle with the white wine, half the garlic, the nutmeg, the blue cheese, and the optional tomatoes. Finish with a layer of white cheese.

♦♦Sprinkle with the remaining garlic, then broil until the cheese melts and the edges of the bread become toasty, crisp, and browned.

♦♦Serve right away.

TARTINE AU CHÈVRE CHAUD

PROVENÇAL

HOT GOAT CHEESE

ON GARLIC TOASTS

WITH COLD TOMATO SALAD

– Serves 4 –

When tomatoes are ripe and flavorful, try this simple fresh goat cheese canapé that food writer Sue Kreitzman prepared for me recently. (As a specialist in low-fat cookery, she didn't brush the canapés with olive oil. Being a glutton, I could not resist adding it.) Sue served roasted whole garlic cloves on the side–sublime.

6 flavorful ripe tomatoes, sliced lengthwise
Salt for sprinkling
8 thin diagonal slices baguette
Olive oil for brushing
1 to 2 garlic cloves, halved
4 ounces fresh white goat cheese at room
   temperature
Several fresh basil leaves, thinly sliced

✦✦Sprinkle the tomatoes with salt and refrigerate.
✦✦Brush the baguettes with olive oil and toast on both sides until golden, then rub each side with garlic.
✦✦Spread the crisp toasts with goat cheese. Arrange 2 on each plate and top with some of the tomato slices. Serve right away, sprinkled with basil.

CHÈVRE CHAUD

AU BEURRE ROUGE

HOT GOAT CHEESE ON TOAST

WITH RED WINE BUTTER SAUCE

– Serves 4 –

One winter weekend we headed for the Saturday marketplace at the little port of Boulogne on the northern coast. By evening, our purchases were stashed away and we were starving. As we wandered through the cobbled streets on that miserable night, looking for dinner, the only restaurant open did not look promising. The tables were empty and the decor had seen better days.

But we were hungry and walked right in.

Within moments of being handed the menu, an overeager chef was sitting at our table offering his advice. We were his only customers and he was frighteningly ready to feed us. Did we like goat cheese? he asked. We timidly answered "Yes . . ."

Then he brought us a plate of goat cheese melted on toast with *beurre rouge*. It was astonishingly good. The night was still cold and damp, the decor was beginning to look charming rather than faded, and our spirits were high with the thrill of good food.

The dish is quick to toss together once the *beurre rouge* is made. Adding balsamic vinegar is a modern twist; its slightly sweet winey flavor deliciously lifts the traditional sauce.

8 baguette slices
8 to 12 ounces aged goat cheese with rind
   (Bucheron, Lezay, or a chabis such as
   Saint-Loup)
4 tablespoons cold butter, cut into small
   pieces
1 shallot, minced
1 garlic clove, minced
½ cup dry red wine such as Pinot Noir,
   Cabernet Sauvignon, Burgundy, Merlot,
   Zinfandel
2 tablespoons balsamic vinegar
Salt, pepper, and sugar to taste if necessary
⅔ to 1 cup young mâche or mixed baby
   greens
2 tablespoons minced fresh chervil

✦✦Preheat the broiler. Place the bread slices on a broiler pan. Broil one side of the bread and remove from the broiler. Slice the goat cheese and arrange it on the untoasted side of the bread. Dot the tops with 1 tablespoon of the butter and set aside.

✦✦In a small saucepan, combine the shallot, garlic, and wine and bring to a boil. Cook over high heat until reduced to about 3 tablespoons, then stir in the balsamic vinegar.

✦✦Reduce heat to very low, season with salt, pepper, and a pinch of sugar, if needed, and whisk in the remaining 3 tablespoons butter until the sauce thickens slightly. Remove from heat.

✦✦Broil until the cheese lightly browns in spots. Cut each slice of toast into quarters or halves.

✦✦To serve, spoon some of the hot sauce onto warm plates. Top the sauce with the hot goat cheese toasts and garnish with a scattering of mâche or baby greens and chervil.

✦✦Serve right away.

CERVELLES DES CANUTS

GARLIC-SEASONED
FRESH CHEESE

– Serves 3 or 4 –

In Burgundian bistros, this irresistable fresh cheese mixed with garlic and herbs might be served in a little pot as a prelude to the meal, or after the meal as the cheese course. In the Savoy, a similar mixture is warmed and spooned over boiled potatoes as a first course or supper dish.

To serve as a first course, garnish the cheese with a sprig or two of fresh thyme and serve it surrounded by a dish of raw and cooked vegetables, such as Salade Aixoise (pages 46–47).

8 ounces fromage frais, or a mixture of half
*   ricotta cheese and half sour cream*
2 to 3 tablespoons butter at room
*   temperature*
2 garlic cloves, minced

2 tablespoons minced fresh chives
2 tablespoons minced fresh parsley
½ teaspoon minced fresh dill or a pinch
*   of dried dill weed*
½ teaspoon minced fresh tarragon or a
*   pinch of dried tarragon*
Salt and pepper to taste
½ teaspoon fresh lemon juice or to taste

✦✦Combine the fromage frais or ricotta cheese mixture with the butter and mix well. Add the garlic and herbs, then season with salt, pepper, and lemon juice.

✦✦Cover and refrigerate until ready to use. For a firmer, more spreadable consistency, place the cheese mixture in a cheesecloth-lined strainer and suspend it over a bowl for several hours, checking every so often to pour off the liquid that trickles out.

✦✦This zesty mixture is at its best prepared at least 1 day ahead and lasts up to 1 week in the refrigerator.

CHEESE FOR DESSERT

There is nothing quite as enticing, quite as—well, quite as French—as ending a meal with cheese.

It keeps you satisfied with eating smaller portions, and it is a delightful way to finish your red wine. A chunk or two of cheese, eaten with knife and fork, while sipping the last of your Bordeaux, or Cahors, or Côtes-du-Rhone, is a rare pleasure.

Mousse au Chèvre Frais (Seasoned Fresh Goat Cheese from the Pyrenees) Use olive oil instead of butter, and fresh white goat cheese instead of ricotta. Season with dried herbes de Provence and/or dried thyme instead of dill weed and tarragon.

Fromage Frais de Biot (Fresh Cheese with Assorted Provençal Flavorings) In a little *auberge* in the Provençal village of Biot, the fromage frais was brought to the table and served with a variety of little bowls, each filled with various ingredients: local lavender honey, sugar, a mixture of minced fresh herbs: chives, chervil, and tarragon. The diner can mix these ingredients as he or she likes, creating either a savory or sweet cheese.

Le Fromage Blanc Niçoise (Fresh Cheese, Niçoise Style) Add a finely chopped green bell pepper and chopped fresh basil to taste.

FROMAGE DE BREBIS

SHEEP'S MILK CHEESE

WITH ONIONS

– Serves 4 –

I was recently served the following little plate for dessert in a funky Parisian bistro-bar. It was my birthday, and the owner-waiter pulled a poster off his wall and rolled it up as a gift, handed me a long-stemmed rose, and grabbed me and bestowed a big smacking kiss. My husband was frightened the fellow would kiss him next, and he just might have, but a slender wraith of a woman suddenly stood up and began to sing in a clear, hauntingly beautiful voice,

and we all joined in. (The cheese was such a wonderful finish to our meal that I ate my husband's plateful as well.)

Use any fresh, slightly salty sheep's milk cheese; feta is fine as long as it's sheep's milk feta. Soaking removes the excess saltiness; soak longer if your feta is quite salty. If it's mild and not salty, you need not soak it at all.

8 ounces sheep's milk feta or other fresh sheep cheese
½ red onion, chopped
2 to 4 tablespoons olive oil
¼ teaspoon paprika
A few fresh parsley leaves

✦✦ Cut the cheese into 4 thick slices and put in a nonreactive pan with cold water to cover. Let sit for 30 minutes to 2 hours, depending on how salty the cheese is.

✦✦ Drain and pat the cheese dry with paper towels. Place each slice on a plate and scatter with onion, drizzle with oil, sprinkle with paprika, and garnish with parsley.

Fromage de Brebis au Melon (Fresh Sheep Cheese with Melon) In summer when the weather is sultry, omit the onion, paprika, and olive oil garnish, and omit soaking the feta–you want it salty to refresh you in the heat. Serve shards of the salty white sheep cheese with wedges of iced sweet melon: watermelon, Cavaillon, honeydew, or another favorite. Serve with a chilled Tavel or Bandol rosé.

THE CHEESE BOARD

A cheese board can consist of one large cheese, aged to its state of milky perfection, such as one unctuous Vacherin, served in its round wooden box with the crust removed to expose the soft cheese. Offer spoons and crisp bread to spread the cheese onto. A tiny plate of two or three cheeses gives the diners a selection and variety, and is good with a garnish of salad, or perhaps fruit and nuts, or a little pot of butter for the stronger cheeses.

The cheese board can also be a delight of largesse, a sumptuous selection of types of cheese, set either on a tray or a basket. Or, for a truly lavish selection, sometimes restaurants will have a *chariot de fromages,* or a cart of trays filled with an irresistible variety of cheeses. At my favorite, a big flat basket is toted from diner to diner at the end of the meal, the wondrous assortment thrilling to choose from. Madame cuts off a slice of this one, murmurs something about that one, encourages me to taste just a sliver from the one right here, in its perfect state.

For any cheese board, remove the cheeses from the refrigerator at least 1 hour before serving and arrange them on a bed of edible leaves such as grape, citrus, or fig, if possible.

Encourage each guest to begin his or her tasting with the mildest cheese and finish with the most pungent. Cheese should be cut in such a way so as not to interfere with the integrity of the cheese's shape and to ensure that each diner gets a similar shape and ratio of inside to crust.

Whether or not to eat the crust is a matter of personal taste. Many think it's the best part; how bland Camembert and Brie would be without their crusts! Aged hard cheeses, however, generally have crusts that are hard to chew and are not really edible.

The glory of the cheese board needs no artifice, though a few bunches of grapes or pears make a fresh counterpoint, and a slice or two of bread or some crisp crackers are always welcome. Fine cheese needs only to be presented in its finest state and savored for its complex depth of flavor.

Here are three suggested cheese boards:

Vignottes or Saint-Andre, a chunk of Roquefort, goat Camembert, ash chèvre, pungent Mariolles, fresh bouton-de-Culotte, and perhaps a Pont l'Evêque.

Sheep cheese from the Pyrenees, Livarot, Pelardon, cabécou de Rocamadour (sheep or goat), and blue fourme d'Ambert.

Saint-Marcellin, Reblochon, bleu d'Auvergne, Brie or Coulommiers, Beaufort, and several chèvres ranging from young to aged and crumbly.

les pains

CHÈVRE FRAIS À LA SAUCE DE NOIX AU JUS DE CÉLERI

GOAT CHEESE IN WALNUT SAUCE WITH CELERY VINAIGRETTE

– Serves 4 –

Walnuts and celery are delicious paired with fresh milky chèvre in this dish from the Dordogne. Goat cheese shares the plate with a rich walnut sauce, suave celery juice, and a crunchy relish of celery and vinaigrette. You could, of course, simplify the dish and serve the chèvre simply resting on a plate drizzled with walnut oil and sherry vinegar, and garnished with celery, herbs, walnuts.

> *2 tablespoons minced mixed fresh herbs:*
>   *chervil, chives, tarragon, thyme, parsley*
> *¼ cup walnut pieces*
> *½ shallot, minced*
> *½ garlic clove, minced*
> *¼ cup heavy cream*
> *Salt and pepper to taste*
> *1 celery stalk with its leaves, finely*
>   *chopped*
> *3 tablespoons water*
> *2 tablespoons walnut oil*
> *1 tablespoon sherry vinegar*
> *Salt and pepper to taste*
> *4 small round fresh or slightly aged goat*
>   *cheeses, each weighing about 2 to 3*
>   *ounces*

✦✦ Make the walnut sauce by combining 1 tablespoon of the mixed herbs with the walnuts, shallot, garlic, and cream in a blender or food processor. Purée until smooth. Add salt and pepper and set aside.

✦✦ Combine half the celery and its leaves in a small saucepan with 3 tablespoons water. Bring to a boil, then remove from heat. In a blender or food processor, purée to juice. Strain and set aside.

✦✦ Combine the remaining celery with the remaining herbs, the walnut oil, and vinegar. Season with salt and pepper.

✦✦ Place a goat cheese on each plate and garnish the plate with several spoonfuls of walnut sauce, celery vinaigrette, and a drizzle of celery juice.

PLATEAU DES FROMAGES ET SALADE PAYSANNE

AN ASSORTMENT OF COUNTRY CHEESES WITH SALAD AND WALNUTS

– Serves 4 –

A tangle of lightly dressed greens and crisp walnuts is the perfect accent for that bistro standby, a plate of luscious cheeses. I was served the following plate recently in Paris, with a slice or two of slightly brown pain levain alongside, and the last of the dinner's wine.

> *1 Pelardon cheese or other small, slightly*
>   *aged goat cheese*
> *½ to 1 goat Camembert cheese or a ripe*
>   *brie*
> *½ to 1 brebis, Felicien, or Saint-Marcellin*
>   *cheese or other runny sheep's milk*
>   *cheese with an aromatic rind*
> *1 Chabis Saint-Loup cheese or fresh mild*
>   *goat cheese*

2 to 3 handfuls mixed baby greens

1 tablespoon walnut oil or as desired

¼ teaspoon strong Dijon mustard

1 teaspoon white wine or raspberry vinegar (for a milder dressing, use a sherry vinegar)

2 tablespoons walnut pieces

✦✦ Cut the cheeses into equal portions as desired and arrange them around the outside of 4 chilled plates.

✦✦ Toss the baby greens with the walnut oil. Mix the mustard and vinegar together, then toss with the greens.

✦✦ Place a portion of salad in the middle of each plate, then sprinkle with the walnuts.

✦✦ Serve right away.

MOUSSE DE FROMAGE BLANC ET EAU DE FLEURS D'ORANGER

SWEET WHITE CHEESE WITH ORANGE FLOWER WATER

– Serves 4 –

This simple sweet sometimes appears in homey little bistros in Corsica or in the hill country behind Nice. It is little more than a delicate low-fat white cheese, sweetened and whipped to a fluffy consistency, then flavored with orange flower water or grappa, the Italian brandy. If available, serve the little cheeses with a garnish of fragrant orange flowers.

In France, a good fromage frais of cow's, sheep's, or goat's milk would be my choice; in the United States I usually use ricotta cheese beaten with sour cream, as below.

1 cup (8 ounces) ricotta cheese

⅓ cup sour cream

3 to 5 tablespoons sugar

1 to 2 teaspoons orange flower water or grappa or to taste

Fresh orange blossoms for garnish (optional)

✦✦ In a blender or food processor, purée the ricotta cheese with the sour cream until it forms a smooth, thick cream.

✦✦ Stir in the sugar and flower water or grappa. Cover and refrigerate for at least 1 hour, or until ready to serve. Garnish with the flowers, if you like.

Niçoise Fromage au Café (Coffee-Scented Cheese "Mousse") Instead of orange flower water or grappa, flavor the sweetened cheese with a spoonful or two of cooled very strong espresso coffee.

Délice de Fromage et Fruit (Concoction of Sweet Cheese, Soaked Cake, and Fruit) For a more elaborate dessert of layered soaked cake, fruit, and sweet cheese, prepare the ricotta and sour cream as above, sweetening it to taste and flavoring it with brandy and vanilla. Soak slices of sponge cake in brandy and fruit juice, syrup, or coffee, then layer with the sweetened cheese and sliced fruit of choice: Sweet peaches, pears, or berries are most delicious. Cover and refrigerate for at least 1 hour. Serve topped with chopped unsalted pistachio nuts.

Brie au "Pumpernickel" (Brie or Camembert and Black Bread) Toast thinly sliced black bread or pumpernickel until crisp, then top with a thick layering of Brie or Culommiers. Place under a preheated broiler just long enough to warm the cheese, not to melt it.

Fromage Chèvre à la Don Camillo (Goat Cheese with Sun-Dried Tomato, Balsamic Vinegar, Olive Oil, and Thyme) In Nice's Don Camillo, the chic little bistro that serves a personal rendition of the local cuisine that I can only describe as "thrilling," my cheese course was a tiny round of absolutely perfect goat cheese topped with a few shreds of sun-dried tomato and a sprig or two of fresh thyme. The plate was sprinkled with drops of balsamic vinegar, Jackson Pollack style, and a cruet of olive oil accompanied it all, to drizzle on as desired.

Tartines de Rigotte de Condrieu au Thym (Crisp Melted Cheese with Thyme on Little Toasts) Brush thin slices of baguette with olive oil and broil until crisp and golden on each side. Top with little slices of the Lyonnaise cow's-milk cheese Rigotte de Condrieu, sprinkle with minced fresh thyme, then broil until the cheese melts. If Rigotte de Condrieu is not available, use Saint-Marcellin or Port-Salut.

Fromage, Noix, et Compote de Fruits (Cheese Board with Soaked Dried Fruit and Toasted Nuts) Soak dried apricots, golden raisins, and/or prunes in hot tea to cover until they plump, then drain (save the liquid for another use) and pour Armagnac over them. Let soak for at least 1 hour.

Serve a selection of aged fresh cheeses on a plate: perhaps one of each, and garnish with several of the plumped fruits and a scattering of toasted almonds or pistachio nuts.

Coings Glacés au Parmesan (Preserved Quinces with Parmesan) Serve slices of preserved quince with a chunk of Parmesan or other aged cheese, and let each person cut into both as desired, pairing the sweet preserved fruit with the salty cheese.

Fromage Frais au Miel de Lavande (Fresh White Cheese with Lavender Honey) Drizzle fromage frais, Mexican queso fresco, or a fresh Greek mizithra) with lavender honey and scatter with the petals of edible blossoms. (To make lavender honey: Gently combine about ½ cup honey and several pinches of lavender blossoms in a jar. Cover tightly and submerge about halfway to the top in hot water in a saucepan. When the honey melts, remove it from heat and let cool. Let sit for several days, then reheat gently and strain.)

Fromage Pain de Noix, Raisins (Cheese Board with Walnut Bread and a Selection of Grapes) Serve sourdough walnut bread with a pungent semi-soft or monastery-type cheese such as Sainte-Nectaire, tomme de Savoie, or the strongly scented Livarot. Garnish with a selection of grapes, such as tiny purple Champagne grapes, Red Flame or fragrant Muscat.

Chèvre Frais au Armagnac (Fresh Gascon Goat Cheese with Armagnac) Sweeten a fresh goat cheese (or fresh goat cheese mixed with ricotta or sour cream) to taste and flavor it with Armagnac.

Desserts

♦♦♦

Desserts

The moment comes when you have nibbled hors d'oeuvre, eaten your first course and main plate, and perhaps a few bits of cheese. You do, however, have just enough space left for a sweet finish. As you're handed the dessert menu, the waiter or waitress asks: *"Comme dessert?"* ("What would you like for dessert?")

The word *dessert* comes from the French word *desservir,* to clear or take away, signifying the clearing of the table before the sweet dish is brought in.

La confiture

Desserts in bistros tend to be homey and rustic. You might find baked apples or poached pears, chocolate mousse or fruit compote; in more fashionable bistros, however, desserts are more elaborate: tarts, ice creams, and fresh fruit macerated in liqueurs or wine in the summer, baked with sweet cookie crumbs in the winter.

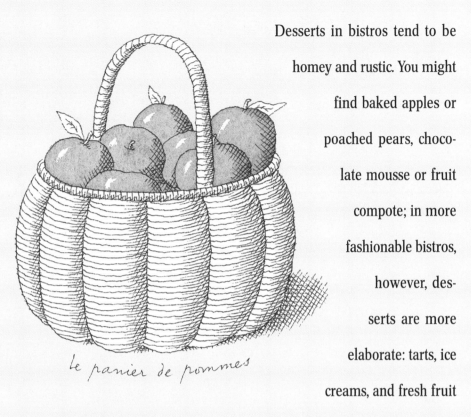

le panier de pommes

Since I can never decide on dessert (and often opt to finish with cheese), I admit to sticking my spoon into everyone else's dessert for a taste. But in Burgundy I discovered a course close to my heart: the dessert *dégustation.* Tiny portions of dessert, beginning with a bright fruit dish, then meandering through custardy, chocolatey, pastry and/or ice cream delights. Then there is that dessert *chariot* at Paris's Chez Eux . . .

PISTACHIO TART

WITH ALMOND-CITRUS CRUST

– Serves 6 to 8 –

A crisp crust of citrus-scented ground almonds filled with puréed pistachio nuts makes an unusual tart. Since it is so rich, a fresh berry coulis or tart sorbet is a good accompaniment.

CRUST
1 cup plus 1 tablespoon all-purpose flour
3 tablespoons ground blanched almonds
¼ cup sugar
Pinch of salt
Grated zest of 1 orange and 1 lemon
6 tablespoons unsalted butter
1 egg yolk
Juice of ¼ lemon

FILLING
⅔ cup (5 ounces) pistachio nuts, ground
1 cup milk
½ cup heavy cream
3 tablespoons unsalted butter
8 tablespoons sugar
1 tablespoon cornstarch
3 egg yolks
½ teaspoon almond extract
2 egg whites
*Crème Anglaise, whipped cream, or ice
   cream for serving*

✦✦ To make the crust: Using either your fingers or a pastry cutter, combine the flour, almonds, sugar, and salt, then mix in the orange and lemon zests, butter, egg yolk, and lemon juice. The mixture should be crumblike but hold together when pressed; if it does not, add a tiny amount–beginning with no more than 1 teaspoon–of cold water. When the mixture just holds together, wrap it in plastic and refrigerate for at least 1 hour.

✦✦ To make the filling: Grind the pistachio nuts in a blender or food processor until they form a fine meal; set aside.

✦✦ Combine the milk, cream, butter, and 6 tablespoons of the sugar in a small, heavy saucepan. Heat over medium-low heat until the butter melts, then stir in the ground pistachio nuts, cornstarch, and egg yolks. Heat to medium and cook, stirring, until the mixture slightly thickens. Remove from heat, stir in the almond extract, and set aside.

✦✦ Beat the egg whites until foamy, then add the remaining 2 tablespoons sugar and beat until stiff, glossy peaks are formed. Stir one third of the egg whites into the pistachio mixture, lightening the pistachio mixture with about one third of the egg, then fold in the remainder.

✦✦ Preheat the oven to 375°F.

✦✦ On a lightly floured board, flatten the chilled dough with a rolling pin, then roll the dough out to a 20-inch circle. Fit the dough into a 12-inch tart pan, wetting the edges and piecing it together if it falls apart. Trim the edges.

✦✦ Carefully pour the filling into tart crust, then bake for about 40 minutes, or until puffed and browned.

✦✦ Let cool to room temperature, then refrigerate for at least 2 hours.

✦✦ Serve the tart cut into small slices, with crème anglaise, gently whipped cream, or ice cream.

TARTE AUX PÊCHES ET CERISES

PEACH AND CHERRY TART

WITH ALMOND PASTE

– Makes one 9-inch tart –

Here, a layer of almond paste is topped with the fruit of the season. While peaches and cherries are quintessential summer fare, nectarines and raspberries, apricots and blackberries are also; in autumn, pears are a traditional bistro favorite.

1 cup almond paste
1 egg, lightly beaten
¾ cup sugar
½ teaspoon almond extract
One 9-inch unbaked tart shell (page 203)
4 fresh peaches, halved and pitted
1 cup fresh dark red or black cherries,
*   stemmed and pitted*
2 tablespoons unsalted butter, melted

✦✦Preheat the oven to 375°F.

✦✦Blend together the almond paste, egg, ½ cup of the sugar, and ¼ teaspoon of the almond extract until smooth.

✦✦Spread the filling over the bottom of the tart shell. Top with the peaches and cherries. Brush the fruit with the melted butter and sprinkle with the remaining ¼ teaspoon almond extract and remaining ¼ cup sugar.

✦✦Bake for 1 hour, or until the crust is golden and the fruit is tender.

Tarte aux Poires **(Pear Tart)** Use 4 to 6 cored, peeled, and sliced firm but ripe pears in place of the peaches and cherries. Choose a fragrant pear like the Bartlett.

TARTE TATIN À L'ANANAS

FRESH PINEAPPLE TARTE TATIN

– Serves 6 –

This tart combines the appeal of two traditional upside-down desserts: the French tarte Tatin, with its crust baked on top, and the American pineapple upside-down cake. The fruit stews in its own juices, gilded with butter and sugar, to form a delicate caramelized sauce.

Mint has a particular affinity for pineapple; here its freshness lightens the sweetness of the tart. Serve the pastry with a refreshing mint sorbet, if you like.

3 to 4 tablespoons unsalted butter
3 to 4 tablespoons packed light brown
*   sugar*
½ ripe pineapple, peeled, cored, and thinly
*   sliced*
¼ to ½ teaspoon vanilla extract
Pastry for a tart shell (pages 202–203)
5 to 8 leaves fresh mint, thinly sliced

✦✦Preheat the oven to 400°F. Melt the butter in the bottom of a heavy 12-inch skillet and sprinkle with the sugar. Caramelize slightly over low heat, then remove from heat.

✦✦Arrange the pineapple in a single layer in the carmelized mixture and sprinkle with the vanilla extract.

✦✦On a lightly floured board, roll out the dough to form a 15-inch circle. Place the dough on top of the pineapple and tuck it in around the edges of the fruit.

✦✦Bake until golden brown, with brown splotches in places, 25 to 30 minutes.

✦✦Loosen the edges of the crust from the sides of the pan. Place a plate on top of the tart and invert it onto the plate, giving a firm hit to the bottom of the pan to make sure that all of the pineapple comes off onto the tart. If it doesn't, just arrange it with your fingers. Drizzle any glaze from the bottom of the pan onto the tart. ✦✦ Serve, sprinkled with the thin shreds of fresh mint.

Tarte Tatin de Pêche (*Peach Tarte Tatin with Sweet Basil*) Instead of fresh pineapple, use 4 to 5 peeled and sliced peaches and prepare according to the above recipe. Garnish with leaves of fresh basil in place of the mint.

Tarte Tatin aux Brugnons (*Nectarine Tarte Tatin with Apricot Coulis*) Prepare the tarte Tatin as above using 4 to 5 unpeeled sliced nectarines and serve in a puddle of apricot coulis (pages 205–206).

BABAS AU MIEL ET RHUM

HONEY-RUM YEAST CAKES

– Makes 8 to 12, serves 4 to 6 –

These little yeast-risen cakes are quintessential Parisian bistro fare, arriving at your table with a variety of flourishes and variations. At Chez Paul, the babas are filled with jam and flambéed; at Monde des Chimères, they are accompanied with juicy wedges of fresh orange. At Polidor, the babas sit in a pool of custard, and at Les Gourmets des Ternes, a whole bottle of rum is brought to your table, to pour over your babas as you like.

Babas were concocted in the town of Nancy by Stanislas Lescyska, the former king of Poland who was also Louis XV's father-in-law.

Though sumptuous, babas are easy to prepare.

La baguette

¼ cup milk
4 tablespoons butter
1 package active dry yeast
¼ cup warm (105° to 115°F) water
2 egg yolks
1 egg
¼ cup sugar
1 teaspoon grated lemon zest
1 to 3 tablespoons dark raisins, golden
    raisins, or dried cherries
1¾ cups unbleached all-purpose flour

SYRUP
½ cup honey
½ cup sugar
1 cup water
1 cinnamon stick
Almond or vanilla extract
½ cup dark rum

GARNISH
Whipped cream or ice cream
About 1 cup fresh fruit: sliced peaches,
    berries, sliced apricots

♦♦ Scald the milk; remove from heat and stir in the butter. Set aside.

♦♦ Sprinkle the yeast into the lukewarm water, then stir and set it aside until foamy, about 5 minutes.

♦♦ Lightly beat the egg yolks, whole egg, and sugar together. Add the cooled milk mixture and the yeast mixture, then stir in the lemon zest, raisins or cherries, and flour.

♦♦ Place the dough in an oiled bowl and turn the dough to coat it. Cover and let rise, covered, in a warm place until doubled, about 1 hour.

♦♦ Stir the dough down and spoon it into buttered or nonstick muffin tins, filling the cups two-thirds full.

♦♦ Let rise in a warm place until the dough reaches the tops of the cups, about 30 minutes.

♦♦ While the dough is rising, preheat the oven to 350°F.

♦♦ Bake the babas for 15 to 20 minutes, or until they are golden and risen to a smooth round shape.

♦♦ While the babas are baking, make the syrup by boiling the honey, sugar, water, and cinnamon stick in a small, heavy saucepan until reduced to about ½ cup. Remove from heat and stir in the almond or vanilla extract and rum. Remove the cinnamon stick and set aside.

♦♦ Unmold the babas and transfer to a shallow pan. Prick the bottoms with a fork or a bamboo skewer and pour the hot syrup over them. The little holes will help them absorb the liquid. Use the leftover syrup to baste onto the babas as they cool.

♦♦ Serve with a dollop of whipped cream or ice cream and fresh fruit.

FONDANTS AU CHOCOLAT

WARM LITTLE CHOCOLATE CAKES

– Serves 4 –

These exquisite soufflélike concoctions are irresistibly chocolatey. They are wonderful warm, when they sigh at the first spoonful, and just as good at room temperature, when they have fallen into a deep and dense swoon, with crisp, ethereally light edges and fudgey insides.

Serve in a puddle of heavy cream or a dollop of unsweetened whipped cream, with a few tart fresh berries around the edge of the plate. Or, for a completely indulgent chocolate experience, try assembling a *tout chocolat* (see page 188), in which the little cakes are surrounded by an array of other luscious chocolatey foods.

> 5 tablespoons unsalted butter
> 5½ ounces semisweet chocolate, chopped
> Pinch of salt
> 5 tablespoons unsweetened cocoa powder
> ½ cup sugar
> 1 teaspoon vanilla extract
> 3 egg whites

♦♦ Preheat the oven to 400°F.

♦♦ Melt the butter in a small saucepan over low heat, then stir in the chocolate, salt, cocoa, and 3 tablespoons of the sugar. Stir until the chocolate mixture is smooth. If it is slightly grainy, do not worry, as this will not affect the final result. Remove from heat and stir in the vanilla. Set aside.

♦♦ Beat the egg whites with the 2 tablespoons sugar until stiff, glossy peaks form.

♦♦ Lighten the chocolate mixture by folding in a third of the egg whites, then fold this mixture into the remaining egg whites, as if you were making a soufflé.

♦♦Butter 4 to 6 custard molds and sprinkle with 1 tablespoon sugar. Spoon about 2 tablespoons of the chocolate mixture into each mold, so that they fill the cups by about two thirds.

♦♦Place the molds in the oven and bake for 8 to 10 minutes, or until puffy.

♦♦Serve right away or let cool and chill before serving.

Sauce au Chocolat et Café (Bittersweet Coffee-Chocolate Sauce) Heat ½ cup strong coffee in a small saucepan with 1 tablespoon confectioners' sugar. When the coffee is bubbling around the edges, remove from heat and stir in 6 ounces chopped bittersweet chocolate until the chocolate has dissolved, then stir in 1 or 2 tablespoons heavy cream and mix well. Season with vanilla extract, a tiny pinch of salt, and confectioners' sugar to taste, if it is needed.

Tout Chocolat (A Plate of Chocolate Delicacies) Serve the little cakes as part of a plateful of chocolate treats. Prepare the plate by sifting confectioners' sugar or cocoa powder around the edge to form a border. Place a puddle of bittersweet chocolate sauce in the middle of the plate and set an unmolded cool *fondant au chocolat* on it. Place a small scoop of slightly bitter good-quality coffee ice cream on one side of the plate, alongside a drift of whipped cream that has been slightly sweetened and enriched with a little brandy. Decorate the plate with a few bits of chocolate whimsy: chocolate-covered espresso beans, chocolate twigs, shaved dark chocolate.

Chocolat et Framboises (Chocolate and Raspberries) Serve Fondants au Chocolat (page 187), in pools of chocolate sauce and raspberry coulis (page 190), accompanied with a scoop of dark chocolate ice cream and a scattering of fresh raspberries. Garnish with more chocolate: a crisp candy, a grating of bittersweet chocolate around the edge of the plate, etc.

PETITS SOUFFLÉS DES FRUITS

LITTLE FRUIT SOUFFLÉS

– Serves 6 –

Areas famous for their fruits give their names to many soufflés: Wild strawberries make a simple soufflé a soufflé Plougastel, bananas become a soufflé antillais, and peaches a soufflé rouissillonnais.

Cherries, apricots, peaches, ripe pears–all are luscious made into soufflés. No matter which fruit you use, it is simply crushed with a little sugar, mixed with the egg yolks, then folded into beaten egg whites and baked. A simple trick to make both soufflé and sauce is to reserve half of the mashed fruit to serve as a coulis.

> *6 to 8 tablespoons sugar*
> *6 eggs, separated*
> *Pinch of salt*
> *2 cups fresh fruit of choice, or a combination: raspberries, strawberries, apricots, peaches, bananas, kiwi, blackberries, etc.*
> *½ teaspoon vanilla extract, or ¼ teaspoon vanilla and ¼ teaspoon almond extract*
> *Crème fraiche or whipped cream for serving (optional)*

♦♦Preheat the oven to 425°F.

♦♦Butter 6 individual soufflé dishes and sprinkle the insides evenly with 2 tablespoons sugar, turning them so that the sugar coats all of the sides, then tipping out the excess. Set aside.

✦✦ Beat the egg whites with the salt until they form stiff, glossy peaks.

✦✦ Mash the fruit with a fork or masher; add the remaining sugar and vanilla or almond extract. Reserve half the fruit mixture to serve as a coulis and mix the rest with the yolks.

✦✦ Stir one third of the egg whites into the fruit mixture, then fold this lightened fruit mixture into the rest of the egg whites. Gently pour into the prepared soufflé dishes.

✦✦ Bake for 40 minutes, or until the soufflés have risen and turned golden. While the soufflés are baking, purée the reserved mashed fruit to make a coulis.

✦✦ Serve the soufflés with the fruit coulis and a little crème fraîche or lightly whipped cream, if desired.

CRÊPES AU FROMAGE
À L'ALSACIENNE

BAKED CHEESE CRÊPES

– Serves 4 –

These tender crêpes, filled with raisins and creamy cheese, sizzling in butter, and fragrant with cinnamon sugar, are reminiscent of childhood blintzes, albeit very light and delicate ones. Alsace once housed a large Jewish community, whose origins in Eastern Europe had a distinct influence on its cuisine, especially its sweets. This dish of crêpes is reminiscent of Jewish cheese-filled blintzes.

This hearty and warming wintertime dessert is also elegant and lovely served with a Cham-pagne or a chilled sweet wine such as a late-harvest Riesling.

> ¼ cup golden raisins
> 3 tablespoons Marsala, Madeira, or port
> 1 cup ricotta cheese
> ¼ cup sour cream
> 5 tablespoons sugar
> 3 egg yolks, lightly beaten
> 8 crêpes (pages 203–204)
> Ground cinnamon for sprinkling
> 1 to 2 tablespoons butter

✦✦ Combine the raisins and spirits in a small saucepan and place over medium-high heat. When bubbles form around the edge of the pan, remove from heat. Let sit for about 15 minutes, or long enough for the raisins to plump up.

✦✦ Mix the ricotta cheese and sour cream with 4 tablespoons of the sugar, stirring to mix well. Mix in the egg yolks and stir until smooth.

✦✦ Drain the raisins, saving any soaking liquid to drizzle on top of the crêpes. Add the drained raisins to the cheese mixture.

✦✦ Preheat the oven to 375°F.

✦✦ Into a buttered 12-by-18-inch gratin dish, spoon about a quarter of the cheese mixture, then fill each crêpe with

Les brioches et le croissant

about 2 tablespoons of the remaining cheese mixture, then roll it up to enclose. Since it is very soft, you will have to work quickly once the crêpes are filled. Arrange each stuffed crêpe in the pan to make a single layer. If any of the cheese leaks out of the crêpes, just let it bake along with the filled crêpes.

◆◆If there is any leftover cheese mixture, pour it between the filled crêpes. Sprinkle the top of the crêpes with the remaining 1 tablespoon sugar, and the cinnamon, and dot it with butter. If there is any leftover soaking liquid, drizzle a tiny amount onto the top of the crêpes.

◆◆Bake the cheese-stuffed crêpes for 25 to 30 minutes, or until the top of the crêpes are sizzling and lightly browned. Eat right away, hot and sizzling.

ILES FLOTTANTES, COULIS

À LA FRAMBOISE

POACHED MERINGUES

WITH RASPBERRY COULIS

AND PISTACHIO NUTS

– Serves 4 –

Little islands of meringue, floating in a pool of raspberry coulis, are garnished with crushed pistachio nuts and a scattering of rose petals in this dreamy dessert. *Iles Flottantes* are classically served in a pool of crème anglaise, but more and more often you will find this replaced by an elegant fresh-fruit coulis.

If your islands turn out a little flat, don't worry–they will still taste quite nice.

RASPBERRY COULIS

2 cups fresh raspberries

½ cup sugar

2 tablespoons framboise or other berry liqueur

6 egg whites

1¼ cups sugar

Pinch of salt

½ cup water

⅓ cup unsalted pistachio nuts, coarsely chopped

Petals from 2 unsprayed roses (optional)

◆◆To make the coulis: In a blender or food processor, purée the raspberries. Add the ½ cup sugar and liqueur. If desired, strain this mixture to eliminate the seeds. Cover and refrigerate.

◆◆Beat the egg whites with the salt until foamy. Gradually beat in ¾ cup of the sugar to form stiff, glossy peaks.

◆◆Fill a large skillet with water and bring it to a boil; reduce heat to simmering. Using a ladle or a deep spoon, gently form a ball of beaten egg white. Ease the meringue mixture off the spoon or ladle into the simmering water. Cook on each side for about 1 minute, then transfer to paper towels to drain. They will deflate somewhat. Repeat to use all the beaten whites.

◆◆To make the caramel: Combine the remaining ½ cup sugar and the water in a small, heavy saucepan. Cook over medium-low heat until the sugar dissolves, then turns from golden to golden brown. Remove, let cool slightly, then drizzle a very thin stream over the egg whites. (Any extra can be drizzled over the bottom of a buttered copper bowl, or a buttered chilled pan, marble slab, or waxed paper. When cool, peel off the crisp caramel strands and use for another dish.)

✦✦To serve: Cover the bottom of 4 shallow bowls or plates with the raspberry coulis. Top with several poached meringues and garnish with a sprinkle of pistachios and a scattering of rose petals.

CHOCOLATE MOUSSE

– Serves 4 –

Some things, when they are good, cannot be bettered. I feel that way about chocolate mousse. But no little airy flights of whimsy, please–I like my chocolate mousse dark and strong like this one: unashamedly heavy, proudly and deliciously so.

Serve it in individual pots, each topped with a dollop of lightly whipped cream or crème fraîche.

6 ounces bittersweet chocolate, chopped
2 tablespoons strong brewed coffee
2 tablespoons unsalted butter
1 tablespoon heavy cream
2 eggs, separated
2 tablespoons sugar
Vanilla extract
Pinch of salt
4 to 6 tablespoons lightly whipped cream
  or crème fraîche

✦✦Combine the chocolate and coffee in a medium, heavy saucepan and heat over a medium-low heat until the coffee is hot and the chocolate starts to melt, about 5 minutes. Do not let the coffee boil or the chocolate could become grainy.
✦✦With a wooden spoon, stir the chocolate mixture until it is silken and shiny and well combined, then stir in the butter, cream, egg yolks, and 1 tablespoon of the sugar, mixing until it is well combined and shiny, then stir in the vanilla and set aside.

✦✦Beat the egg whites and salt until foamy, then gradually beat in the remaining 1 tablespoon sugar to form stiff, glossy peaks.
✦✦Stir one third of the beaten whites into the chocolate mixture, then fold the lightened chocolate into the remaining beaten whites.
✦✦Pour into individual pots, cover, and refrigerate until ready to serve.
✦✦Serve topped with a little whipped cream or crème fraîche.

MOUSSE OF PURÉED APPLES

WITH WHIPPED CREAM

– Serves 4 –

This little mousse tastes of Normandy's best: tender baked apples puréed with a bit of cream and Calvados. Any firm apple is good here, even apples you might not usually use for cooking, such as Golden Delicious; or you might try a combination of apples: one chosen for its flavor, another for its fragrance, another for its juice, and so forth.

6 firm apples such as Golden Delicious or
  Granny Smith
6 tablespoons honey
6 tablespoons sugar
1 teaspoon ground cinnamon
1 to 2 tablespoons butter
¼ cup crème fraîche or sour cream

¾ *cup heavy cream*
½ *teaspoon vanilla extract, or to taste*
1 *tablespoon Calvados or brandy (optional)*

♦♦Preheat the oven to 350°F.

♦♦Core the apples but do not peel them. Set them upright in a baking pan and fill the hollows with the honey, 3 tablespoons of the sugar, and the cinnamon. Dot with the butter and bake until tender, about 40 minutes. Let cool to the touch.

♦♦Chop the apples coarsely and purée them in a blender or food processor along with the crème fraîche or sour cream.

♦♦Beat the cream until it forms soft peaks; add the remaining 3 tablespoons sugar and beat to form stiff peaks.

♦♦Stir one third of the whipped cream into the apple–sour cream mixture, then fold this lightened apple mixture into the remaining whipped cream. Season with vanilla and Calvados or

La table de ferme

brandy, if using. Spoon the mousse into wine-glasses and serve right away, or refrigerate until ready to serve.

Mousse au Poire Williams **(Pear Mousse)** Substitute pears for the apples in the above recipe and the eau-de-vie Poire Williams for the Calvados. Serve the mousse surrounded by raspberry coulis (page 190) or Sauce au Chocolat et Café (page 188).

SOUPE AUX FRUITS DE FORÊT
À LA CRÈME
FRUIT OF THE FOREST SOUP
WITH CREAM

– Serves 4 –

There is something so comforting about eating a bowl of sweet berry soup. Sitting at the table, spooning up this soothing bowl of berries floating in sweet crimson cream, I felt so young, so full of my childhood that I was surprised to find my feet actually reached the floor.

This Gascon favorite can be made with or without cream. The cranberry juice is my adaptation; the original uses all wine.

1 *cup dry red wine*
1 *cup cranberry juice*
½ *cup fresh black or dark red cherries,*
   pitted
¼ *cup sugar*
½ *teaspoon cornstarch*
One 2-inch cinnamon stick
½ *teaspoon vanilla and/or almond extract*

2 cups mixed fresh berries
1 cup crème fraîche or equal amounts of
sour cream mixed with heavy cream

✦✦Combine the wine, cranberry juice, cherries, sugar, cornstarch, and cinnamon stick in a medium saucepan and bring to a boil. Reduce heat to a simmer and cook, stirring, until slightly thickened. Remove from heat and stir in the vanilla and/or almond extract. Let cool.

✦✦Mix the berries with the cooled cherry mixture and the crème fraîche or sour cream. Refrigerate for at least 2 hours. Remove the cinnamon stick and serve.

Soupe aux Fruits de Forêt (*Fruit of the Forest Soup*) You also can make the soup without the addition of cream and instead serve it with a scoop of ice cream. In Arles, a bowl was brought to me with a big spoonful of pastis-flavored ice cream. At home I scent the ice cream with cardamom, so sweetly fragrant with the berries. (To make either: Soften vanilla ice cream and mix in either 1 to 2 tablespoons of any type of pastis or anisette, or crushed cardamom seeds to taste. Return to the freezer until it is firm enough to scoop.)

POIRES AUX VIN ROUGE

POACHED PEARS IN RED WINE

– Serves 4 to 6 –

Pears, poached to a ruby red, are a classic dessert of bistro fare. This recipe takes the classic one step further and reduces the poaching liquid to a dark and deeply flavored syrup.

To further gild the lily, add a little cassis to the finished syrup.

Serve a whole pear, sitting upright, nestled beside a scoop of vanilla ice cream or frozen yogurt, or a drift of whipped cream.

4 to 6 ripe but firm Barlett pears, peeled
and cored but stems left on
1 bottle dry but fruity red wine such as
a Beaujolais or a Zinfandel
½ to ¾ cup sugar
1 cinnamon stick, or ¼ to ½ teaspoon
ground cinnamon
3 tablespoons brandy or Cognac
1 strip orange zest, or ⅛ teaspoon grated
orange zest
¼ teaspoon vanilla or almond extract
2 to 3 tablespoons crème de cassis
(optional)
Vanilla ice cream for serving

✦✦Put the pears in a heavy saucepan just large enough to accommodate them in one layer, then add the red wine, ½ cup sugar, cinnamon stick or cinnamon, brandy or Cognac, and orange zest.

✦✦Bring to a boil, then reduce heat, cover, and simmer for 20 to 30 minutes, or until the pears are just tender but still firm.

✦✦Set aside and let the pears cool in the poaching liquid.

✦✦Remove the pears from their poaching liquid; cover and chill.

✦✦Cook the poaching liquid over high heat until reduced to a thick, syrupy sauce.

✦✦Add the remaining ¼ cup sugar to balance the natural bitterness of the wine, if needed, then stir in the vanilla or almond extract and cassis, if using.

✦✦ Serve the pears drizzled with about half of the syrup, alongside a scoop of ice cream drizzled with more of the wine syrup.

Poires et Prunes au Vin Rouge **(Pears and Prunes in Red Wine)** When the pears are half tender, add 12 pitted prunes to the poaching liquid. Remove when you remove the pears, then serve the pears and prunes with ice cream, frozen yogurt, or whipped cream.

FRAISES AU CITRON

STRAWBERRIES

IN LEMON AND SUGAR

– Serves 4 –

This is the classic way to serve strawberries in any homey bistro, alongside a bowl or crock of crème fraîche to ladle on.

The simple combination of sugar and lemon juice makes a flavorful glaze that enhances the berries brilliantly. Since all berries vary according to their sweetness and acidity, you'll need to adjust the sugar and lemon juice to taste.

2 pints fresh strawberries, hulled and sliced
Juice of ½ lemon, or to taste
¼ cup sugar, or to taste
Crème fraîche or sour cream for serving

✦✦ Toss the strawberries with the lemon juice and sugar. Cover and chill until ready to serve, at least 30 minutes or up to 3 or 4 hours. Serve with crème fraîche or sour cream for topping.

RAISINS ET MELON BEAUMES

DE VENISE

MUSCAT GRAPES

AND HONEYDEW MELON WITH

BEAUMES DE VENISE

– Serves 4 to 6 –

Beaumes de Venise is one of the fragrant flowerlike Muscat wines so beloved throughout the south of France. You will see tasting signs for a wide variety of these wines along country roads in Provence and the Languedoc. They make a light and refreshing sweet to end a meal with, and are perfect with late-summer fruit such as the sweet local Cavaillon melons or the first grapes of the season. A handful of red summer berries, currants, or little purple grapes makes a nice color contrast to the pale green palette.

1 to 2 cups Muscat grapes
1 ripe sweet honeydew or other melon
½ cup Beaumes de Venise or other sweet
Muscat wine

✦✦ Cut the grapes into halves and remove their seeds.
✦✦ Peel the melon and remove its seeds; slice about ½ inch thick.
✦✦ Arrange the melon and grapes on plates or on a platter, then drizzle with Beaumes de Venise or other sweet Muscat wine and chill until ready to serve.

PAMPLEMOUSSE À LA MENTHE

GRAPEFRUIT WITH MINT

– Serves 4 to 6 –

Citrus fruit, stripped of its tough membranes and macerated in a little sweetened wine, is one of the most refreshing dishes to end a meal with.

4 grapefruit, preferably a selection of pink
    and white
3 tablespoons packed light brown sugar
1 cup dry white wine such as Chardonnay,
    or the juice of ½ lemon
1 tablespoon shredded fresh mint, plus
    4 fresh mint sprigs

✦✦Peel the grapefruit by hand and section the fruit using a small, sharp paring knife, cutting next to the membranes to remove the flesh and leave the membrane. Carefully remove the seeds from the grapefruit flesh.

✦✦Arrange the grapefruit sections in a large shallow bowl or in individual shallow bowls and sprinkle with the sugar, then drizzle with the wine. Scatter the shredded mint over the top, then cover and refrigerate for at least 3 hours and preferably overnight.

✦✦Serve garnished with the mint sprigs.

Les Deux Oranges à la Menthe (Two Types of Oranges with Mint) Peel and segment 2 oranges and 2 blood oranges and arrange in shallow bowls. Sprinkle grated orange zest over the top, and sprinkle with an orange liqueur such as Grand Marnier or Cointreau and a little sugar to taste. Cover and refrigerate. Serve garnished with mint leaves.

FROZEN DESSERTS

DESSERTS GLACÉS

Frozen desserts, whether rich and decadent or light and fruity, make wonderful bistro sweets. Almost always there is at least one on the dessert cart. Homemade ices and sorbets add a distinctive flavor to your menu, but good-quality, store-bought ice cream or sorbet is terrific as a base. Simply dress it up with the finery of the season's sweetest fruit and add a drizzle of heady liqueur.

FRUITS ROUGES SORBET ET GLACE

MACERATED SUMMER FRUITS WITH MANGO SORBET AND VANILLA ICE CREAM

– Serves 4 to 6 –

This makes a beautiful and refreshing dessert: The berries are so lush, the mango sorbet so delicately orange in color, the vanilla so gently creamy.

2 cups assorted summer fruits: blackberries,
    strawberries, cherries (pitted and
    halved), currants, raspberries
½ to ¾ cup Muscat wine such as Beaumes
    de Venise
2 to 3 tablespoons orange liqueur
Sugar to taste
½ pint mango sorbet
½ pint vanilla ice cream

♦♦Combine the berries, wine, orange liqueur, and if needed, sugar. Cover and refrigerate for up to 2 hours.

♦♦Serve the berries and their juices on plates or in a bowl, garnished with small scoops of tangy mango sorbet and creamy vanilla ice cream.

GOURMANDISE DU CHEF

AN ICE CREAM AND FRUIT

CONCOCTION OF THE CHEF

– Serves 4 –

I have freely adapted this dessert from one I spooned up in Paris's Restaurant Bleu, a tiny bistro near Montparnasse.

A scoop of sweet peach ice cream in a pool of blackberry coulis is surrounded with nuggets of fresh peaches and blackberries. Poke a few crisp cookies into the assembly in a jaunty manner, et voilà!

Any berry could be used in place of the blackberries, and nectarines could nicely take the place of peaches. And peach frozen yogurt or sorbet can replace the richer ice cream.

2½ cups fresh blackberries
8 tablespoons sugar, or to taste
¼ to ½ teaspoon raspberry vinegar,
*   or 1 tablespoon cassis, or any berry*
*   liqueur or eau-de-vie*
2 ripe peaches, peeled, pitted, and diced
1 pint peach ice cream or frozen yogurt
8 crisp little cookies for serving

♦♦Make the blackberry coulis by puréeing 2 cups of the blackberries with 6 tablespoons of the sugar and the raspberry vinegar, or liqueur, or eau-de-vie. Use right away or cover and refrigerate. (For a smooth consistency, strain the mixture through a sieve.)

♦♦Toss the peaches with the remaining 2 tablespoons sugar. Use right away or cover and refrigerate.

♦♦When ready to serve, make a puddle of coulis on each plate, place a scoop of ice cream in the center, and scatter the peaches and remaining berries around the edge of the plate. Serve with cookies.

♦♦Insert a cookie or two into each ice cream scoop at a jaunty angle and serve right away.

BONBONS AU SORBET

ICED SORBET "JEWELS"

COVERED IN DARK CHOCOLATE

– Serves 4 –

These little frivolities are utterly delicious, tiny bites of deep dark chocolate with the tart fruit taste of sorbet inside. Serve with a cup of black coffee after the meal.

1 pint good-quality very tart fresh-fruit
*   sorbet*
About 12 ounces semisweet chocolate,
*   chopped*

♦♦Slightly soften the sorbet just enough to spoon into it. Spoon little morsels onto a waxed paper–covered baking sheet and insert a toothpick into each. Refreeze immediately until rock hard.

◆◆Melt the chocolate gently over barely simmering water. Dip each sorbet morsel into the melted chocolate, then place immediately back on the waxed paper and back into the freezer. Serve when all of the bonbons have been dipped and refrozen for about 15 minutes.

GLACE DE RIZ
ET EAU DE FLEURS D'ORANGER
RICE AND ORANGE FLOWER
ICE MILK

– Serves 4 to 6 –

The hills behind Nice up toward Grasse are famous for the sweet fragrance of the flowers that are used to make the perfumes of the area. The fountain in the main square of Grasse says it all, as it is shaped like a large perfume bottle.

The flowers that grow so aromatically for the perfume trade traditionally figure prominently in the foods of the area, such as in its hauntingly perfumed ice creams. Lavender ice is a local specialty, as is the following rice and orange flower ice cream, which was once served to me decorated with a scattering of white orange blossoms.

Whole milk makes a predictably rich ice cream, but low-fat milk is refreshingly light.

¼ cup Arborio rice, whole or
*   coarsely broken up in a*
*   blender or food processor*
1 cup water
1 cup sugar

Small pinch of salt
2 cups milk
1 vanilla bean
1 egg yolk
3 tablespoons orange flower water

◆◆Combine the rice, water, sugar, and salt in a small, heavy saucepan. Cook over low to medium heat until the rice is tender, stirring all the while. The rice should cook at a simmer; stir so that it doesn't stick, and to break the grains somewhat, encouraging a sticky, slightly starchy consistency to the mixture. This should take about 30 minutes.

◆◆When the liquid is nearly evaporated, add the milk and whole vanilla bean and continue to cook and stir until the rice is tender.

◆◆Remove the vanilla bean and rinse it under cold water. (Let the bean dry and store it in jar of sugar to use again; meanwhile, it will be perfuming the sugar.)

◆◆Beat the egg yolk, stir a few spoonfuls of the hot rice mixture into it, then stir it all back into the rice mixture.

le cageot de poires

✦✦Cook the rice mixture gently over low heat until it thickens slightly.

✦✦Let cool, then stir in the orange flower water.

✦✦Freeze, either in an ice cream maker according to the manufacturer's instructions, or in a shallow Pyrex bowl or tray, stirring the mixture from time to time.

La citrouille

ANANAS GRILLÉS, ANANAS EN SORBET

GRILLED FRESH PINEAPPLE WITH PINEAPPLE SORBET

– Serves 4 –

Having the same fruit prepared in two strikingly different ways is an almost thrilling sensation: Fire and ice bring out very different qualities of the juicy fruit.

The grilled pineapple and the sorbet are each good on their own; the sorbet is especially refreshing.

1 large juicy sweet pineapple, peeled and
*   cored, juices reserved (see Note)*
About ½ cup pineapple juice
8 tablespoons sugar
Juice of ½ lemon
½ teaspoon vanilla extract

✦✦Cut the ripest part of the pineapple into 4 thick slices and set aside.

✦✦Cut the remaining pineapple into small chunks. Place in a blender and purée with the pineapple juice, 5 tablespoons of the sugar, lemon juice, and vanilla, adding more pineapple juice as needed to make a smooth purée.

✦✦Pour the purée into an ice cream maker or ice cube tray and freeze, either according to manufacturer's instructions or by periodically scraping the ice crystals until a fluffy sorbet consistency is reached. One way to achieve a fluffy light consistency is to chop up the frozen sorbet and whirl it in a food processor.

✦✦To serve, preheat the broiler. Sprinkle the reserved pineapple slices with the remaining 3 tablespoons sugar and broil until the sugar is lightly caramelized, about 5 to 7 minutes on each side.

✦✦Serve the hot pineapple with a scoop of sorbet on the side.

NOTE A quick and lovely sorbet can be made with canned pineapple. Proceed according to the above recipe; serve it without the grilled pineapple, however, as that needs to be fresh to be wonderful.

SORBET AU CARAMEL

CARAMEL SORBET

– Serves 2 or 3 –

The simple act of heating sugar gives you that delicacy known as caramel, a flavor terribly chic now in Paris's modern bistros.

This is a lovely and unusual ice, one to make when you think there's nothing to eat in your kitchen.

¾ cup sugar
2 cups water
Juice of ½ lemon

✦✦Combine the sugar and ¼ cup of the water in a medium, heavy nonreactive saucepan. Heat gently until the sugar melts, then raise the heat to medium high and boil the syrup until it turns a light caramel. Do not let it become dark or even medium caramel, as it will continue to cook a few moments afterwards and in that time could burn and taste bitter instead of sweet.

✦✦Meanwhile, heat the remaining 1¾ cups water in a small saucepan until it boils.

✦✦Pour the hot water into the golden brown syrup, stirring to dissolve the caramel, which hardens frighteningly fast. Let cool, stirring ever so often. By the time it reaches room temperature, the caramel should be dissolved into a light brown liquid.

✦✦Add the lemon juice and freeze in an ice cream maker according to the manufacturer's instructions, or in an ice cube tray by repeatedly scraping the frozen ice crystals or puréeing the frozen mixture in a food processor.

SOUFFLÉ GLACE À L'ANISETTE

FROZEN ANISETTE SOUFFLÉ

– Serves 4 –

The licoricelike scent of aniseed is one of the quintessential flavors of France, from the pastis sipped before a meal to the sweet anisette to finish. This frozen soufflé, flavored with anisette, is utterly refreshing.

The icy little soufflés are very nice surrounded by fruits cooked in sweetened red wine (see Soupe aux Fruits de Forêt, page 193).

½ cup sugar
¼ cup water
3 egg whites
Small pinch of salt
4 tablespoons anisette liqueur
1 cup cold heavy cream

✦✦Combine the sugar and water in a small, heavy saucepan and cook, stirring, over medium heat until the sugar dissolves. Raise the heat and bring it to a boil, then cook it without stirring for 10 minutes, or until it thickens and turns slightly golden. Take care it does not burn.

✦✦Beat the egg whites with the salt until they are stiff and glossy. Beat in the hot syrup in a steady stream, then add 2 tablespoons of the liqueur.

✦✦Beat the chilled cream until soft peaks form, then whisk in the remaining 2 tablespoons liqueur.

✦✦Fold the whites into the cream, then carefully pour it into a 4-cup soufflé dish or four 1-cup soufflé dishes. Cover and freeze until firm, about 6 hours.

Fonds de Cuisine
✦✦✦
Basics

Bistros keep a few basic foods on hand. The legendary pot of stock bubbling away on the back burner may not exist in a vegetarian kitchen, but there are vegetable stocks, simple purées such as coulis, and traditional sauces such as béchamel. And oil and vinegar to combine for a savory vinaigrette at a moment's notice.

Pastry is used to wrap almost any vegetable or cheese for a crisp indulgent dish, and cooked beans are not only delicious and nutritious on their own, they are good in soup and puréed into sauces.

FOND DE LÉGUMES À LA MINUTE

QUICK VEGETABLE STOCK

– Makes 1½ to 2 quarts –

Stocks play a large part in bistro cooking. Vegetable stock can easily be made using the bits and trimmings from your daily vegetables as well as the cooking water you might otherwise discard. Vegetable trimmings can be saved in the freezer during the week, then used when you have enough to make a pot of stock. So, too, can the vegetable cooking water. You can replace homemade stock with canned stock, or use canned stock to intensify the flavor of your simmering vegetable broth. One or two bouillon cubes may be added to your stocks as there are several good-quality ones that are low in salt.

8 cups water
2 vegetable bouillon cubes, or 1 to 2 cans
    vegetable broth (decrease liquid in
    recipe accordingly)
1 onion, coarsely cut up
5 garlic cloves, coarsely chopped
1 carrot, peeled and diced
1 bay leaf or 1 tablespoon minced fresh
    parsley
Assorted vegetable trimmings
Any reserved cooking liquids from mild
    vegetables: spinach, zucchini (if not
    bitter), peas, asparagus, etc.

✦✦Combine all of the ingredients in a large stockpot.

✦✦Bring to a boil, then reduce heat and simmer until the vegetables are tender and the liquid is flavorful (about 30 minutes). Cover and store in the refrigerator for up to 3 days, or in the freezer for up to 2 months.

NOTE Freeze all liquids left over from cooking vegetables. When you are ready to make stock, pull them out and pop them into the pot.

FOND DE LÉGUMES

BASIC VEGETABLE STOCK

– Makes 2 or more quarts –

2 tablespoons butter or olive oil
3 onions, chopped
1 carrot, chopped
1 leek, including green tops, cut into dice
¼ celery root, peeled and cut into dice
6 cups water
3 bay leaves
½ teaspoon fresh thyme or ¼ teaspoon
    dried thyme
1 head garlic, unpeeled, but cut in half
3 tablespoons coarsely chopped parsley
Several grindings coarse black pepper
About ¼ pound mushroom stems or other
    mushroom trimmings, chopped
Salt to taste
Any leftover cooking liquids from other
    vegetables such as spinach, zucchini,
    parsnips, etc.; cabbage and other strong-
    smelling vegetables should not be used
    (optional)

✦✦In a stock pot, melt the butter or warm the olive oil and gently sauté the onion, carrot, and leek until vegetables are softened and just golden, about 10 minutes.

✦✦Add the celery root, water, bay leaves, thyme, garlic, parsley, pepper, and mushrooms, and bring the mixture to a boil.

✦✦Reduce the heat and simmer, uncovered, for about an hour. If using leftover vegetable cooking liquid, add it when stock is about half cooked. Strain stock, pressing on vegetables to squeeze out all of their flavor. Discard the vegetables, and season the stock with salt to taste.

✦✦Stock may be kept for 2 to 3 days in the refrigerator or may be frozen.

CRÈME FRAÎCHE

– Makes about 3 cups –

C rème fraîche is an indispensable flavor of France, spooned out of ceramic crocks in *fromageries* or, less picturesquely, purchased in the supermarket.

Crème fraîche is wonderful in sauces, with its slightly acidic flavor balancing its richness and its body giving it a certain authority. And there's nothing like crème fraîche with desserts: In most bistros when you order strawberries, a big bowl of the creamy stuff will be offered. Crème fraîche will not curdle when added to acidic sauces, and can cook in a sauce without separating.

1 cup sour cream
2 cups heavy cream

✦✦Stir the sour cream until it is smooth, then whisk in the heavy cream.

✦✦Cover loosely and let sit at room temperature for 8 hours or overnight.

✦✦Refrigerate for at least 4 hours to firm and thicken. Crème fraîche will continue to develop a tangy flavor as it ages, and will keep, covered and refrigerated, for about 1 week.

PÂTE BRISÉE

PASTRY DOUGH

– Makes pastry for one 9- to 10-inch tart shell or four 3-inch tartlet shells –

I add a small squeeze of lemon to my pastry dough, whether for sweet or savory tarts–it's my belief, though it may just be a fanciful thought, that this makes the crust more tender.

The less water you use, the flakier the crust; the same goes for the less you handle the dough and the cooler you keep it. Once it warms, the tiny fragments of fat work their way into the flour and act as a sort of glue that makes a tough rather than light flaky crust.

Always make dough ahead of time so the gluten can relax, making a more tender result. Thirty minutes will do in a pinch, but 1 to 2 hours will give more reliable results. Luckily, pastry dough freezes well; keep a double or triple batch in the freezer.

1¾ cups all-purpose unbleached flour
¼ teaspoon salt
½ cup (1 stick) cold unsalted butter,
    cut into bits
1 to 2 teaspoons fresh lemon juice
2 to 3 tablespoons ice water, or as needed

✦✦Combine the flour, salt, and butter in a bowl. Rub the butter into the flour using your fingertips, a pastry cutter, or 2 knives.

✦✦When the mixture looks like coarse grains, sprinkle in the lemon juice and just enough water to form a soft ball of dough. You do not want the dough to be sticky.

✦✦Wrap in a plastic bag and refrigerate it for 1 to 2 hours, or up to 2 days. If you need to store it longer, freeze it.

Le marché

UNBAKED TART SHELL Place the dough on a lightly floured board and roll it out into a circle about 12 inches in diameter and ⅛ inch thick. Fold it gently into quarters then place the corner in the center and unfold. It should fit right into the tart shell. Trim the edges. If there is extra dough you can save it in the freezer or refrigerator, or make tartlets.

PARTIALLY BAKED TART SHELL Preheat the oven to 400°F. Prick the bottom of the dough, then cover it with a sheet of baking parchment or aluminum foil and fill with dried beans or pie weights. This keeps the dough from rising and puffing while it's baking.

Bake for 8 to 10 minutes, or until shrunk from the sides of the pan and lightly brown. Remove from the oven and remove the beans or weights and paper or foil.

FULLY BAKED TART SHELL Return the partially baked crust (with its paper or foil and beans or weights removed) to the oven and bake for another 5 to 10 minutes, or until the pastry is a light golden brown.

CRÊPES

– Makes about twelve 9-inch crêpes –

Crêpes are just thin pancakes, made from a simple batter of eggs, milk, flour, and oil.

They are eaten on the streets of Paris as a snack, in *crêperies* as main courses and desserts, and in bistros as a first course or dessert, especially in the north.

3 eggs, lightly beaten
1 cup milk
⅓ cup water
1 cup all-purpose flour
3 tablespoons oil or melted butter
Pinch of salt
Oil for coating pan

✦✦ Whisk together all of the ingredients except the oil for the pan, or purée in a blender or food processor until smooth. If you are using a blender or processor, let the batter sit for 30 minutes to relax the gluten in the flour.

✦✦ Heat a 9-inch crêpe pan over medium-high heat until almost smoking. Add a few drops of oil to the pan and swirl until it coats the entire pan, then ladle in 3 to 4 tablespoons of the batter. Swirl the batter to coat the pan, then pour the excess back into the rest of the batter.

✦✦ Cook until the batter is firm on top and lightly browned on the bottom, then turn and cook a few moments on the second side. Turn out onto a plate.

✦✦Repeat, stacking the crêpes as they cook. Wrap in foil and keep warm in the oven if eating right away; otherwise leave them uncovered at room temperature. To keep, wrap in plastic and store in the refrigerator for up to 5 days, or in the freezer for up to 3 months.

Crêpes Sucrées (Dessert Crêpes) Add 1 to 2 tablespoons sugar to the batter mixture.

GALETTES

BRETON BUCKWHEAT CRÊPES

– Makes 4 crêpes –

Buckwheat crêpes are eaten throughout Brittany in both savory and sweet dishes, rolled around a filling or simply sprinkled with sugar and doused with liqueur.

½ cup all-purpose flour
⅓ cup buckwheat flour
½ teaspoon salt
2 eggs, lightly beaten
1½ cups water, or as needed
2 to 3 tablespoons butter for cooking

✦✦Mix the flours and salt with the eggs, then stir in the water, pouring and stirring until the mixture is the consistency of thick cream or a thin custard sauce. Or, combine all the ingredients in a blender or food processor and blend until smooth. If you have used a blender or food processor, let the batter rest for 30 minutes to relax the gluten in the flour.

✦✦Melt 1 or 2 teaspoons of the butter in a 9-inch crêpe pan over medium-high heat and swirl 4 to 5 tablespoons of the batter to cover the bottom of the pan in a thin layer, then pour the excess back into the rest of the batter.

✦✦Cook until the crêpe is lightly browned on the bottom, then turn it over and brown on the other side. Transfer to a plate and repeat to use the remaining batter, stacking the crêpes as you make them. They can be eaten right away or covered and stored in the refrigerator or in the freezer.

ŒUFS DURS

HARD-COOKED EGGS

✦✦For firm yet tender hard-cooked eggs, place eggs in a saucepan with cold water to cover. Gradually bring the water to a boil, then reduce the heat and cook at a simmer for 6 to 8 minutes. Remove from heat, then remove the eggs from the hot water and immediately rinse them in cold water; this makes them easier to peel. If you are going to peel them shortly, let them rest in a bowl of cold water for 5 to 10 minutes beforehand.

ŒUFS POCHÉS

POACHED EGGS

✦✦Heat about 3 inches of water in a large skillet. When bubbles form around the edge of the pan, add 1 teaspoon wine vinegar. (The vinegar keeps the whites from spreading through the water in a raggedy fashion.) Reduce heat to low.

✦✦Crack an egg into a cup, then slide it into the simmering water. Cook for 3 to 4 minutes, until the white is firm but the yolk still soft. Remove from the water and drain on paper towels.

> ### COULIS
>
> A coulis is a purée of vegetables or fruit to be used as a sauce. It should taste of its own freshness, and can add flavor to other sauces and vinaigrettes or be served as a sauce on its own accord, spooned around a simple tart, omelet, or soufflé.

COULIS DE TOMATES

AUX POIVRONS ROUGES

RED PEPPER AND TOMATO

COULIS

– Makes 1½ cups –

Red pepper and tomato coulis is a bright, fresh-tasting sauce that adds a ray of sunshine to whatever it is served with. Its also easy to prepare and freezes nicely, and if you have only a few tablespoons left, it makes a marvelous garnish to spoon into soup.

This can be multiplied at will, in quantities as large as your pot.

1 onion, coarsely chopped
1 tablespoon olive oil
3 garlic cloves, minced
1 red bell pepper, seeded. deribbed, and
  chopped
2 fresh or canned tomatoes, diced
¼ cup tomato juice
Salt and pepper to taste
Tabasco sauce or cayenne pepper to taste

Pinch of sugar if tomatoes are acidic
A large pinch of dried thyme, marjoram,
  savory, or herbes de Provence

✦✦In a medium, heavy saucepan over medium heat, sauté the onion in the olive oil until softened, then add the garlic and red pepper. Continue to cook for about 5 minutes, or until the pepper begins to soften, then add the tomatoes.
✦✦Cook until the mixture is chunky and almost saucelike, then add the tomato juice and bring to a boil. Reduce heat, cover, and simmer for about 5 minutes, or until the pepper and tomatoes are very soft.
✦✦Let cool, then purée in a blender or food processor. Season with salt, pepper, Tabasco or cayenne, sugar if needed, and thyme or another herb of choice.

Coulis de Tomates (Fresh Tomato Sauce) For a fresh unseasoned raw tomato sauce, grate raw flavorful summer tomatoes using the big rasps of a grater. This not only purées the tomato flesh, it removes the skin, too.

To intensify the flavors, place the coulis in a saucepan and cook over medium-high heat until mixture has been reduced to the consistency desired.

Out of season, a quick tomato coulis can be made by puréeing diced canned tomatoes in a blender or food processor. I also like to use the diced tomatoes that are preserved in cardboard boxes rather than cans.

Coulis de Fruits (Fruit Coulis) Poached or raw fruits can be used to make coulis. Simply purée in a blender or food processor and sweeten to taste. A dash of eau-de-vie or liqueur adds vibrancy, and a squirt of lemon can balance any flavors that seem a little flat.

Poached fresh or dried apricots, poached or ripe peaches, berries of all types, poached cherries, pineapple, and kiwi are among the fruits you can use to make this simple sauce.

BÉCHAMEL

WHITE SAUCE

– Makes 1 cup –

Béchamel adds body to any dish, but is less rich than cream. Using olive oil instead of butter is particularly good with Provençal dishes; the same holds true for simmering whole garlic cloves or chopped onion in the milk.

A béchamel can be the basis for a gratin, spread on top of a layer of vegetables and topped with crumbs and/or cheese; or béchamel can be the basis for that bistro classic, the soufflé: Stir in the yolks, beat the whites until stiff, then fold in. Pour into a soufflé dish and bake: Voilà!

This sauce can be prepared and multiplied at will. For a thicker sauce, add more flour; for richer sauce, use a milk with a higher cream content. I generally use low-fat milk, and sometimes even use half low-fat and half nonfat.

To add to its general usefulness, béchamel freezes exceedingly well.

1 cup milk
1 tablespoon butter or olive oil
1 slightly heaped tablespoon flour
Pinch of salt
Pinch of grated nutmeg
Pinch of cayenne pepper

✦✦ Heat the milk until bubbles form around the edge of the saucepan. Remove from heat and keep warm.

✦✦ In a small, heavy saucepan over low heat, heat the butter or olive oil, then sprinkle in the flour. Cook for 2 or 3 minutes, stirring, until the flour is slightly golden but not brown.

✦✦ Remove from heat and pour in the hot milk all at once. Stir well, then return to heat, and cook, stirring all the while, for 30 to 40 minutes, or until thickened.

✦✦ Season with salt, nutmeg, and cayenne.

Béchamel à l'Ail (*Garlic Béchamel*) Increase the amount of milk to 1½ cups. Peel the cloves from 1 head garlic and simmer with the milk until the milk reduces to 1 cup. Use this liquid in the above béchamel recipe.

La vache

Three Gratins to Make with Garlic Béchamel

Gratin d'Asperges **(Asparagus Gratin)** Layer tender-crisp asparagus spears with garlic béchamel, then sprinkle with Parmesan and bread crumbs to taste. Bake in a preheated 425°F oven until crisp and golden, about 30 minutes.

Gratin d'Endives **(Endive Gratin)** Arrange 8 to 12 blanched Belgian endives in a baking pan and cover with a layer of garlic béchamel. Sprinkle with ½ to ¾ cup grated cheese and bake in a preheated 425°F oven for 15 to 20 minutes, or until the top is golden and lightly browned in places.

Gratin d'Aubergines **(Eggplant and Cheese Gratin)** Beat 3 eggs into the garlic béchamel and season with grated nutmeg to taste; layer it with browned sliced eggplant and 1 to 1½ cups grated cheese, ending with a layer of grated cheese. Bake in a preheated 375°F oven for 30 minutes, or until the top is golden brown. Serve warm, or let cool.

Sauce Meurette

Burgundian Red Wine Sauce

– Makes 3 to 4 cups –

This classic sauce can be spooned over poached eggs for a bistro supper of *œufs en Meurette*, or puddled onto a plate and topped with baked goat cheese. It's also delicious with boiled potatoes or layered into a macaroni gratin.

Meurette sauce freezes well.

1 bottle dry red wine, such as a Côtes-du-Rhône or a Cahors
2 cups vegetable stock (page 201–202)
1 onion
2 whole cloves
Bouquet garni: 1 bay leaf, 1 sprig fresh parsley, 1 sprig fresh thyme, 1 sprig fresh rosemary, tied in cheesecloth bag
2 carrots, peeled and cut into very thin slices
3 garlic cloves, coarsely chopped
1 celery stalk, chopped
6 peppercorns
1 green onion, including the green part, diced
1 tablespoon tomato paste
4 tablespoons butter
3 tablespoons flour
Salt and pepper to taste
Dash of balsamic vinegar

✦✦ Combine the wine and stock in a large saucepan. Cut the onion in half, then stick each half with 1 clove and add to the pan, along with the bouquet garni, carrots, celery, pepper, and green onion. Bring the mixture to a boil, then reduce heat to medium and cook until it has reduced by about half and the vegetables are very soft, 40 to 45 minutes.

✦✦ Strain this wine mixture and press hard with the back of a large spoon to extract the flavorful juices from the vegetables; if the vegetables do not press easily, whirl them in a blender, then strain them. Discard the vegetables once they have been squeezed.

✦✦ In a large, heavy saucepan over low heat, melt 3 tablespoons of the butter and sprinkle in the flour; cook, stirring, until lightly golden, then remove from heat and add the wine mixture, tomato paste, and remaining butter all at once. Whisk well, then return to the heat. Cook, stirring, until smooth, thickened, and glossy.

✦✦ Season with salt and pepper and add a dash of balsamic vinegar to sharpen the flavors.

VINAIGRETTE

– Makes ¼ to ⅓ cup –

On the table of many bistros, especially old-fashioned ones, stands a cruet of oil, another of vinegar, and a little pot of mustard. From this you can mix your own vinaigrette.

But other, more stylish bistros, make their own vinaigrette, little sauces of oil and vinegar flavored with herbs and aromatics.

Here is a good basic one. Note: The addition of sherry, fruit, or balsamic vinegar cuts the sharpness of many wine vinegars.

> *2 teaspoons sherry, fruit, or balsamic*
> *vinegar*
> *2 teaspoons red or white wine vinegar*
> *½ teaspoon salt*
> *Large pinch of coarsely ground black*
> *pepper*
> *3 to 4 tablespoons olive oil, as desired*

✦✦ Whisk together the vinegars, salt, and pepper, then slowly whisk in the olive oil until it forms an emulsion.

✦✦ If vinaigrette sits, it separates; simply whisk together before using.

VINAIGRETTE À LA MOUTARDE

GARLIC-MUSTARD VINAIGRETTE

– Makes about ½ cup –

This makes a thick dressing, as the mustard emulsifies the vinaigrette. Whichever mustard you choose–strong, mild, herbed, wholegrain, and so on–will determine the flavor of your vinaigrette. Don't use all strong mustard, however, as it's a bit too hot.

> *1 shallot, minced*
> *1 garlic clove, minced*
> *2 tablespoons Dijon mustard of choice or a*
> *combination*
> *1 tablespoon red or white wine vinegar or*
> *fruit vinegar*
> *Salt and pepper to taste*
> *4 tablespoons olive oil*

✦✦ Combine the shallot, garlic, mustard, and vinegar and mix well; season with salt and pepper, then slowly whisk in the olive oil until it forms a thick dressing. Taste and adjust the seasoning.

PISTOU

GARLIC-BASIL PASTE

– Makes about ¾ cup –

A good basil pistou is little more than fresh basil puréed with olive oil and garlic. To add a Provençal flavor, add a few tomatoes; for a more Italianate taste, add freshly grated Parmesan as desired. Blue cheese and goat cheese are delicious in pistou as well.

This freezes extremely well and can be defrosted and tossed with pasta or stirred into vegetable soup to make *soupe au pistou.*

2 cups fresh basil leaves, stemmed
5 garlic cloves, minced
⅓ to ½ cup olive oil
Salt and pepper to taste
2 or 3 diced ripe tomatoes (optional)
½ to 1 cup (2 to 4 ounces) grated Parmesan
  cheese (optional)

✦✦ Purée the basil and garlic in a food processor or a mortar, then slowly add in the olive oil until you have a thick green sauce. Season with salt and pepper and add the tomatoes and/or cheese if you like.

HARICOTS SECS

DRIED BEANS

– Makes 2 cups –

Dried beans, to be at their most tender, should be soaked overnight. If you don't have the time, however, the quick-soak method works well. It is very important not to add salt or acid foods to the beans as they cook, as this retards the cooking process. A bay leaf, on the other hand, always adds a lovely flavor to cooking beans, especially white beans or chickpeas.

Cooked beans, by the way, freeze extremely well.

½ cup dried beans or chickpeas
1 bay leaf

✦✦ Place the beans or chickpeas in a saucepan with water to cover. Soak overnight, or use the quick-soak method: Bring to a boil, boil for 5 to 10 minutes, then remove from heat, cover, and let soak for 1 hour.

✦✦ Drain and add fresh water to cover the beans by about 1 inch. Add the bay leaf and bring to a boil. Reduce heat, cover, and cook at a very low simmer until the beans are tender, about 1 to 3 hours, depending on the type and age of the beans and the mineral content of the water.

✦✦ When the beans are tender they may be flavored with onions, garlic, tomatoes, salt, and other flavorings.

LENTILLES

LENTILS

– Makes about 4 cups –

Most lentils do not need to be soaked before cooking, but soaking green lentils softens them and lets them cook at a gentler pace so that they grow tender but do not fall apart during their cooking.

1 cup green lentils (preferably lentils de
  Puy)
3 bay leaves
1 onion, chopped
Salt and pepper to taste

✦✦ Put the lentils and water to cover in a medium saucepan and let soak for 1 hour.

✦✦ Drain the soaked lentils and add fresh water to cover by about 1 inch, along with the bay leaves and onion. Bring to a boil, then reduce heat, cover, and simmer until tender, about 30 minutes.

✦✦ When the lentils are tender, remove from heat and season with salt and pepper.

Preparing Vegetables and Legumes

Blanched Artichoke Hearts and Bottoms Pull back each leaf until it crisply breaks off; fresh artichokes are best, as the softer, less fresh leaves will break off with more difficulty and take more of the tasty heart with it.

When all of the leaves are pulled off, peel the stalk and trim the tough ends. If artichokes are young, tender, and free of a choke, they may be prepared whole. If they have a choke, cut them into quarters or halves and scoop out the choke with a paring knife and spoon, then pop each cleaned artichoke heart into water that has been acidulated by the addition of the juice of half a lemon.

Drain and blanch in boiling water for 1 or 2 minutes. Rinse well and dry on paper towels.

To make artichoke bottoms: Prepare as above using the largest artichokes you can find. Trim all of the leaves to the edge of the heart and hollow out the insides using a grapefruit spoon, or a spoon and a paring knife.

Roasting and Peeling Peppers Roasting peppers until their skin chars makes them easy to peel and gives the flesh a soft, velvety texture. If you've cooked them over an open flame, you will have the luscious scenty smoke as well. Any pepper can be roasted and peeled; peppers with the thickest flesh work best.

Lay whole peppers directly over a gas burner and turn the heat to low-medium, turning several times so that the peppers char evenly. You want black char marks and large blistered areas.

Or, to roast under a broiler: Arrange whole or halved peppers in a single layer and cook the skin side until it chars and blisters.

Place the charred, blistered peppers in a plastic bag or a bowl. Seal the bag or cover the bowl and leave for 15 to 30 minutes. Peel off the skin, core the peppers, remove the seeds, and leave whole or slice, as desired.

Rehydrated Dried Mushrooms Place dried mushrooms in a bowl and pour hot but not boiling water over them. Cover and let sit to absorb the hot liquid for about 30 minutes.

Remove the mushrooms from their liquid and squeeze them tightly to extract their extra liquid, letting the juices drip back into their soaking liquid. This liquid is packed with flavor and should be used in the sauce, soup, or stew you are making. Use all but the last inch of the liquid, which will contain some grit.

Rehydrated mushrooms are often sautéed in a little butter or olive oil to further enhance their flavor. Sometimes they are combined with ordinary domestic mushrooms to bring out the latter's flavor.

Occasionally, dried mushrooms may be simmered in soups or sauce without rehydrating them in advance.

Steamed Rice Place 1 cup white or brown long-grain rice and 2 cups water or stock in a heavy saucepan. Bring to a boil over medium-high heat, then reduce heat to low, cover, and simmer for about 25 minutes for white rice and for brown, 40 minutes, or until the rice is tender. Check the rice after about 20 minutes for tenderness and moisture. Add more liquid if it appears dry. Fluff the rice with a fork when tender. Makes 3 cups white rice and 2 cups brown rice.

TOASTED NUTS AND SEEDS Preheat the oven to 375°F. Arrange the nuts or seeds in a single layer on a baking sheet or in a shallow baking pan. Bake for 10 to 15 minutes, or until toasted, turning once or twice. Remove from the oven and let cool.

TOASTED AND PEELED HAZELNUTS Toast as above, or toast on top of the stove in a single layer in a large, heavy skillet over medium heat, turning every few minutes. When the hazelnut skins begin to split and fall off and the nuts smell fragrant, pour them into a clean towel and wrap them up. Rub the nuts together vigorously, using your hands to agitate the outside of the towel-wrapped parcel. The skins should rub right off, leaving the peeled toasted hazelnuts.

PEELED AND SEEDED TOMATOES To peel tomatoes, use a sharp paring knife to cut the core out of each tomato, then turn each over and score with an X shape. Bring a large pot of water to a boil, then put the tomatoes in the boiling water and boil for about 15 seconds, or until the skin begins to pull away at the X. Remove each tomato from the hot water using a slotted spoon and plunge each into a bowl of cold water. Soak for about 15 seconds, then remove. With the help of the paring knife, the tomato skin should peel off relatively easily. To seed tomatoes, cut the peeled tomatoes in half across their equator (consider the cored stem end as the North Pole). Hold each half over a bowl, cut side down, and lightly squeeze to remove the seeds, using the tip of your paring knife if needed.

CLARIFIED BUTTER Clarified butter is long-keeping butter without the debris of milk, which is what causes butter to go rancid or, when using it to fry, to burn. To clarify butter, slowly melt a lump of butter in a heavy saucepan over very low heat. When foam rises to the surface, skim it off and discard. Let the melted butter stand a few minutes after you have skimmed all the foam, then carefully pour off the liquid, letting the sediment of milk particles that have settled to the bottom of the pan remain there. (For an even finer result, pour this hot butter liquid through a cheesecloth.) Pour the filtered butter into a jar and cover it with a lid. It may be kept at room temperature or in the refrigerator for several months.

CRÔUTES (TOASTS) Crisp pieces of bread are a delicious addition to bistro salads, rustic soups, or alongside savory nibbles and cheeses. They are also an excellent way of using up stale bread. Cut into small bite-sized *crôutes,* they become croutons. *Crôutes* are only delicious made with good quality bread such as a pain levain or good baguette.

Preheat the oven to 400°F. Slice slightly stale bread (about ½ to ¾ inch thick). Brush lightly with olive oil on both sides, then arrange on a baking sheet in a single layer.

Bake, turning once or twice, for 10 to 15 minutes, or until the toasts are crisp and golden brown. Let cool.

For a garlic favor, toss the warm toasts with chopped garlic to taste and let them absorb the garlic flavor as they cool.

Restaurants in France

. . . .

The following restaurants, though not vegetarian, often offer vegetarian dishes. Most of the chefs I spoke with echoed the sentiments of the patron of Au Chien Qui Fume, when I enquired as to whether or not a vegetarian could eat happily at the restaurant: "No customer of mine will ever go hungry!"

PARIS

Au Chien Qui Fume
33, rue de Pont-Neuf
Paris (1st arr.)
Tel: 42-36-07-42

Baracane-Bistrôt de l'Oulette
38, rue des Tournelles
Paris (4th arr.)
Tel: 42-71-43-33

Chardenoux
1, rue Jules-Valles
Paris (11th arr., métro: Charonne)
Tel: 43-71-49-52

Chez Georges
273, boulevard Pereire
Paris (17th arr., métro: Villiers or Ternes)
Tel: 45-74-31-00

Chez Eux
2, avenue Lowendal
Paris (7th arr.)
Tel: 47-05-52-55

Fermette Marbeuf 1900
5, rue Marbeuf
Paris (8th arr., metro: Franklin D. Roosevelt)
Tel: 47-20-63-53

L'Œillade
10, rue de Saint-Simon
Paris (7th arr., métro: rue de Bac or Solferino)
Tel: 42-22-01-60

La Cafetière
21, rue Mazarine
Paris (6th arr.)
Tel: 46-33-76-90

La Maison du Valais
20, rue Royale
Paris (8th arr., métro: Concorde or Madeleine)
Tel: 42-60-23-75

For raclette, including a very nice version with steamed vegetables (maraîchère)

La Tour de Montlhéry (Chez Denise)
5, rue des Prouvaires
Paris (1st arr.)
Tel: 42-36-21-82

Le Bistrôt d'Henri
16, rue Princesse
Paris (6th arr., métro: Mabillon)
Tel: 46-33-51-12

Le Restaurant Bleu
46, rue Didot
Paris (14th arr.)
Tel: 45-43-70-56

FRENCH COUNTRYSIDE

Auberge des Vignes
Place de l'Eglise
Sauternes
Tel: 56-63-60-06

Chez Bruno
Lorges
Tel: 94-73-92-19

Truffles, olive oil, and other quintessential flavors of Provence meet on Chef Bruno's passionate plates. Call ahead to inquire about vegetarian offerings.

Don Camillo
5, rue des Ponchettes
Nice
Tel: 93-85-67-95

Wonderful food that is simple yet refined down to its flavor essence. Though pricey, the prix fixe lunch is reasonable, and though the offerings will probably feature nonvegetarian items, the bistro is very amenable to the choices to suit your tastes and desires. If raw cèpe salad is on the menu, don't pass it by.

Ferme Auberge du Bruel
Saint-Illide
Cernin (Auvergne)
Tel: 71-49-72-27

Ferme-Auberge René Laracine
Ordonnaz (Jura)
Tel: 74-36-42-38

Super potato gratin; call ahead to confirm availability of vegetarian offerings, since it is farm fare and dependent on the seasons.

La Bonne Etape
Chemin du Lac
Château-Arnoux (Alpes de Haute-Provence, the hillside area north of Nice)
Tel: 92-64-00-09

La Petite Auberge
Lascabanes, Montcuq (Quercy)
Tel: 65-31-82-51

Call ahead to inquire about what is growing in the garden and what vegetarian speciality they can offer. I once ate braised leeks with truffles here, and a mushroom tart, and both were luscious. They bake their own bread from wheat they have grown.

La Table du Marché
38, rue Clemenceau
Saint-Tropez (Côte d'Azur)
94-97-85-20

La Merenda
4, rue de la Terrasse
Nice

No telephone–stop by in the morning and have your name placed on a list for a table at lunch. Fabulous pasta au pistou.

La Mère Poulard
Grande Rue
Mont-Saint-Michel
Tel: 33-60-14-01

Famous for its omelets, but don't pass up the zucchini crêpes if they are available (they are served as an accompaniment to other dishes, so you might have to ask).

Le Faitout
25, rue Tour Carrée
Cherbourg
Tel: 02-33-04-25-04

Traditional specialites of Normandy.

Les Arcades
16, place des Arcades
Biot (Provence)
Tel: 93-65-01-04

A cozy, artistic ambience and delicious daily offerings.

Les Viviers
Port de Larros
Gujan-Mestras (Bordeaux)
Tel: 56-66-01-04

Lou Pistou
4, rue de la Terrasse (directly next door to La Merenda)
Nice
Tel: 93-62-21-82

Delectable ratatouille and soupe au pistou.

Index

Table of Equivalents

· ·

The exact equivalents in the following tables have been rounded for convenience.

ABBREVIATIONS

US	Metric
oz=ounce	g=gram
lb=pound	kg=kilogram
in=inch	mm=millimeter
ft=foot	cm=centimeter
tbl=tablespoon	ml=milliliter
fl oz=fluid ounce	l=liter
qt=quart	

WEIGHTS

US	Metric
1 oz	30 g
2 oz	60 g
3 oz	90 g
4 oz (¼ lb)	125 g
5 oz (⅓ lb)	155 g
6 oz	185 g
7 oz	220 g
8 oz (½ lb)	250 g
10 oz	315 g
12 oz (¾ lb)	375 g
14 oz	440 g
16 oz (1 lb)	500 g
1½ lb	750 g
2 lb	1 kg
3 lb	1.5 kg

OVEN TEMPERATURES

Fahrenheit	Celsius	Gas
250	120	½
275	140	1
300	150	2
325	160	3
350	180	4
375	190	5
400	200	6
425	220	7
450	230	8
475	240	9
500	260	10

LIQUIDS

US	Metric	UK
2 tbl	30 ml	1 fl oz
¼ cup	60 ml	2 fl oz
⅓ cup	80 ml	3 fl oz
½ cup	125 ml	4 fl oz
⅔ cup	160 ml	5 fl oz
¾ cup	180 ml	6 fl oz
1 cup	250 ml	8 fl oz
1½ cups	375 ml	12 fl oz
2 cups	500 ml	16 fl oz

LENGTH MEASURES

⅛ in	3 mm
¼ in	6 mm
½ in	12 mm
1 in	2.5 cm
2 in	5 cm
3 in	7.5 cm
4 in	10 cm
5 in	13 cm
6 in	15 cm
7 in	18 cm
8 in	20 cm
9 in	23 cm
10 in	25 cm
11 in	28 cm
12 in/1 ft	30 cm